THE
DEATH
OF RUGBY

THE
DEATH
OF RUGBY

Neil Back MBE with Dean Eldredge

First published by Pitch Publishing, 2015

Pitch Publishing
A2 Yeoman Gate
Yeoman Way
Durrington
BN13 3QZ
www.pitchpublishing.co.uk

A CIP catalogue record is available for this book
from the British Library.

ISBN 978 178531-054-6

Typesetting and origination by Pitch Publishing

Printed by TJ International, Cornwall, UK

Contents

Acknowledgements

I F it wasn't for the support my parents gave to me, and the values they set, there is no way I would be here today, looking back over my career in rugby and my life outside of the sport in the form of an autobiography. Vanessa and Keith, or Mum and Dad as I know them, have done so much for me and I'd like to thank them for everything.

My wife, Ali, has constantly supported me, but more importantly, I would like to thank her for everything she has done for our children, Olivia and Finley, who I am so proud of. Ali has at times during my career, taken the role of two parents, supporting the kids academically, emotionally and with their respective sporting achievements. As I selfishly pursued my goals, she supported our family, and it's only now that I can look back and really appreciate what she did, and also what my parents sacrificed for me when I was younger.

They say that behind every successful person, there is a rock they depend on, and Ali is that rock for me, as I couldn't have achieved even half of what I did in the game without knowing she was there, by my side.

I'd like to thank my first coach, Jack Carnell, who inspired me to take up this wonderful sport of rugby football at a young age, and his inspiration continued in to my coaching days, through to the present day. You simply can't be successful in sport, or in life, on your own without the help of others. There are too many people to thank from my career, but many of them will be mentioned throughout the book, for their contributions.

I want to mention Pitch Publishing for believing in this book, and ultimately for their support and for publishing it. Of course, I must mention the co-author of *The Death of Rugby*, Dean Eldredge. This is the first book that Dean has written, and I am certain that it will be the first of many; that's if he ever wants to write again after working with me for over six months! Seriously though, he has done a tremendous job and I have enjoyed working with him throughout the process.

Thank you also to my former colleagues for generously giving their time up for this book; Clive, Johno, Jonny, Hilly and Lol, plus Andy Key and Glen Thurgood for their invaluable contributions on my time at Leeds and Rugby respectively. Your help is really appreciated. That goes for everyone I have played alongside, worked with in the game, and the fantastic supporters, especially at Leicester Tigers, who helped me throughout my career, as well as Tim and Rose Buttimore, my good friends and first professional agents, and Adidas, my personal sponsors. Thank you to all of you.

Finally, sincere thanks also to my media agents, Champions (UK) Plc, and my rugby agent David Ricketts of Legion Sports for everything they have done, and continue to do for me, and also Dean's company, Oporto Sports, for their support, as well as Templars of Rothley, where the bacon sandwiches and coffee helped to get us through every Wednesday morning and each chapter.

I hope you enjoy the read.

Neil Back

Dedications

THE reason for revisiting my professional career, and picking up where my last autobiography finished, was to tell the story of my time as head coach of The Rugby Football Club (2011) Ltd, for the people affected by the actions of Michael David Aland and his associates during that emotional season.

I could have easily written a whole book about our year with Rugby, and for me, chapter 11 is why this book has been published, but I wanted as wide an audience as possible to read this and to understand what happened to us, so everything else in my career from 2001 onwards is included.

I know that I don't owe anyone anything, but I feel like I do. This book, *The Death of Rugby*, is dedicated to the players and staff of the club during the 2011/2012 season, as well as the supporters, local community and businesses who supported us during that period.

I have listed all of the players as follows: Nick Adams, Joss Andrews, Sam Bennett, Joe Bercis, Alex Bibic, Will Brock, Robert Brown, Ben Buxton, Adam Canning, Beau Carney, Dave Clements, James Collins, James Daniel, Matthew Davies, Neil Davies, Paul Davies, Harry Ellis, Frankie Fenwick-Wilson, Jon Fitt, Ben Gollings (player-coach), Steve Goode, Phil Greenbury, Ade Hales, Gareth Hardy, Oscar Heath, Leigh Hinton, Stuart Lee, Emyr Lewis,

Matthew Mountford, Nigel Mukarati, Tim Murphy, Dan Needham, Ben Nuttall, Dan Oselton, Sam Overton, Stewart Pearl, Santiago Pulgar, Allan Purchase, Sam Raven, Jack Riley, Michael Rust, Wayne Saunders, Joey Shore, Fraser Tait, Callum Tucker, Simon Tunnicliffe, Andy Vilk, Peter Wackett, James Wadey, Nick Walton, Danny Wright, Jack Young.

And the staff: Brad Ainslie, Geoff Buck, Alan Collins, Milly Dahl, Clive Davies, Martin Dundas, Mark Ellis, Fred Empy, Richard Gee, Lauren Gollings, Nadio Granata, Thomas Hames, Andy Key, Steve King, Fred McKenzie, Rhys Morris, Jon Newcombe, Charlie Parker, Blake Sporne, John Tarrant, Steve Tucker and Glen Thurgood.

I want to thank you all for your unwavering professionalism in extraordinary circumstances, as you helped us to succeed against all the odds and deliver an unbeaten season of 31 wins from 31 games, gaining automatic promotion and cup success, while laying solid foundations for the club to go on and deliver our shared vision, which we all know, all too painfully, didn't materialise. I hope this book, in some way, will shine a light on what happened to you all and will bring us some closure.

Sir Clive Woodward OBE
England head coach 1997–2004

'GREAT teams are made of great individuals' – this is one of my favourite lines in sport and you need look no further than England's World Cup-winning team of 2003 for evidence of its truth. As head coach, I was lucky to work with a remarkable group of players and Neil was one such player – truly remarkable.

When I started as England's head coach in 1997, I was determined to break away from the stereotypes of English rugby. I wanted to play an all-court game that could get 70,000 England fans at Twickenham on their feet going nuts. This meant playing with relentless speed, keeping the ball alive and attacking the opposition with and without the ball. To play the game like this, your back row has to be at the heart of it and Backy took to it brilliantly.

He was the quickest loose forward across the ground and his sevens experience gave him the passing game, handling skills and spatial awareness that put him ahead of his time at openside flanker. On top of this he was unbelievably fit, playing 80 minutes of flat-out rugby without being the slightest bit distressed. That is just gold dust for a head coach. With the ball in hand, he was the complete rugby player who I fancy could have played as well at scrum half or centre. But it was Backy's sheer bloody toughness which took his game to a whole new level.

I think it is no exaggeration to say he was the player in the game that everyone was afraid of, even Johno. As gifted as Backy was with ball in hand, it was what he did on the ground that made him the toughest player in the game. Backy's courage and grit was just something else and when combined with his speed of thought and dynamism to get into the right place at the right time to chop down the opposition, or steal the ball, it made him a number seven unlike any other.

In 2003, I was lucky to have a number of fine players to choose from; Lewis Moody, Joe Worsley and Martin Corry were all outstanding in their own right – but my starting back row, barring a real drop in form, was always Richard Hill, Lawrence Dallaglio and Backy. Between them they exhibited everything you are looking for. Pace, power, stamina, handling skills, line-out capability, ferocious tackling, strength in the contact area, tenacity over the ball, poaching skills par excellence and flinty temperaments. Together they were a mighty force and the best back-row combination I have seen in the game.

At a time when the likes of New Zealand, France, South Africa, and Australia all had great back rows, the way Backy, alongside Lawrence and Hilly, fronted up, snarled, smashed and raced across the field was amazing to watch and something the whole team fed off. The game that stands out most to me is the 2003 semi-final against France. Imanol Harinordoquy, Olivier Magne and Serge Betsen were a great trio for France in the back row – but Lawrence, Neil and Richard tore them apart. Our pack smashed the French that day, with our back row totally unplayable. When the final whistle blew, the three of them just left the field with no ceremony or celebration, the performance spoke for itself, their job well done. We were in the World Cup Final and the rest is history.

Neil's career boasts countless Premiership titles, two European Cups, a grand slam among three Six Nations Championship wins, three Lions tours including a series win against South Africa, and a World Cup triumph. That is some career, for one of the nation's great players. But as long as I've known Neil, whether he be in Leicester's, England's, the Lions' colours, or in his recent coaching roles, it is his love and dedication for the game and his family which has shone through. For this my admiration and pride in Neil will only continue.

Martin Johnson CBE

Leicester Tigers and England captain

I FIRST really noticed Backy in an England Schoolboys trial in 1987. It was my first real big game of rugby and I really wasn't sure if I was good enough to be there. During a pause in the game a blonde head appeared in our forward huddle and started to vigorously encourage and berate us all in equal measure. The thing that struck me most was not just his passion, but the fact that he had one of his teeth knocked out and either hadn't noticed or just wasn't that bothered. I found that to be deeply impressive.

Neil didn't stop being deeply impressive over the best part of the next 20 years and I can honestly say I never saw him play anything remotely close to a bad game. He set standards for fitness and professionalism that we all strived to equal and was an integral part of hugely successful Leicester Tigers, England, and British & Irish Lions teams, and is one of a unique group of players who have won European and World Cups, and played on a winning Lions tour.

Neil is one of the greats.

Jonny Wilkinson CBE
England and British & Irish Lions

RUGBY is a brilliant way to learn about life. It is also schooling in team values, mainly what it means to take responsibility for your own actions and how best to use the power we all have to influence the success of the group. It can, at times, seem to be a school of hard knocks though. At other times it can feel like a complete celebration of all that is good about the world and the people whom inhabit it with us.

Every school needs teachers qualified to preach such a strong message and if the sport of rugby is the headmaster in this case, then Neil Back is the more than able deputy.

For me, Backy was always the enforcer of our team and individual standards. After the players had decided upon what was and what was not acceptable in terms of performance, on and off the field, guys like Neil made it their mission to make sure that expectations were heavily respected and met.

He did this by setting examples for others to aspire to. First, with obvious passion, he made it very, very clear how he believed things were going to have to be, then, more importantly, he more than backed his words up with actions which motivated and inspired others to believe just as fiercely. Whereas he was vocally the enforcer of exceptional standards, he was, through the way he went about his business, the re-inforcer of everything it takes to be a winner.

The incredible Martin Johnson was our leader, but Neil was his right-hand man and he illustrated to us all exactly what the word ruthless looks like when put in a white rugby shirt, with a rose on the chest.

A more professional athlete and competitor I do not believe you will find; he pushed back the barriers of daily intensity to such an extent that it could strike fear in you if you didn't know him better. Yet, as with all the purest champions, it was the sheer regularity with which he dominated the game in his position, which underlined his excellence. On the field he was machine-like; unbreakable, unstoppable and simply horrible to play against.

Off the field, there is a very endearing human side to him. This only drove me to respect him more as I realised that this consistency of performance and fierce, no-nonsense attitude was something that, as for all of us, had to be worked on daily and resulted from his sweat and sacrifices.

People sometimes ask me to recount the most treasured memories of my time in the game. At the top of the list, not surprisingly, there are a few which involve Neil Back.

My favourite will stay with me as perhaps the greatest mark of respect a man could be awarded in rugby. It happened when we were heading back into the changing rooms at half-time in the Stade de France during the Six Nations Championship of 2000. I had completely drained myself of energy during the first 40 minutes trying to unload all I had into every tackle and Backy, as the messiah of all things defence and determination, popped up next to me, put his arm around me and spoke.

'Great workrate. You're a man after my own heart Jonny!'

I suddenly felt completely re-energised. As he sprinted off past me (always first into the dressing room!) he wouldn't have seen the schoolboy smile I was trying to suppress, reach right across my face. When Neil Back puts you in the same ball-park as himself then you know you've pretty much made it.

'I always aspire to give 100 per cent each day, to ensure that I never fail through lack of effort.'

Neil Back

1

We've Only Gone And Done It!

AUSTRALIA 17 England 17. Extra time in the 2003 Rugby World Cup Final, and a quick glance at the clock at the Telstra Stadium, Sydney, told us all we needed to know. It was our kick-off and there was time left to win this, but equally, there was time left to lose it. Ninety seconds remained and we kicked long down the middle of the field, but not too long, so we could still apply pressure.

George Gregan passed to Mat Rogers inside their 22, with Lewis Moody, who had replaced Richard Hill, putting Rogers under massive pressure. None of this was new to us though. We'd already completed hundreds, if not thousands, of drills with Phil Larder, our defensive coach, working on a strong defensive line, with one player applying huge pressure to the kicker by focusing on closing down their kicking foot, not just the ball. So, if you missed the ball, you at least smothered the man, in a legal fashion. Consequently, rather than taking a line-out in our own half, we had one around 30 metres from their try-line, as Rogers sliced his kick, so 'Moodos' had done his job.

This was our moment. There was little communication at this stage, as we all knew exactly what we needed to do. We had a pattern called 'zig-zag', where we aimed to move up the field between the 15s, to get us in to position, either to make a line break and score, to get a penalty, or to provide Jonny Wilkinson with the opportunity to kick a drop goal.

I was tired, but I knew that this was what all the sacrifice was about. Hundreds of people, the players, staff and families, had all given everything over a number of years, building up to this moment. We just had to focus. We had a team call, where if you made a mistake someone would shout out 'next job', to ensure you moved on, forgot about it and focused on the next play, but making a mistake was the last thing on our minds at this stage.

From the line-out, most people would have bet on us throwing the ball to our captain, Martin Johnson at the front of the line-out, as there would be a higher percentage chance of us retaining and securing possession in the Australian half, and we could build an attack from there. Ben Kay, who was in the middle of the line-out, made the call for Steve Thompson to throw to the back, meaning there was one last lift, one last effort for me. Lawrence Dallaglio was the front lifter for 'Moodos' and I was at the back. Thommo hit just below double-top, with a near-perfect throw for Lewis to catch, and immediately get the ball away off the top to Matt Dawson for us to launch an attack.

Mike Catt, who had come on for Mike Tindall at inside centre at the end of normal time, burst forward with the ball in hand and smashed in to the Australians, with Will Greenwood in support from the outside and myself from the inside. Front jumper Johno had joined the move as soon as the ball went over his head from Thommo's throw and we were pushing forward with all of our remaining energy. The drill had happened in the blink of an eye, but had been executed perfectly. If the hosts didn't know already, we were threatening and we were ready to strike.

The great thing about our team was the familiarity we had with every move. It was almost autonomous. Our communication had evolved from verbal to visual, as we'd worked so hard together for so long, analysing previous games and facing similar situations, so much so that game scenarios were ingrained in to all of us. We knew what we had to do, and we knew we could do it even under the most intense of pressure. Catty looked after the ball like it was the most precious thing he'd held in his life, and we all gave him the support he needed. At this stage, one of the props would normally come in to have a sniff at the contact and both arrived, probably looking for a breather, but they ensured that the ball was ours.

Jonny was waiting. Probably 38-40 metres out, so it would have taken a huge drop kick from him. The Australians were offside and were edging forward, so it could have quite easily been a penalty for us, but we knew, with the way the game was being refereed, that we wouldn't be given a thing. Sir Clive Woodward had introduced a mantra to the ethos of the team, T-CUP (Thinking Correctly Under Pressure), and this passage of play was one of the best examples of this. Matt Dawson could have taken the obvious option and passed the ball to Jonny for him to drop kick us to glory from distance. Instead, he followed T-CUP, and also the great work we had done with Dr Sheryll Calder, on visual skills and scanning a situation, and with ProZone, and Daws got his head up and saw the space. George Smith was ready to put pressure on Jonny, as the Australians were expecting the kick, but Daws had dummy passed and was gone in a flash and broke through their defensive line, with me, Will and Jason Robinson close by, and we gained crucial yards.

After Matt's break, I found myself in the scrum half position. We'd all practised passing skills intensely over the years, and I, probably more than most, had worked closely with the nines who had played for England. Sometimes when we went in to wide areas, I would cover that role for Daws, or for Kyran Bracken, or Andy Gomersall when they played, so I was used to being there. I knew that Jonny was in the pocket and we had great blockage around the contact area, but before there was time to think, this great, imposing hulk of a man, Martin Johnson, appeared. In that moment he could have just become an extra blocker, allowing me to pass to Jonny, but that wasn't what our team was about. We always found a way to put the best people in their best positions, and there was never a more crucial time to do it.

Daws was our best passer, and a hugely experienced scrum half, and we needed him on the ball to make the final pass. Johno took the ball off a short pass from me, and probably only gained us a matter of inches, but what he enabled us to do was to bring Daws back to his feet, to scrum half and set us up for a shot at glory. At that moment, under massive pressure, everyone seemed pretty cool and there was no real rush. We were set and we were ready. When I look back today at video footage, the Australians were up, they were offside, but as I've said, we couldn't count on this and we had to make something happen ourselves, rather than look for a decision from the referee.

Having cleared Johno out, bent on one knee, I'm powerless. There's nothing left to do, but to trust in my team-mates. These guys, these warriors, who I would run through walls for. I can see Daws shaping to pass, and I can see Jonny waiting, and I can hear nothing. Over the years we had all learnt from those painful defeats, those nearly moments, especially the grand slam attempts, in order to not make the same mistake more than once. We'd got to the stage where we were doing things and making decisions on instinct, and we had a track-record to support that. We'd already beaten the Australians at home in autumn 2002 and again away in the summer before the World Cup, so there was no reason why we couldn't do it for a third time. The World Cup Final is just your next game, and it's about winning. We had incredible levels of expectation on us as we were ranked number one in the world, and then the criticism such as the Aussie press labelling us as 'Dad's Army', and I was definitely one of them at the age of 34 during the tournament!

When the ball left Matt's hands on its way to Jonny, there's the blur of the crowd in the background, and I'm still on one knee. Jonny takes the ball cleanly and kicks with his wrong foot, although in fairness, he could always kick with both feet. I still can't hear a thing. I'm in a bubble, and yet there is so obviously noise everywhere. People forget that Jonny has already missed three drop kicks and this is his fourth attempt, but it's Jonny, and this is everything we have been building towards. If you give a man of his calibre enough chances, then he will make you pay.

I'm still looking at him and Jonny makes contact with the ball. Good contact, perhaps not the best he's ever struck, but certainly the most important. I can see the referee, André Watson, and as the ball sails towards, and then clearly between the uprights, I see his arm lift to acknowledge the score, but I know it's over anyway. I turn my eyes to the scoreboard and the time. We're ahead, but there's time left. Time for Australia to come back again. I'm sprinting to get in to position to receive the kick-off, and the referee will give them the time to try and build an attack, I'm sure of that. Twenty seconds remain, but it doesn't feel as if we are getting back as quickly as we normally would. We were fitter than people gave us credit for, but we were obviously tired, both physically and emotionally. This was it. The Webb Ellis Trophy was within touching distance, but we weren't there yet. For all the euphoria in the stands, and on the other side of the world in the pubs and the living rooms across England, we are just shouting at each other to get in to position. On the biggest of stages, all we need is to execute the basics of rugby, just one last time.

Australia raced in to place and kicked short, to give themselves a chance of getting the ball back for one last assault on our defence. Nearly 100 minutes of going toe-to-toe with each other, two of the best sides in the world, and there's just one more battle to face, one more challenge to win and we're there. The short kick from the Aussies reaches our loose-head prop, Trevor Woodman. I always say that what Trevor did, right then, securing possession for us by cleanly catching the ball, was just as important as Jonny's winning drop goal, if not quite as memorable. Whether they kicked to Trevor intentionally I'm not sure, but with no disrespect to props, especially if they've been on the pitch for over 99 minutes, they wouldn't be your first choice to take a crucial catch in a World Cup Final. Australia certainly kicked short deliberately though, and with five seconds remaining it was the only option they had to force an error or recapture the pill.

Once Trevor claimed the ball, we were like bees to a honeypot. We all swarmed to him to help retain it. We knew that we just had to win the ball, keep it and kick in to the seats, over the touchline and the trophy would be ours. Catty, who had a superb game against Wales in the quarter-finals and France in the semi-finals, was ready and waiting in the pocket. The management team's introduction of Catty in the Wales game at half-time was a real masterstroke, and his kicking game was perfect that day. This, together with the fact he had previously been used to take the pressure off

Jonny against France, kept Mike Tindall out of the number 12 shirt for the semi-final.

With the stadium clock past 100 minutes, Catty received the ball from Daws and with one true, sweet kick to touch, he cleared the management bench, reached the seats in the stand, and all I can do is look to the referee. I still remember to this day thinking, 'The game's not over until the referee blows the final whistle.' I didn't have to wait for long. Ben Kay has a double-take to check that the whistle is gone, and we all leap for the sky. England, our team, our country, our staff, all of us together – are the world champions. Everything we have worked for over the years, the final professional piece of the jigsaw of possible trophies to be won, is no longer a dream; it is right in front of our eyes as a reality.

No one can ever really have a perfect game; players, management, the referee, but this was as close as I had to a perfect feeling. Looking back, for example, we, or should I say Clive and his staff, removed Phil Vickery on 80 minutes. Phil was absolutely smashing their scrum, time after time, but he was being penalised unfairly by the referee. Only he can answer why he was doing that to Phil. So Jason Leonard replaced Phil, and using his previous experience told the referee that at scrum time he would not go forward, back, up or down, but just stay in there and not scrummage, so he couldn't be penalised. That takes real discipline to do, but Leopard (as we called him) did it perfectly and we didn't give any further penalties away! That's what I mean about a perfect game being difficult to achieve. Phil had a great 80 minutes, he was tremendous, but because of someone else, the referee, he had to be replaced and that was hard on him, but Leopard's experience was just what we needed. We had an incredible level of trust in each other; in ability, but also in character. I'm probably giving Australia too much credit for picking out Trevor, for example, but I never doubted for one second that we would hold on to the ball, and that Catty would smash the ball and us to victory.

Once I heard the final whistle, I just went ballistic. My emotions were all over the place. I jumped in to Johno's arms, and for the first time ever I was taller than him, as he lifted me up. It was just unreal, incredible, and so difficult to explain. We were so disciplined throughout, that the final whistle was like a huge release for us all. I knew, personally, that this was going to be my last World Cup, as I was 34 and I wasn't going to be playing four years later at the age of 38. I'd been fortunate enough to play in two World Cups previously, reaching the semi-finals and the quarter-finals, so this was my way of completing the jigsaw. As a club and international player, I had won everything I could win, apart from the World Cup and now we were world champions for the next four years.

Around 30 seconds later, I turned my attention to my family. In the heat of the moment, and my focus, I remembered that I didn't know where they were. At Leicester Tigers or England games at Twickenham, I knew exactly where to look, and I would wave to them, but on this day, of all days, I hadn't a clue where they were. My four-year-old daughter Olivia and my 14-month-old son, Finley, along with Dorian West's wife and children, were the only kids at the ground from the players' families, alongside my wife, Ali, and her sister Linda, who was a great support during an emotional time for us all. It took me a couple of minutes of staring and searching, but I found them. I just wanted to share this achievement with them, as they had always been there for me, supporting and motivating me. Perhaps I should credit Dr. Sherylle Calder, for giving me the sharpness of eye to pick them out? It was like looking for a needle in a haystack.

In sport and business, and in life in general, there is always sacrifice, but I can only tell my own story. I'd missed out on so much family time over the years in pursuit of sporting achievement, and I'm not moaning about that, it was my choice and was something that we all bought in to as a family. I missed the Uruguay game in the group stages of the tournament to be at the bedside of Olivia, who was very ill, and she joyfully came in to my arms on the pitch, but Finley didn't know who I was. That was the price of being away on tour and missing out on getting to know my son. I mean, he was so young, it was an 8pm kick-off, then extra time, and there were no real provisions for families, so he wasn't in the best of moods and to be fair to him, he regrets it a bit now! But that moment hit home for me. I guess the fact I was a sweaty, smelly, blood-stained, horrible man with a thug's haircut, didn't really help in endearing me to my son. But the sacrifice was worth it. If we hadn't won the final, I think it would have been the worst trip Ali had ever been on. Two young children, although she had her sister Linda to help, all the travel, firstly over to Australia and then while we were out there, the accommodation which was provided wasn't great either, so I think if we hadn't lifted the trophy I would have been in serious trouble with the missus!

In a matter of moments, I went from the euphoria of winning the trophy and celebrating with everyone, to bawling my eyes out. We all knew what we had been through to get here and crying was just a release. I couldn't have been happier, and all I wanted to do was celebrate and share the moment with my family. We had beaten Australia 20-17, on their own patch, to win the 2003 Rugby World Cup; the first northern hemisphere side to do it in the history of the competition. Against all the odds and the doubters, we were the best in the world and no one could take that away from us. We had the medal and the cup to come, but I didn't need them to know what we had achieved. Rugby, for me, was always about enjoyment, working hard and winning. My mantra was always to never fail through lack of effort, and I was always driven to succeed at anything I put my mind to.

I stood on the pitch, holding my daughter Olivia, who had attended her first game at the age of just two weeks, having been born the day before we met up for the 1999 Rugby World Cup. I remember thinking back to her birth, which fortunately I was there for, but then had to dash off to meet up with the squad. I'd been up all night and was shattered, arrived and booked in to the hotel after a two-hour journey and went to my room and dumped my bags before going to the toilet. The phone then rang to tell me that I had to go to reception to meet drug testers and give a urine sample. I went down to reception, tried to explain the circumstances, and even asked the testers to sit with me while I slept, so when I woke I could give the sample. Thankfully, Phil Larder and Clive sorted the situation with me, and I was able to give the sample the following morning. I suppose it shows my mindset after the final, that I was thinking back to key moments in my life, and everything seemed to be flashing in front of my eyes. It really was like an out-of-body experience.

Typically, Johno, being the great leader of men, calmed everything and lightened the mood. He also showed more emotional intelligence than John Howard, the Australian Prime Minister of the time, who was about to present him with the Webb Ellis Trophy on the podium in the centre of the pitch, with the eyes of the stadium and the world on him. You would think that with a young child on there with him, he would have been aware and engaged, but he was emotionless. I suppose he was disappointed with losing. Johno turned to Olivia and said, 'Shall we go and get the trophy?' and she replied, 'Yeah, I'll do it Johno!' which is when I stepped in and suggested we let Johno handle this one on his own. He epitomised what our team was about, and what rugby should be about as a team sport, not about the individual. I couldn't express how proud I was to be stood behind this man who had led us so well, who we all respected so much. There were plenty of guys in that team who captained their club sides, and who could easily have been England captain, but there was only one Johno. To his credit, Jonny Wilkinson understood that as well. He was the star of the team, but he put the hard yards in as everyone else did over the years, and we suffered and eventually triumphed, together. I trusted all of those guys and as I looked them all in the eyes, as we waited for Johno to lift the trophy, I knew what a special moment this was and how I would have done anything for any of them.

As I look back now, I can appreciate and understand, having been a coach myself, how Clive and his staff must have been feeling at this moment. All of their work and sacrifice, just like ourselves as players, built up to this crowning glory. I can also appreciate the challenge he must have faced in trying to get articulate messages across to the players, in pressure-cooker atmospheres and he must have felt powerless at times, either sat in the stand or stood on the sideline. I was pleased for him, and for his wife, Jayne, who was great in the background with the families and was always supportive. I'm sure that Clive, himself, when Jonny's kick sailed over, wasn't thinking that we'd done it. He would have been anxious and thinking how long is left and eager to see us all get back in to position. No one would have heard a thing at the time, but Clive had done everything he could over the years leading up to the final. In fact, Jason Leonard was quoted as saying after the final that Clive didn't really need to be there. That is the greatest accolade you could pay to a coach, in saying that their job has been done, their preparation complete and that was how we all felt with Clive at the helm. We were in control of our own destiny and he had helped to make everything as certain as possible. I'm not taking anything away from him and the changes he made during the game, and the things said at full time, to prepare us for extra time, but we knew what we needed to do. We got in to a huddle before extra time and I think that anything said to us by the coaching staff, like 'play in their half' or references to territory, or possession, was kind of met with a 'no shit' reply. As I say, we knew what we had to do and the staff had created that culture, along with the players, for us to take responsibility ourselves.

My words to my family, for challenges we achieved throughout life, were, 'We've only gone and done it!' and they were the first words I said as I reached the touchline, and we celebrated. I looked at Ali, who was in tears, and hugged and kissed her and Linda, and I held Olivia, with her hair in bows and an England flag painted on her face, and it was hard to know what to say, and Finley, bless him, didn't really know where he was. We were all overcome and I suppose I felt relief more than anything. We'd dealt with the pressure and the expectation.

I was privileged to be in this position. I didn't want to sound greedy, but having won everything else I could in the game, I just wanted this. I wanted it for my family, for my parents who had supported me so much. My mind wandered back years, to my first coach, Jack Carnell. I joined my first junior club when I was around four years old, and my older brother played, as well as my next-door neighbour's son, and they were slightly older and I was encouraged to go along. Jack played until in to his 70s, he was around 50 when he coached me, and is sadly no longer with us, but he made rugby enjoyable, about praising each other and skill acquisition. In fact, the tackle technique that he taught me I used throughout my playing days, and I still use that as a coach today. I thought back to presenting one of my first international shirts to Jack, and you think back to all the people who helped you, and you almost have to pinch yourself to believe where you are.

We had some group photos to take, and it was time for me to return Olivia to Ali. We were still on the pitch, but Ali needed to get the children back to the hotel. I arranged to meet them later, a lot later. I got my hands on the Webb Ellis Trophy on the pitch; held it, kissed it and said a few private words to it, which was great. I didn't want to touch it until then, until it was ours for certain. Then it was about spending time with each other, the players and staff, so we could be together and celebrate the achievement. I'm not just saying this, but everyone involved was as important as Jonny, Johno, Clive and the rest of us; and the supporters were something else. We had to try and focus and block the noise out of our minds as it could have become a distraction, but we all knew they were there, and it felt as if we could hear them back home in England too.

In the dressing room, we were able to celebrate privately. I think Prince Harry was there, and the then Sports Minister, Tessa Jowell was there too, and Moodos told her in no uncertain terms that the photos were for those involved, and not her. There were a lot of people trying to get involved in photos, and I realise that in some way, the Sports Minister would have made a contribution to our sport, but this was our time and Moodos wasn't having any of it. We sipped some champagne, drank a few beers, went along to a media function and it wasn't until around 1am that we finally got to our after-party and I was reunited with Ali, as Linda had offered to take care of the kids with a friend, so we could celebrate as a couple. It was hard for Linda, as they had to get a cab and communication was down in Sydney as the phone networks were overloaded. I think they had to get a ferry too, it was manic for them trying to get the kids back to the sanctuary of the hotel, but once we knew they were safe and settled we could enjoy this amazing, once-in-a-lifetime evening, or early hours as it was. We were with the team and the management, and we had a good drink, until around 6am.

We had to leave as Ali was boarding a flight at around 11am to go back home to the UK, and we were walking through the streets trying to get a taxi, while keeping in the shadows and trying to avoid being mobbed by everyone who was still out celebrating.

I couldn't resist speaking to one fella though. This England fan was stood outside a bar, with his replica shirt on, with my name and number on his back. I tapped him on the shoulder, he turned around and nearly fainted. We had a laugh and then we were jumped on by his mates and had one last celebration with the fans. I finally navigated the streets and cabs of Sydney, got Ali home to the hotel to pack for her flight, and I had my next challenge to face – more drinking and celebrating, before we returned home ourselves, as the world champions.

2

The Hand Of Back

I NEVER once took my eye off, or undervalued, representing my country. That was an honour and a privilege, but 2001/02 was a season where club rugby, and helping to drive Leicester Tigers on to further unprecedented success, was my priority.

With England, everything was building towards the 2003 Rugby World Cup, and there was plenty to play for at international level in 2002, but at Tigers, we had our eyes on more than one prize.

Looking to record a fourth straight Premiership title, both for the club and for myself, with Dean Richards at the helm, we were also attempting to become the first club to retain the European Cup in the competition's history, following our dramatic victory over Stade Francais the previous season. Deano decided to strengthen the ranks and ensure we had a stronger squad to cope with the demands and pressures of striving for success on all fronts. We needed to replace Pat Howard, who was a key player and was returning to Australia to play for the ACT Brumbies. As Johno recalled in his self-titled autobiography, Rod Kafer, the ACT centre, pretty much crossed with Pat in mid-air to sign for us, as did Josh Kronfeld.

The signing of Josh had a few people questioning the balance of the squad and whether there would be enough places for the likes of myself, Josh, Lewis Moody and other talent in the back row such as Martin Corry, Will Johnson, Adam Balding and Paul Gustard. Deano spoke to me about signing Josh, and I felt that he would provide greater competition for places, and that would improve the quality of the squad and ultimately, the team. I wanted that pressure on me to deliver. Josh was a world-class player and was an All Blacks legend, so I felt that he could help me to develop, and help to bring Lewis's game along too. Plus, it was always going to be a demanding year with so many competitions, international rugby, and we were just coming off the back of the 2001 British & Irish Lions tour of Australia, which was physically and emotionally draining.

Deano decided to rest those Lions players at the start of the season, and we were given a reality check on the first day as we lost 19-16 away to Newcastle Falcons. Despite keeping the Lions players on the bench for the second game against London Wasps, we were on top, but with the likes of Johno, Austin Healey, Martin Corry and myself to come on, we eventually smashed them 45-15, to start a five-match winning run, which ended when Leeds Tykes beat us 37-16 in November.

It seemed that during that season, each time we lost a game or were given a warning, we stood tall and reacted in the right way. The Leeds defeat saw us then record ten wins on the bounce in the league, taking us through to the end of March. We were simply tearing teams apart. Unfortunately, Josh had picked up an injury in pre-season, which gave Lewis a chance to shine and he developed rapidly, being rewarded with a place in the England squad as well, and he never looked back.

To little surprise, we wrapped up our fourth consecutive Premiership title with relative ease. We took our responsibilities seriously as a team, and we never felt that the title was ours until it was mathematically assured, but the media and the general public had pretty much crowned us by Christmas, and the statistics back that up. We finished the season with 18 wins and four defeats from our 22 league matches, and were 14 points clear of our nearest rivals, Sale Sharks, in second place. We had the best defence, the best points difference, most tries scored and least tries conceded. We were dominant, pretty much from start to finish of that season and to record four consecutive league titles was, and still is, a remarkable achievement, one which I am very proud to have been a part of.

During the season, much debate took place on the introduction of the play-off system to the English Premiership. Halfway through the season, it was announced that the champions would be decided via the play-offs, and eventually, after much pressure, the decision was reversed and an eight-team play-off championship took place at the end of the season, including a 'wildcard' entry in to Europe for the winner. We lost our home quarter-final 13-27 to Bristol Shoguns, who went on to reach the final before losing 28-23 to Gloucester at Twickenham. I think it took everyone involved in rugby time to get used to the play-off system, and we as players were not very well prepared for this new introduction to the sport. I can sort of understand it now, and agree with the system, as the fact that international fixtures clash with domestic fixtures, can really distort the league table, so the play-offs is a fair way of deciding the eventual champion, while also ensuring excitement right up to the final day. Sadly, I feel like the current championship play-off system is unjust against the team that wins the division, as they aren't really affected by internationals, and it's harsh on recruitment at that level too. If you are running away with the division, looking to plan for next season around November, December or January time in preparation for reaching the Premiership, then you can't, as you won't know what division you will be in until right at the end of the season. I experienced this during my time coaching at Leeds, and it was hugely frustrating.

Getting back to my playing days and Ian 'Dosser' Smith, the former Tigers flanker, who retired as I joined Leicester Tigers and later became one of our coaches, once said to me, probably with the aim of motivating me, 'It's a massive game at the weekend,' and I replied, 'The next game is always the massive game.' It was always about winning for me, whoever we played against, and that included that play-off game against Bristol in 2002. I was hugely disappointed as we'd won the league, but if you could pick a competition to lose, as a sacrifice to ensure you won the major trophies on offer, then this would be it. We also bowed out of the Powergen Cup at the quarter-final stage, losing 22-20 to Harlequins. We had an incredible culture at the club at that time where we didn't just want to compete, we always wanted to win. When we won, we loved it and when we lost, we hated it, but probably learned more from those disappointments, which helped us to go on to achieve further success.

Despite our continued domestic dominance, with that fourth consecutive title, the 2001/02 season will always be remembered for the Heineken Cup and specifically my role in the final. As a northern hemisphere rugby club player, success in Europe is the biggest challenge and you want to test yourself against the best of the best. Success at that level is the highest accolade for a club player and in some cases European games were even harder than international games, such was the quality of the opposition. We were all aware of just how difficult it had been to win the trophy in 2001; that game against Stade Francais, winning 34-30, has to rank as my favourite game, alongside the 2003 World Cup Final. The way we won, with a late try from Leon Lloyd, and Tim Stimpson's assured kick from the tightest of angles, and then an unforgettable moment, celebrating with the Tigers fans on the streets of Paris, was something I would always cherish.

To repeat that success we knew we would have to become the first side in history to win the European Cup back-to-back. In fact, no side had actually won the trophy more than once since the competition's inception in 1995, and English and Scottish teams only joined the competition a year later, when we lost in the final against French club Brive, at the Millennium Stadium. We were drawn in Pool One against Llanelli of Wales, Perpignan of France and Italian side Calvisano. With only the six group winners and best two group runners-up to go through, there was once again little room for error, and the pressure was all on us as the holders, but we felt confident and believed that we were up to the task.

We won five games on the bounce, meaning we had already qualified by the time we went to Wales for the final group game, against Llanelli. It wasn't as comfortable as it sounds though, as they gave us a real scare at Welford Road in the opening match, and we hung on for a 12-9 win under intense pressure. That was probably the test we needed, against players like Scott Quinnell and Stephen Jones, and then a tight 31-30 win against Perpignan in the third game, showed that we had the ability and the nous to see out a game and get the points. In the final group fixture Llanelli needed the win to qualify as one of the best runners-up and they outplayed us for a 24-12 victory, which left us sweating on a home quarter-final, but results had gone our way and we were to face Leinster at Welford Road.

Leinster had won Pool Six with the same record as us and it was only points difference and tries scored that saw us at home, rather than travelling to Ireland. We won 29-18 to set up a third mouth-watering clash against Llanelli in the semi-final, to be played at Nottingham Forest Football Club's City Ground stadium. It underlined what a tough pool we had progressed from, as we faced the runner-up in Llanelli, and the third-placed side, Perpignan, reached the final the following season.

The semi-final was tight and cagey, which was no surprise as we knew each other very well, and had won our respective home matches. Make no mistake, they were a quality side, and this was a game where we needed to summon all of our experience to get over the line. All looked lost as we trailed 12-10 approaching the final whistle, but despite piling forward and exerting real pressure on them, we just couldn't get a penalty in their half. With seconds left on the clock, we were awarded a penalty inside our own half, and before Johno or any of the senior players had the chance to discuss what to do, Tim Stimpson pointed towards the posts. It was a huge call from Stimmo as it would take a monumental kick to get the three points we needed to reach the final. He was nearly 60 metres from the posts but he calmly stepped up and smashed the ball towards the target. As time seemed to stand still, and with our hearts in our mouths, the ball dropped rapidly, hit the crossbar, bounced up against the left-hand post and dropped over the bar, to give us the win. It was a simply incredible kick and a moment I'll never forget.

Stimmo showed real character, firstly in making the decision to kick for goal rather than for touch, and secondly for achieving the almost impossible with his kick, and win us the match. He was quite a character anyway, to be honest. He'd once mentioned to me that he found it helpful talking to trees on a hilltop, which was certainly different, but whatever his methods, the end result took us to a second consecutive European Cup Final, which only Brive had done before. They failed to win the second time, but we wanted to create history.

There was a feeling of relief at reaching the final, but also at the manner in which we achieved it. Johno talked about feeling sorry for Llanelli, especially as they had lost in a similar manner to Northampton in 2000, but I can honestly say I didn't feel sorry for them at all. That's just sport at the elite level, and we had faced our fair share of unlucky results and decisions, as well as criticism and pressure, so I felt we deserved our bit of luck. Little did I know what was to come.

We were determined to take our chance and hold on to the trophy we'd worked so hard to secure in the first place. Back in 1997, we'd beaten the best French side of the time and the holders, Toulouse, in a fantastic semi-final and then we lost the final 28-9 to Brive at Cardiff Arms Park. We had prepared poorly, were not focused mentally, and it took us four years to get another shot at glory. Now, we were back in Cardiff, at the Millennium Stadium, and we weren't ready to let go of our crown.

Munster had reached the final by winning five of their six pool matches, finishing in second place to Castres Olympique. They beat the previous year's runners-up, Stade Francais, 16-14 in Paris, and then returned to France to beat Castres 25-17 in the semi-final. The final four teams had all come from Pools One and Four, and Munster had certainly done it the hard way, underlining what a challenge we were set to face.

The Millennium Stadium was packed, with over 74,000 people and the atmosphere and sense of occasion was incredible. When you look back at the teamsheet and replacements on the day, it was a real world-class calibre match, and it was always likely to be a tight game, coming down to one or two key moments. We trailed 6-5 at half-time, with a Geordan Murphy try our only score, and as much as it pains me to say it, Austin Healey scored a superb breakaway try in the second half and with Stimmo's conversion and a penalty ten minutes later we led 15-9 going in to the final ten minutes. As for Austin, and why it pains me to praise him, I'm often asked why people take an instant disliking to him and my answer is simple – because it saves time! He is a character, and his skill and guile put us firmly in the driving seat to retain the trophy.

With moments remaining in the game, a game we had deserved to win, I put my head down for one last push at the scrum. I'd done this a thousand times, but just as Munster's scrum half Peter Stringer was about to put the ball in, I glanced towards him and with sleight of hand, I tapped it away from him towards Dorian West, giving us possession and ending any Munster hopes of a last-minute victory. Peter Stringer was not only Munster's number nine, he was Ireland's number nine, and a very accomplished player. He was fuming. He chased the referee after we had cleared to touch, and once we won the resulting line-out, we cleared to touch again and in the blink of an eye we were European champions for the second year in a row. We were history-makers.

Sadly, victory was overshadowed by a hysterical reaction after the match in the media regarding my illegal tap at the scrum, which was named as 'The Hand of Back' in reference to Diego Maradona's infamous 'Hand of God' moment in the 1986 football World Cup in Mexico, against England.

For the first time, in writing, I wanted to explain how I viewed the incident at the time and how I feel looking back today. The analogy I would use to describe what happened is this; imagine someone who enjoys a fat cream cake, and then imagine that cream cake being placed right in front of their face. The person takes a look around to check that no one is looking, and then they grab it and take a huge bite. There was no one around me. The touch judges and the referee were both unsighted, so I took the cream off the top of the cake, so to speak.

If what happened had happened at any other point of the game, we just wouldn't be talking about it today. There were many incidents that happened during that game, and in other games, that were far worse than that, which are never mentioned. We were bemused, for example, when Johno scored a perfectly good try, after we pressurised Munster and won the ball from their short line-out just a few metres from their line. We did nothing wrong, but the French referee, Joël Jutge, ordered the line-out to be retaken six inches away from where it was taken! That incident, for example, had more of an impact than what I did at the end of the game, yet it's never mentioned because of when it happened. We also felt that Peter Clohessy was scrummaging illegally throughout the whole 80 minutes, but we just had to get on with it. Illegal things happen and mistakes happen, but we never complained, despite the retaken line-out directly costing us points.

Although the Munster players were upset that they had lost the game, and protested to the referee about the incident, no one player in the Munster team had a go at me after the game. None of their management said a word to me about it. It was the media who created a massive story out of it. I think Brian Moore, who was commentating on the game at the time actually stated that it was a piece of brilliance, or words to that effect. It was autonomous behaviour, not something I'd planned or been coached to do, but something that happened in the moment. I suppose that if I'd thought about it, I wouldn't have done it.

My wife, Ali, gave her opinion on the incident, and the effect the aftermath had on the family for the book and said, 'What stands out to me about the whole "Hand of Back" thing, was that it didn't decide the game. What I do remember more than anything about it though, were the death threats that we received to our family home. I know that letters were sent to the club, but to get them sent to our home when you have a small child, and I was hormonal as I was heavily pregnant with Fin, was absolutely terrifying. It was a real invasion of our privacy, and it brought it home to me that whatever he did would be judged in the public eye. I didn't think of him as a particularly dirty player, I mean, Johno was always getting in trouble wasn't he? I was so surprised with the impact it had. I remember speaking to my sister Linda about it, and she reassured me that this kind of thing happened in the celebrity world as such, but I never saw us as being part of that world. I suppose it would have been so much worse if it had happened during the days of social media.'

When I'm asked about the incident today, I always attempt to make light of it, not out of arrogance, but out of trying to bring some perspective to the situation. The upside, ironically, is that I helped to develop Peter Stringer to become a better scrum half as he has never allowed anything like this to happen to him again, and I'm not trying to claim credit there, it's just factual. The downside of 'The Hand of Back' is that I have to spend an extra bit of time polishing another European Cup medal! That's the way I try to look back at the day, and the decision I took, in that split second, to tap the ball away from Peter, and secure possession. I don't regret what I did, I want to make that clear. It was part of the game and it was the decision I took at the time.

In that game, players at the contact area illegally fished the ball out with their hands, yet weren't penalised. Another way of looking at this, is that if I had been caught doing it, it wouldn't necessarily have resulted in Munster winning the game. They would have been awarded a penalty, but they still would have had to get past us, which they hadn't done once in the game leading up to that final minute, and three points would have been of no use to them as they trailed

15-9. Even if I'd been sin-binned for the offence and we had gone down to 14 men, there would have been no guarantee that with little time left on the clock, they could have beaten us. New Zealand couldn't manage it a year later with our England side down to 13 men, and they were one of the best sides in the world.

To summarise, what I did was illegal, but the game is full of acts that come close, or often cross the line, in terms of the rules and regulations we play within. If you don't sometimes, just sometimes, and at the right time, go close to the edge or past it, then you won't be part of a winning team. No one adheres to all the rules in sport, or in life in general. We make decisions in the heat of the moment and we make errors of judgement, or do things that perhaps others wouldn't do, and that's life. Ideally, no one would cheat, no one would gain a competitive advantage, but they do and you have to accept it.

In over 500 senior games and 17 years in the professional game, playing in a highly-pressured and competitive environment, I only stood in front of a disciplinary committee twice. Once was eight years in to my career and the second time was for my last club game against Wasps at Twickenham, so I can look back without regret and stand by my record.

In the days and weeks following the game, the club received a few letters addressed to me, from passionate Munster supporters and even a few from Leicester Tigers fans, who felt what I had done was wrong. There were threatening letters too, but for me, these people who threatened my life, or those around me, weren't true supporters of the game of rugby. Anyway, I've spoken with a couple of Irish friends since then, who assured me that if the threats were real, I wouldn't be here today to tell the story. Trust me, I believed them. In fact, at the time, the president of Munster said that if one of their players had done what I did, they would have named him Mayor! I'm still waiting for the invitation from Leicester.

3

Of Bottlers And Nearly Men

ENGLAND, 2002. Nine matches and an incredible eight wins. But only remembered for our failure; for being classed as bottlers and nearly men.

At the end of 2002 we were ranked number one in the world, but losing one game, just one game to France, was an absolute travesty. We should have been elated about where we were, to look at the bigger picture and see that we were standing on the edge of glory, but instead we were gutted to once again come so close and yet finish so far from the prize. There was a reason for that though; a backstory of years of coming so close, winning game after game and then missing out at the final hurdle, when it mattered most.

We'd had the heartache of 1999, 2000 and 2001, and we were sure that this was the year to put it right. In 1999 we lost 32-31 to Wales at Wembley in the final minutes, which cost us the grand slam and the last-ever Five Nations Championship. That was a key result, as through that defeat, we learned the lesson of how to build a score; three, six, nine points, meaning the opposition would have to score twice, instead of us kicking to the corner and trying to force a try as we did at Wembley. We learned the hard way. They scored a brilliant try through Scott Gibbs and then Neil Jenkins's conversion sent Wales wild and broke our hearts. I guess it was like a rite of passage for us, but there was more to come.

In 2000, the first Six Nations Championship, including Italy making their debut in the competition, we smashed Ireland 50-18 at home first up, and then we beat France on the road and Wales at home, and then smashed Italy too. That Italy game included a drop goal from yours truly! I'm the only England forward to ever kick a drop goal. Beat that Jonny!

Anyway, we finished the competition at Murrayfield against Scotland, knowing a win would seal a grand slam. Again, we learned harsh lessons. Our training all week had been in perfect, dry conditions, but when we lined up for the national anthems, and it may surprise people to learn that I love listening to 'Flower of Scotland', we soon realised that the rain was coming down, and within 20 minutes of the game there was a quarter of an inch of rain on the surface of the pitch. We continued with our normal style of play, while Scotland kicked, chased, hacked and harried and got a result, and once again our hearts were broken. They played the conditions and they taught us a lesson.

Later that year, we played Argentina in similar conditions to the Scotland game, this time at Twickenham, and we adopted the right tactics and learned from the heartbreak of Murrayfield, winning 19-0. That showed real strength and character within our team. We weren't always the prettiest of teams, perhaps we 'won ugly' at times, but we learned from our errors and each time we lost, which in fairness wasn't very often, we always attempted to put things right immediately.

In 2001, as a result of the foot and mouth outbreak, Ireland's three matches against Scotland, Wales and ourselves were delayed until the autumn. We absolutely destroyed Wales, Scotland, Italy and France back in the spring and just needed to win in Dublin to end this run we were on of failing the final test, to achieve the grand slam. Crucially, Ireland had the momentum of having played two matches, including a great win at the Millennium Stadium against Wales, before playing us and we lost 20-14. For the third year running we had fallen at the final hurdle. Heartbreak once again. Perhaps if we had played Ireland in the spring, it would have been different? Who knows? We were flying though and the delay of six months between the France and Ireland games, albeit with a tour of Canada and the USA in between, must have played a part in us missing out on another grand slam. I think all of the pain and heartache of coming so close to success helped to bond the team together, and increase the collective hunger to get it right, eventually, whatever it took.

Having missed out for three years running in the final game of the competition, we went again in 2002 hoping to go one step further, but circumstances seemed to conspire against us. After disposing of Scotland at Murrayfield, 29-3, and then Ireland two weeks later at Twickenham, 45-11, our chances seemed to hinge on the third match of the tournament in Paris against the French. Johno was given a 21-day ban for punching Saracens hooker Robbie Russell while playing for the Tigers, which caused a great deal of controversy and debate as to whether he had been singled out, due to his stature within the game, almost to make an example of him. In the end, Leicester Tigers appealed the decision, which then allowed Johno to lead us out for the crucial game in France. The media storm seemed to suggest that this flouted the rules, but it didn't, as Tigers and Johno were well within their rights to appeal the decision.

Johno had missed the 2000 defeat to Scotland and the loss in Ireland in 2001, with the results and performances on those days no coincidence in my mind. He would say that one man doesn't make a difference, being the kind of guy he is. He would always push the fact that rugby is a team game, and we were a good enough side to win without him, but we knew just how key he was and I was sure he would have made a difference.

So Johno was eligible to play against France, but this time, it didn't make a difference. I often think about that game, and the image of me slumped on my haunches in despair, as another grand slam attempt was left in tatters. I was absolutely devastated. Again. This time it was over for us after three games, rather than five, and in some ways that was harder to take, as without being arrogant we were used to going in to the final day with the grand slam still at stake. Taking nothing away from that French side, they scored two tries and were 14-0 ahead before we knew what had hit us, and they were an accomplished defensive unit, so it was too long a road back for us. Ben Cohen screamed in for a late try, but that flattered us really as we weren't good enough to cope with the French on the day.

After that game, we were labelled 'nearly men' and quite harshly as 'bottlers' by the media, for our failure to deliver under pressure and our failure to cope with the tag of being the favourites. We had lost four years on the spin, to four different nations; Wales, Scotland, Ireland and now France, and people were ready to use that as a stick to hit us with. Despite being a consistently good side, one mistake per year was enough for us to be lambasted. It was hard to take and I remember a lot of soul searching at the time, as we summoned the inner desire to prove people wrong, and achieve our dreams.

After the disappointment of losing to France, Johno was then banned for our next game, against Wales at Twickenham. I was asked to captain the side, the third time I'd been given the honour, after leading us to wins over Australia and Romania the year before. With Johno suspended and Daws, who had led the side against Scotland and Ireland in those failed grand slam attempts, out too, I was the skipper and had the job of lifting the team after the dejection of Paris.

People had forgotten that in the previous autumn, we had beaten Australia, Romania and South Africa, after the disappointment of losing to Ireland. I knew we had that level of professionalism within the squad, and we just had to remind ourselves of that. It was my job for the first of those two games, to make sure we were on the ball. For example, and it sounds simple, rather than just going down to the training pitch and warming up in a leisurely manner and throwing the ball around, with a few laughs and jokes, I asked the squad to walk up to the white line as if we were playing a Test match in front of 80,000 people, with millions watching on TV around the world. I wanted them to visualise and feel that moment and get their minds and their actions in to good habits. I felt it would help us, and even if it only made a 1 per cent difference, it was worth it to me. Getting the mentality right, and treating the experience the same whether there's one man and his dog watching, or the eyes of the world on you, was something I felt was important, and I was delighted that the lads adopted it. We beat Australia 21-15 and I lifted the Cook Cup as captain, which was an incredible honour.

The next week we faced Romania, and with all due respect to them, we were always going to beat them. If we'd have won by 70, 80 or 90 points to ten, people would have said that was expected. To prevent any complacency and to challenge the team leading up to the game in training, we disciplined ourselves to concentrate and to perform at the highest level, regardless of the score. So, every time we scored against Romania, we ran back ready to start again. We didn't want to concede a try, or even a penalty, and I felt that game, by winning 134-0, showed how ruthless we could be, by showing no weakness at all. We were like programmed machines. We were in a no-win situation, so to win the way we did made it a moral victory, as well as an actual win for us. That professionalism would stand us in good stead for finishing the 2002 Six Nations Championship strongly, as despite the France defeat, there was still an important job to be done.

We had to pick each other up for Wales. We'd only lost one game out of six at that stage in 2002, and we could still claim the triple crown for the first time since 1998, so there was plenty to play for. We beat them comfortably, 50-10, which just left Italy to play, in what was to be the final of my four games as captain of England. I'd won three out of three as the skipper, so I was desperate to keep my 100 per cent record going, to finish the tournament as strongly as possible, and it was also my 50th cap for England. It should have been a celebratory day, but our display in Paris had meant it was a day of 'what might have been'.

In theory, we had nothing to play for in Rome, just our own pride, as France had already claimed the championship and the grand slam the day before. As I looked across our bench at the likes of Johno, Lol, Daws and Jason Leopard, 252 caps of quality, who all entered the pitch together, Lawrence coming on for me, I wondered what the Italians were thinking. We were doing okay without them, but to bring that wealth of experience and quality on must have been a shock to the system for the hosts. We ran out 45-9 winners and finished second in the championship. Another year gone, and sadly, another near miss for us.

There was nothing we could do now but learn from our failures. It was agony, but we had to stay strong and continue to believe in ourselves. Clive had set down, early in his tenure, that we could be honest, brutally honest, with each other. We were used to having open discussions and then all buying in to how to put things right. That approach helped us grow and mature as a team and as individuals, and is one of the reasons why we eventually enjoyed the success we had. In everyone's eyes, we'd failed though and we had to rectify that. We couldn't keep talking about it; we had to prove to the rugby world that we had it in us.

The grand slam that had eluded us was so important because it illustrated that you could win five games on the bounce, and to win a World Cup, you needed to win seven, so we knew what it signified. The fact that we kept losing one out of five, each year, showed that we were close, but that something critical was missing. We didn't need status to prove anything, we just wanted to win. Like my 100 per cent record as captain – I didn't just want it for me, I always wanted to win for the team.

At this point in time we were strongly labelled as 'bottlers'. The media really went to town on us but we'd only lost one game in 2002 so far. We sent a young squad to Argentina, which was led by Phil Vickery, and had the likes of a younger Benny Kay, Joe Worsley, Steve Thompson and Lewis Moody there too. That showed the strength in depth we had, that some players could be rested, but we still had quality to bring in to the side, and youth to freshen things up. The Heineken Cup Final was just before that tour, so my focus was on the Tigers, but the young side won 26-18 in Buenos Aires, which was a fantastic result considering, and helped to keep the momentum going from the Wales and Italy wins.

We then faced the big three southern hemisphere giants in the autumn internationals; New Zealand, Australia and South Africa. I was absolutely gutted to miss out on selection for the starting XV against the All Blacks. Clive, on the back of Lewis Moody's try-scoring performance in Argentina, went with him instead of me, but I understood. I guess it showed the strength in depth we had, that I could go from being captain, to being left out, and that level of competition brought the best out of us all. I enjoyed the week leading up to the New Zealand game, helping to prepare the guys that were starting, and playing a part in the squad ethic that we had built. I often talk about the role of players who are left out, and the support staff, in how they can help to create a positive atmosphere and give the 15 guys who are starting the best chance of bringing home the win. For example, I always agreed that everyone on a tour should be paid the same, regardless of whether they started or not. We were all in it together was my view. I was brought on as a blood replacement in the first game, for Richard Hill, for 11 minutes. We won 31-28, which was only the fifth time England had ever beaten New Zealand, so it was a tremendous achievement. We had found a way to win against them. We were actually 31-14 ahead at one stage, but two late tries made it touch and go at the end for us, and we needed Ben Kay, who came on for Danny Grewcock and stole the ball at the end near our line, to see the game out. It wasn't a beautiful game, but it didn't matter. We had put down a marker against a quality side.

The following week, I was back in the team for the visit of Australia and another incredibly tight match. Lawrence was left out this time. I was convinced that Clive was playing us. He was testing us mentally, to work harder and also to see how we would react to missing out. Lol came on for Hilly for a bit, and in this game we showed different skills, to chase a lead down, which was crucial in our development. Australia had pulled away and were 31-19 ahead not long after the half-time break. We came back like a steam train with Jonny's kicking and then a Ben Cohen try after Jason Robinson had whizzed through them, as he did so often for us. We hung on to win 32-31 and extended our unbeaten home record to 17 matches. At the time, I had a responsibility along with Mike

Tindall to help Phil Larder out with the defence, so even though we'd won two huge games, we'd conceded seven tries in the process, four against New Zealand and three against Australia. Our team target was always a maximum of one try conceded per game, so Phil, Tins and I were a bit pale at this time to say the least!

We finished the autumn internationals against South Africa at Twickenham. The Springboks were coming off the back of a 30-10 defeat to France in Marseille, followed by a 21-6 loss to Scotland at Murrayfield. Our feeling at the time was that they would be hurting and would be dangerous if we underestimated them. We were sure there would be a reaction and I know I would much rather have been playing them following a win, as opposed to two humbling defeats. They hadn't become a bad side overnight, in fact they were very strong and were led by Corne Krige, their captain, but they were just in poor form. We knew we would be facing them again, a year later, in a game which would probably decide Pool C of the 2003 Rugby World Cup and we couldn't have sent out a stronger message that day.

Playing against South Africa is always a physical game. They are big and brutal and you have to be prepared for pain, but even we were surprised that day, as they were a total disgrace to the game of rugby. So much happened off the ball, and there was a nasty atmosphere from the first whistle. My cheekbone was cracked, which I can still feel to this day; Jason Robinson's ear was perforated, and the first time Jonny caught the ball he was smashed on the touchline by Jannes Labuschagne, who was sent off on 23 minutes. They had obviously come with the intention of rattling us, but they just ran straight, and as physical as they were, it was honestly just bread and butter stuff to us. We were a better side than them, in good form, and I guess they felt that intimidation was the only way they could beat us. How wrong they were! We ran riot that day, winning 53-3, with tries from Will 'Shaggy' Greenwood (two), Ben Cohen, Hilly, Lol, a penalty try and I grabbed one too.

We were developing that winning environment and we wanted to be ruthless, and within the spirit of the game, we wanted to suffocate and break teams. That was our mentality. In the press after the game, their coach, Rudi Straeuli, tried to claim that they were the victims of our aggression and their skipper, Krige, had a go at us for turning the knife as they were down to 14 men. I couldn't believe what I was hearing! Later, in Krige's book, *The Right Place at the Wrong Time*, he admits that he deliberately set out to injure us that day, mainly as a result of our arrogance. That game has to go down as one of the roughest tests I'd ever been involved in, but we weren't arrogant, we were just getting better and better and they didn't like it, and as such they reacted to it. The red card may have ruined the game, but that was down to their lack of discipline under pressure.

Straight after the final whistle, battered and bruised, but elated that we had beaten all three of the southern hemisphere sides, Krige came marching up to me, shook my hand, looked me in the eyes and simply said, 'See you in Perth.' I must admit that at first I didn't know what he was referring to; Perth? Later I realised, ah, the World Cup and our pool match against them and the penny dropped. That didn't intimidate me at all. We were all left in no doubt about their aims on that day at Twickenham, but we had more than stood up to the challenge. They had failed to beat us and failed to break us. We had the upper hand, and although there was still a lot of rugby to play before the World Cup, we had leaped another huge physical and mental hurdle.

This was a huge game for me too. It was the game where I developed a greater self-discipline needed when a player was simply targeting you. My approach, if I had been smashed off the ball, was to get up, wipe the blood off, smile and get on with the game. Hand on heart, I can't say that I did that throughout my career, but this game was definitely a turning point for me. In 1996, playing for the Tigers, I lost my head when I pushed over referee Steve Lander, at the end of the Pilkington Cup Final which we controversially lost to Bath, which resulted in a six-month ban from the game. The other time I lost it was in my final game for Tigers, the 2005 Premiership Final against Wasps, when I punched Joe Worsley. I was no angel, but I normally managed to hold my nerve and not react. Two incidents in 17 years is surely not too bad?

Looking back at the one defeat of the year, to France, which cost us any chance of the grand slam, it was clear that Jonny had also learnt lessons. The powerful Serge Betsen had targeted him in Paris. He was absolutely relentless that day and Jonny reacted. We lost, but Jonny learned a lesson, in fact we all did. He was taken off of his normal game and that affected us all. However, by the time of the three autumn wins, we were maturing. Each mistake we made was being eradicated in time for the next game. We all wanted to get up after being hit, just to show our opponent that they hadn't got to us. I can't speak for all footballers, but there is often a perception that they pretend to be hurt, whereas rugby players pretend not to be hurt. I know which of the two I did during my career; you only have to look at the state of my face to see how many times I've been hit!

As a team, the England side under Clive never wanted to show that we were either hurt or tired. Very rarely would one of us stay on the ground, have our hands on our knees, or have our hands behind our heads gasping for the next breath. We knew it was important to show to the world that we were strong. Players back in the amateur era would often be caught looking shattered! The image of Dean Richards, bent down with his hands on his knees, would have been typical of that time in the game, but Deano has one leg shorter than the other so he could get away with doing it. Our body language, even though we were sometimes hanging, was incredible. The opposition would have looked at us and felt that we were invincible, but inside we often had nothing left to give. It was this mentality which we had to take in to 2003, for the biggest year of our careers. I was proud of what we did in 2002, more of what we learned and the battles we faced and overcame than of the results as such.

Our time of being branded as bottlers and nearly men was almost over…

4

All Good Things Come To An End

WE began the 2002/03 league season as English rugby's defending champions. We had dominated domestically, winning the Premiership in each of the last four seasons, and also had back-to-back European Cups in our trophy cabinet. It was an unprecedented run of success and as the saying goes, although we didn't necessarily see it at the time, all good things come to an end.

It was business as usual in our first game, as we faced Biarritz in August, in what was billed as the prestigious Orange Cup, between the respective champions of English and French rugby. It was an incredible fixture to be part of and at the time we compared it to the annual rugby league game played out between the northern and southern hemisphere winners. We had lost in the inaugural game a year prior, to Toulouse, and we were determined to come back from France with a new trophy to add to our collection.

It was a colourful affair and was an ideal game for us to test ourselves against a quality side. I set up Steve Booth for a try, for a 14-13 win, and in hindsight you could probably pinpoint this as the final highpoint of an incredible period of time for the club. To maintain the standards we had set, and to put in those performances week in, week out, and to come home with the silverware every time, was, I guess, eventually going to take its toll on us all. Teams were ready for us, raising their game, which meant that every match had a cup final feel that season, not just the Biarritz game. There was a really insatiable appetite to play us and to beat us and we were the yardstick against which everyone compared themselves.

We were an ageing side, who had grown old together and there were younger players, who having been happy to be part of the squad, now had an appetite to further themselves at other clubs if the opportunity didn't arise at Tigers. I say this with a smile on my face, but number ten, a critical position, saw Austin Healey and the young Andy Goode competing for a place, and as most people would have done at that time, Deano kept Austin due to his versatility, and reluctantly let Andy move to Saracens to develop his game. That would have been fine, but Austin suffered a number of injuries that season, and some of the younger guys, like Sam Vesty, had to be thrown in, so we were a little exposed at times. Sam developed brilliantly that year, as well as the experienced Rod Kafer, who was really a number 12, but had to fill in at times and did a competent job. We needed two players in every position, and I think we just lost that extra strength in depth and struggled to hit the high standards we had set over the past four seasons, particularly in such a pivotal position.

Another aspect which affected us was the hunger we all had, and still needed, which had driven us on to our success. It's probably easy to say now, but it was inevitable that we would lose some of it. We had become used to winning everything and we had given everything we had to achieve it. I guess we just ran out of that little bit of steam which makes the difference and the squad was slowly beginning to dismantle. Dorian West had already pushed Richard Cockerill out of the side, who subsequently left to join Montferrand in France, James Grindal left for Newcastle and then we had the injuries; Lewis Moody, who was flying, had to have an operation and only started eight games, and I also only started 16 games that season due to a nagging calf injury. In the past we would have coped with these circumstances and the pressure that brings, and I'm not making excuses here, we should have coped with it all, but we didn't.

The result of all of this was real inconsistency in our performances and our results throughout the season. In elite sport, it is often about fine margins, and we had lost that slight edge. Call it whatever you want; squad depth, desire, availability of key players, luck, whatever it was, we just didn't have it anymore. Another factor was that feeling of coming towards the end of an era. Players who had achieved success, while growing up together at Leicester Tigers, were either leaving or retiring, or even thinking about retiring, and the last group of players from the amateur era were coming towards the twilight of their time in the game. Our whole mindset had changed and we just couldn't adapt quickly enough. I'm not saying our minds were elsewhere, but we always had the 2003 Six Nations and World Cup on the horizon as well. For the likes of Johno and myself, we knew that would be our last chance to win the World Cup. For fleeting moments I would look ahead, knowing that the 2007 World Cup would be beyond me. There was no way they would, or even should, pick a 38-year-old, but in terms of Tigers, I can say, hand on heart, that I wasn't thinking about retirement myself at this stage. I still wanted to continue our success, however unlikely that was looking as the season progressed.

Our opening league game was away to Leeds, with all due respect, a game we would have expected to win, but we lost

26-13 and just put it down as a blip. The following week, we beat Harlequins 30-6 to continue our remarkable unbeaten home run of over 50 games, but then lost 29-16 away to Sale Sharks, and the pattern continued with a 52-9 home win over Newcastle Falcons. We'd won our opening two home games, and lost our opening two away games, and that simply wasn't the Leicester Tigers of the last four years. Perhaps other teams were working us out and we had lost the fear factor that we had cultivated over the years?

Our form picked up a little, in and around the autumn international period, where we perhaps would have expected to struggle as we factored in losing players to their respective countries. We were convinced that we were over the blip and had battled back in to the top three. There was a bit of a siege mentality and the squad rediscovered some of the old battle, ahead of the return of the international players, but there was less cavalry returning than expected, as the likes of myself and Moodos were injured, so fatigue set in as the strain showed on the squad and we lost three games on the spin. We were rooted in mid-table and losing to London Irish, Northampton Saints to end our unbeaten home run, and Wasps away just wasn't good enough for us and our expectations.

We had a history of nicking close games, turning almost certain defeats into improbable wins, but now the tide had turned and we were losing games and in turn, we were losing the intimidation effect we had over our opponents. Looking back, it's hard to blame our loss of form on one thing, it was a combination of factors. Other clubs were catching up with us; they were recruiting better coaches like Warren Gatland at Wasps and Wayne Smith at Northampton, and teams were becoming more professional, fitter and were recruiting on an international level. Teams were better organised, especially in defence, so it wasn't as easy for us to break them down. It seemed as if it happened in the blink of an eye, and I hate saying it, but we just seemed like an ageing side overnight. The likes of 'Wig' (Graham Rowntree), Cockers, Darren Garforth, myself and both of the Johnos, Will and Martin, meant that we just seemed to be slightly off it. I guess that because of the success we'd had, there was always going to be a point where our average age increased, just as our consistency level dropped, and the talented younger players had either moved on in search of first-team rugby, or those still with us weren't quite ready. We needed to replace all of those years of talent, culture and experience and it is very difficult to know when to do it, but perhaps we just didn't move quickly enough at the time. Maybe it was always going to happen to us though? I mean, we couldn't win everything, every year, even though it felt like we could. I think other teams learned from our excellence as well, and I saw signs of us in those teams, which was a big compliment, but didn't help to ease the pain of us sliding down the table.

The Northampton Saints defeat on 30 November was probably the game where we knew our time had come. My fractured eye socket meant I missed the game through injury and sadly we lost 25-12 at home; our first domestic home defeat since losing to Newcastle in December 1997, nearly five years previous, as Saints became the first team to win at Welford Road in 58 league matches. It was a real landmark result, not just for us, but for everyone in the league. Teams now felt they had a chance of beating us at Welford Road and we lost again at the end of the season to London Irish.

We finished the Premiership league season in sixth place, winning 12 games and losing ten. We were 27 points behind first-placed Gloucester, who were thrashed in the play-off final by regular season runners-up Wasps.

In the Heineken Cup we were double defending champions, so to speak, having won the tournament in the previous two seasons. We'd again proved we could compete at this level by securing the Orange Cup at the start of the season, so we still felt we could go far in Europe, if not all the way again.

We won five and drew one of our six pool matches, and stormed to the top of the group to earn a home quarter-final. Even though our domestic form was a struggle, we maintained our standards in Europe and beating Calvisano and Beziers home and away, and Neath at home with a draw away, was no mean achievement, especially given our lack of form in the league.

At this stage though, it felt as if there was a lack of loyalty, a loss of the ethos we had worked tirelessly to build at the club over the past few years. People were distracted by the lure of money, matched with first-team rugby, and I'm trying not to be judgemental here, because leaving the club was totally their prerogative, but things just weren't the same and as I've said, we had lost our edge. It was a sign of a change in the game and in the mentality and approach of players, almost another step away from the amateur era, and I guess just the natural progression of rugby towards the game we know today.

I was faced with that same big decision myself, years earlier. When Bob Dwyer left Leicester and was replaced by Deano as coach, Bob tried to recruit me for his new club, Bristol, with a £1m contract for four years, which was a considerable amount more than I was being paid at Tigers and was a huge offer for the time. I'd been at the club for what felt like a lifetime even then, and I turned down the Bristol offer as for me and my career it was about the club, the people, the meaning of playing for Leicester and everything we stood for. I wanted to be a part of something special. That meant more to me than any financial offer. I went on to play for the Lions, got in to the England squad and the rest is history, whereas things didn't really work out for Bob at Bristol. I'd also turned down an offer from Gary Hetherington at Sheffield Eagles for the chance to play professional rugby league in 1992, four years before rugby union turned professional, but it was never really about the money for me, it was about my career goals.

I couldn't blame people for leaving the Tigers. They were looking after their careers, looking for more money for themselves and their families, while searching for first-team rugby. I would have stayed though, that's all I'm saying. If I hadn't have been in the side, I would have fought to get in and would have given everything to make the position my own, rather than walking away to join someone else. I mean, who in their right mind at that time leaves Leicester Tigers? It was the beginning of the end of the amateur/professional crossover, and that change in mentality within the game was probably one of the reasons that the 2002/03 season didn't yield the success we had craved.

The edge that I had talked about, which had disappeared, we needed more than ever in the Heineken Cup, at the elite level. As fate would dictate and as so often happens in sport, our reward for winning our pool was a home quarter-final against Munster, our opponents in the 2002 final. We'd broken their hearts less than a year earlier, so we knew they would be fired up to beat us, but whoever you play at this stage is always going to be a top rugby side. The media circus around 'The Hand of Back' as we've already discussed, made more of this being a revenge mission for Munster than it was in reality. For us, it was a big game, but my approach was always the same; the next game was always a big game.

As the pool stage was coming to a close, it felt as if it was destined to be Munster, so there was an inevitability about it all. I was asked all the typical questions in the media about the final, about whether I would be targeted, and I tried to laugh it all off. In the build-up to the rematch I felt like a promoter for a title fight in boxing, with everyone clambering to get tickets and the media hyping it up and showing re-runs of my 'moment' in the final. That game at Welford Road would have sold itself twice over and must have been the easiest game the Tigers' marketing and ticketing teams ever had to sell.

Sadly, it wasn't an easy game for us and Munster got their revenge by beating us 20-7 and knocking us out. We knew that our reign as champions of Europe was coming to an end, and it hurt us all, especially coupled with our indifferent league form. I suppose people would have said that having won the tournament two years running, a quarter-final place was no disgrace, and we'd ensured another bumper crowd for the club's coffers, but that was no consolation for us.

Ronan O'Gara, who was a fantastic player throughout his career, inspired them and my old friend Peter Stringer grabbed a try too. They really did get their own back on us that day! Munster were a very good side though, which they had shown in the 2002 final when they pushed us all the way, and this time around they deserved their win. They were edged out 13-12 in the semi-finals by eventual winners Toulouse, who overcame Perpignan 22-17 in an all-French final.

In the Powergen Cup we beat Worcester Warriors 36-9 in the last 16 and then beat Harlequins 19-12 away in the quarter-finals. I didn't play in the semi-final against Gloucester, as I'd torn my left calf at the Millennium Stadium for England, against Wales, in the Six Nations Championship. Gloucester beat us 16-11 and knocked us out, but the game was remembered more for the fact that referee Steve Lander was left with no option but to allow uncontested scrums as Gloucester claimed following injuries to their props, Andy Deacon and Rodrigo Roncero, they had no other players available who could fill the role. We were all over them at the end of the game and were denied the opportunity to use our scrum, on a couple of occasions, to force ourselves over the line. All we needed was a converted try to win the game, and our argument was that Olivier Azam, the Gloucester hooker, had played at prop previously, so he could have done this and then we would have avoided the farce of uncontested scrums in such an important game. Lander couldn't force anything and we were left with another bad day at the office. Gloucester had played to the rules, and they had gained the upper hand. Who was I to question that and take issue after the Munster game last season and my own actions? It still left me frustrated though and that feeling was symptomatic of the season as a whole.

Anyway, the likelihood of uncontested scrums was diminished, with the International Rugby Board announcing in 2009 that a complete front row would need to be named on the bench, so this game certainly had an impact on the game of rugby, long after the final whistle was blown.

All that was left, from an ultimately disappointing season, was a Zurich wildcard play-off to play for, which more importantly, represented our only chance of qualification for the European Cup. After all our years of dominance, it was sad to see us clinging on by the skin of our teeth just to play in Europe. We'd been the kings of Europe, so this was a rapid fall from grace, but we had to be professional and achieve that minimum target at least.

In the semi-finals we played Harlequins over two legs, and lost 26-23 at The Stoop, but two second-half tries from Geordan Murphy and Martin Corry and some solid kicking from Stimmo kept us in the tie. Deano had brought on the likes of Johno, Wig, Dorian West and Darren Garforth late on, which really turned the tie back in our favour, with a home leg to come. I returned to the side in the second leg, grabbed a try and we won 28-13, sealing a 51-39 aggregate victory and a place in the final against Saracens on neutral turf, Franklin's Gardens, for that place in next season's European Cup.

It was my try in extra time that thankfully sealed a 27-20 win, and for most clubs, a couple of decent cup runs, winning the Orange Cup, and a place in Europe would have been enough, but we knew that season had been a failure. It wasn't for a lack of effort; I would never have questioned that at the time, nor now, but we were a shadow of the side that had reached the top on a consistent basis over the past four years, here and in Europe.

The Saracens game was Darren Garforth's final match for the club. 'Garf' looked exactly how a tight-head prop should look. In his last season, his fingers were all curled over, as they had been broken so many times, and his ligaments were all gone. He was on medication to sleep at night, suffered with arthritis and often slept upright in a chair, with the help of a glass or two of red wine, just to help him drift off. His nickname was 'Skin', as he was also from Coventry. We used to share lifts in to Leicester, as I lived close by, and then I eventually moved to Leicester after the game turned professional. Those lifts were expensive for me though, as Garf had psoriasis, and used to leave quite a lot of his 'Cov Skin' all over my car, so I had to invest in a car vacuum. He was as hard as nails though, and had actually started his sporting career as a footballer, playing as a centre-forward. One day, he went off to play, arrived at the ground and the game was cancelled due to a frozen pitch. As he walked home, a minibus passed him, and the guys shouted out of the window asking if he wanted to play rugby. Seven years later, he was playing for England at Twickenham, a remarkable turnaround and achievement.

Garf is a great guy, a real legend of the game. He describes himself as a 'tubular technician', which is a posh term for a scaffolder and he was able to balance those huge, heavy poles on his chin! He was phenomenal on and off the field. He had a great partnership with Johno in the scrum, which was critical to our success, and I was fortunate enough to sit behind them both and carry us over the line on numerous occasions from driving mauls off line-outs. In fact, I remember the bookmakers, Ladbrokes, coming in to Welford Road one season and the odds they were offering on Garf to score the first try was something like 50/1, and I started at 20 odd to one and was soon down to 6/1, as I was scoring a try most weeks. I know you weren't allowed to bet on yourselves, and I never did, but we could have really made some money if I'd just slipped the ball to Garf instead! How dumb were we? We must have made a lot of money for Tigers fans though, as halfway through that season Ladbrokes pulled out! They were running out of money at half-time, with punters heading off to collect and spend their winnings on celebratory beers.

Despite qualifying for Europe, I had time to reflect on a new feeling; the overriding sense of failure. It was something that we weren't used to and was not something I wanted to make a habit of experiencing. I'd been proud to be part of one of the club's best sides in history and in the space of one season we'd been caught by our opponents. We'd lost the fear factor which had served us so well and seen so many sides leave Welford Road with nothing. I knew that we would return to the good days again, as we hadn't become a bad side overnight, and I wanted to taste that success sooner rather than later.

I began to look ahead that summer to the World Cup in Australia; the one trophy that had eluded me. I needed to focus on something positive after the season at Leicester. Rugby was changing, on and off the field, and that may have been difficult for some people to adapt to, but I hadn't changed. I still had my eyes on the final piece in the jigsaw, the William Webb Ellis Trophy, and while there were obstacles in the way, I was more than ready for the biggest seven weeks of my professional life and the moment that would define my career.

5

The Weight Of The World On Our Shoulders

FOR four years, which felt like an eternity to us, the Six Nations grand slam had slipped through our fingers. It began in 1999 with the injury-time loss at Wembley to Wales, was followed by the 2000 defeat to Scotland, which we blew in wet conditions, 2001 was the foot and mouth epidemic when we lost to Ireland and then in 2002 our dreams were shattered by the French in the third game. We knew what was at stake now. 2003, ahead of the World Cup, simply had to be our year for the grand slam. There was no longer any room for errors.

We all felt that having got to where we were, we would need to win a grand slam, on top of beating the three southern hemisphere giants, to prove we could win a World Cup. Winning eight games on the spin, against the best teams in the world, would be an indication that we could win seven in Australia. The confidence that momentum would give us would be immense. Following our defeat to France in 2002 we were on a decent run of form; we won the final two Six Nations games, then the game in Argentina, followed by all three autumn internationals against the All Blacks, Australia and that bitter battle against South Africa.

I remember, when we met up ahead of the Six Nations, there was a real attitude around the place at Pennyhill Park. The management, consciously I believe, put pressure on to us all, as we did ourselves. We were left with no choice but to win, and I'm convinced that brought the best out of us. In the leadership meetings we had, myself and Mike Tindall had responsibility for the defence, working with our defence coach, Phil Larder, and we knew that to be successful we had to have the best defence. We had collectively set rules, since Phil's first involvement in 1997, and we now focused on a few key areas of excellence, which were, per game; team tackle success must be 95 per cent or over, less than ten penalties conceded, and one try or less conceded. If we met all of those criteria, then we knew we would most likely win, as it would make us extremely hard to beat, especially with the attacking prowess we possessed, both individually and collectively. This was emphasised by the autumn games in 2002, which we won, despite conceding lots of tries. It emphasised what a threat we were and that we could beat anyone, even if we were exposed in those matches.

Our self-analysis in the dressing room, and team meetings, was nothing short of brutal. That honesty was developed very early in the Clive Woodward era, and that style of management enabled us all to say exactly what we thought, demand the best of each other, and improve upon mistakes. We could discuss anything and everything. Clive's whole coaching philosophy was that it was our ideas and input that would form the approach, so if things weren't working, yes, he was in charge, but it was our responsibility. We were involved, treated with respect and ultimately we had a hand in decisions. A lot of coaches will dictate style and strategy, not just in rugby, across all sports, but this way if you are a part of the process, the coach has empowered you and you have no one else to blame if you fail. It meant that when it came to the crunch, it was our necks on the line, not just Clive's and I, personally, thrived under that extra pressure.

We headed in to the first game against France, at Twickenham, with huge pressure and the reminder hanging over us of our failings last year in Paris. The first game was always a challenge, as you've only just got together again as a group, having been with your respective clubs. Clive always worked on having a good relationship with the clubs and the RFU though, at least in those days anyway, so we had a great togetherness, even with just a week to prepare. Pennyhill Park was a second home to us and once you walked through that door, you were England again. Nothing else mattered.

Our preparations were shocked though, when on 14 February, the eve of the game, 21-year-old Nick Duncombe, a very talented scrum half for Harlequins who had a bright future ahead of him having played twice for us in the Six Nations the previous season, had passed away suddenly while in Spain. There were a number of Quins players in the squad, and we were a family, so it was a very emotional time. Even though Nick had only been with us briefly, he was an obvious talent, and the group were hurting at hearing such shocking and ultimately sad news. There was no way we could lose the next day, as we all wanted to win that game for Nick.

It wasn't an easy win, but we did battle past France 25-17, although poor Phil Larder lost more hair in the process as the French outscored us by three tries to one. Jonny outgunned Gérald Merceron, kicking 20 points, alongside Robbo's try and we were up and running with a win on the board. We were fitter and stronger than them, and I knew we were the better side, but I still came off the field devastated that we had conceded those three tries, which really took the shine off the victory. That meant that if we were to achieve our statistical targets, there was once again no room for error in the four games to come.

The following week, we took on Wales at the Millennium Stadium. Playing rugby there is a magnificent experience; right in the heart of Cardiff, the passion their supporters have for the game means there is always a sense of occasion. That special backing tends to mean that they come out of the blocks like a 100m sprinter, but we were ready and despite them dominating the first half, we went in 9-6 ahead. They were reacting to their 30-22 defeat to Italy the previous week, so there was a sense of pride at stake for the hosts, and we were under par. Thankfully, in the second half, tries from Will Greenwood and Joe Worsley saw us home 26-9, but unfortunately I had to come off with a calf injury after 52 minutes. I only suffered six injuries in a 17-year career that kept me out for more than a week, so I tend to remember them all! I was absolutely devastated though. I had the ball, and two Welshmen jumped on me, and I tried to power through, but the combined weight was too much for my dainty little calves to take and I knew immediately it had gone. My first thought was about missing the Italy game. When you're in the shirt, you are fighting as hard as you can to keep it, but when you are out injured you should want the best for the team regardless. Young Joe Worsley had come in and done well, so I was pleased for him and the team, and it meant I'd have to be at my best to retain my place once I was back to fitness.

With England our medical team was simply incredible. I went straight over to the physio Phil Pask, the sports nutritionist Matt Lovell, and sports performance coach Dave Reddin and asked them what I had to do to recover and be ready for selection as quickly as possible. Then I phoned my family! I just wanted to get back in and didn't want to miss out on any of the journey we were on as a team. I'd worked so hard to be a part of the success to date, that I wasn't about to allow a calf problem to deny me a part of this grand slam attempt.

Unfortunately, I had to watch the Italy game from the stands at Twickenham, and after just 20 minutes we were 33-0 ahead and cruising. It was a weird and uncomfortable feeling for me, as I wanted the team to win, but I was watching someone else in my jersey. It just didn't feel right and I suppose I realised what an awful spectator I was. Frustratingly, we didn't keep that intensity going and spent most of the rest of the game defending, and allowing the Italians to dominate possession. We only added one further try, and mentally, we had gone off the boil and hadn't put them to the sword. We ran home 40-5 winners, conceding just the one try, but again there was an air of disappointment as we had dropped our intensity, and we knew if we wanted to beat the top sides we wouldn't be able to ease off at all. Jonny captained the side for the first time in his career, as Johno attended the birth of his first child, Molly, so it was a real honour for him, but unfortunately he went off injured in the second half, and then Charlie Hodgson replaced him and was also injured, sadly for a year, which would scupper any chances he had of playing in the World Cup. He must have been gutted. I couldn't have imagined a worse time to pick up a long-term injury.

I kept harking back to the Romania game in 2001, and making sure we didn't concede any tries, so we were frustrated to have conceded the try against Italy, but the job was done and we had three wins from three games, with two weeks until Scotland visited Twickenham. I've always said how much I love 'Flower of Scotland' and the emotion it evokes on the day of an England vs Scotland game. It really is special and must give the Scots more energy, and strangely it always seemed to give me a little more fire too! There is so much history, off the rugby field, let alone on it, which they use to their advantage when they play us. In fact the level of hatred for the English is really something. I remember my parents buying a rose from a florist in Scotland once, before I made my debut against them in 1994, fearing they were going to be spat at. Thankfully they weren't, but they were left in no doubt as to what their support for England meant to the locals, even though they were only buying a rose.

I was back in the side and had worked very hard to recover from the calf injury sustained against Wales. The game, again, probably wasn't the prettiest, and was at times a war of attrition, as each side tried to grind the other down, with two early sin-bins for Scotland, and then Robbo sent to the bench for a high tackle on Kenny Logan. The expectation was that we would beat Scotland, and we were at home, so we had enough pressure on us to deliver the goods. We won comfortably, with two tries from Robbo, one from Ben Cohen and one from Josh Lewsey, and importantly, no tries for Scotland. Being back in the side, and getting our try conceding average down to one per game in the tournament carried a real sense of achievement for me personally, but also for the whole defence. We won 40-9 and were even able to rest people towards the end, like Jonny, and try out Robbo at 13, as Dan Luger came on for Mike Tindall. Robbo lit the place up with his footwork, which was something always worth the entrance fee alone.

Clive and his team were always looking at options, something that would just give us an edge if a game was tight and we needed to make a move. Take the back row for example; Hilly, me, Lol, Moodos, Cozza (Corry) and Worzel (Worsley) were all in the mix, and the competition was strong. People often talk of Hilly, me and Lol, but it wasn't until the World Cup when we became the established combination. Clive was probing and testing us, across all positions, making sure we were prepared for all eventualities. As I've said before, that brought the best out of us all, and also ensured that the lads who were on the bench were going at full pelt to try and get in the side.

The final game was against Ireland at Lansdowne Road, which was a grand slam decider. You don't really get much bigger in northern hemisphere rugby and all the heartache of our recent grand slam failures boiled down to this. England hadn't won a grand slam since 1995, and in some senses we were returning to the scene of a crime, after losing the 2001 grand slam in Ireland, which was still fresh in the memory. A lot was stacked against us; Ireland had home advantage, we had the ghosts of the past four years and no side had ever won an away grand slam decider with both teams going for the honour in the history of the competition. We didn't really pay notice to that sort of thing. We didn't listen to the media branding us as 'bottlers' either. We just believed in our ability and in each other, and weren't prepared to leave anything to chance this time. Our collective intent, belief and intensity, to get across the line this time, simply can't be put in to words. It was incredible. Clive deliberately stepped up the pressure in the build-up to the game and said that if we didn't win the game, there would be nowhere for the team to go ahead of the World Cup. His view was that to increase the pressure would bring the best out of us, and I loved that attitude.

However, I did notice nervousness on the morning of the game, at breakfast in the team hotel. You could sense it from looking around at everyone and no wonder really when you think what was at stake and what had happened to us at the final hurdle in previous years. Flippantly, I said, 'Don't worry lads, we'll win by 40 today,' trying to make light of the situation and relax everyone. We were flying and we felt unbeatable at that stage, but the pressure of the day could easily have got the better of us. I followed up by saying, 'They'll probably get a couple of penalties, so it'll be 40-6.'

The last few minutes before kick-off was always the worst for me, and I'm sure they are for players in all sports today. There are the final few words in the dressing room, then the national anthems and the introductions to dignitaries and all you want to do is run on that pitch, and get things started. This game was no different. Time seems to freeze and your mind slows down, perhaps you are clock watching and that's why it feels like that, as you are itching to get out there. Little did we know that the pre-match would be talked about as much afterwards, as the game itself.

Johno won the toss and selected which way we were going to play, and as such, that's the side of the half that you warm up on and you would line up on for the introductions. We were genuinely unaware that Ireland had a favoured side to line up on, and we were on that side. When Ireland entered the field, all of a sudden there were officials who were hassling Johno and indicating that we needed to move. The same guy who was shouting at Johno had been banging on our changing room door 20 minutes earlier, trying to disrupt our pre-match teamtalk, which Clive and the coaching staff soon dealt with. The line-ups were set behind a red carpet so that the Irish President, Mary McAleese, could walk along it for the handshakes. It was all pretty standard stuff, but no one had told us where to stand, and pretty quickly it became evident that we weren't moving either. I was in earshot of Johno, and there was no way we were going to move. Clive has since jokingly branded me as the culprit for this incident. I was certainly backing Johno's immediate decision not to move and as a team leader I reiterated this to the team, in no uncertain terms!

I've said many times that it wasn't a deliberate tactic for us to stand there in the first place, but once we were there, we didn't want to move and show any weakness, or give even the slightest edge to our opponents. I looked down the line and perhaps with a few expletives, I told the lads to stand firm, and we all did. I guess it was their lucky end or something, but as a result of all this, the President had to walk along the grass to be introduced to the Irish team, as they decided to stand in the same half we were, on the other side of us. When you think about it, you can't predict a coin toss, so how could we have planned to have done this deliberately? In all honesty, it was a lot of fuss about nothing. Groundstaff and officials were coming up to us and telling us to move, but I'm not even certain that the match officials knew what was happening. I'm sure it is now at the top of the agenda for informing visiting teams of expected protocol.

We had won what seemed like the first battle by standing our ground, but then we reserved one of our best wins for the real battle. We tore in to Ireland and smashed them 42-6, with a really dominant and emphatic performance. Finally, we had the grand slam that we'd craved for so long and we laid the ghosts to rest. No longer could we be classed as 'bottlers' or 'nearly men'. The media would have to come up with new names for us. Lol's early try, followed by Tins, two from Greenwood and one from Luges, meant we ran in five tries, with no reply. We had made a statement to everyone in rugby, ahead of the World Cup, and no one could question us now; we were real contenders and we were bang in form.

I think that Lol's early try was absolutely key. It settled everyone's nerves and we were able to play our game, both in an attacking and defensive sense, without feeling like we had the weight of the world on our shoulders. Our defensive coach Phil Larder had a saying that he introduced, 'hit the beach', which was intended as a respectful reference to the Battle of Normandy, that we would shout if we were under intense pressure and needed to all work together to prevent the opposition from scoring. It was a team call to just ask that you gave everything you could for each other, and do whatever it would take to win. I remember that call being made quite a lot on the day, as we were so committed to denying Ireland even a try, leaving them with just a penalty and a drop goal to show for their efforts. At the time, they had come within one game of their first grand slam in 55 years, but in the end they couldn't have been any further from success. We almost reached my light-hearted pre-match prediction as well. If it wasn't for Jonny banging over a late conversion from Dan Luger's try, I'd have been bang on with my 40-6 prediction.

Watching Johno lift the Six Nations Championship trophy, and knowing that we had secured that and the triple crown, as well as the grand slam, gave us great satisfaction, as a reward for all the years of coming so close. Importantly though, it also meant that we were ready to compete mentality with the likes of New Zealand, Australia and South Africa, showed that we could win a major trophy, and also that we could do it away from home, as we would have to do in Australia later in the year. Let's not forget, that was a very talented Irish side as well, so it was a huge psychological boost for us all. I suppose the post-match feeling was a combination of relief, emotion and celebration, and that all came out as the pressure was released. We had also just won 11 games on the bounce, and hadn't lost in 13 months, since the defeat to France in 2002. It was a really special period, as we were still on an upward curve. Even though we had been together for many years, there was such a sense of excitement at what we could achieve together if we were prepared to go the extra mile.

After the euphoria of the grand slam and the superb performance against Ireland, our next challenge was as big as it gets in world rugby; go to New Zealand and Australia, as the number one side in the world, and win. Throughout history, these two nations, along with South Africa, would most likely be classed as the best, so at any time you play them, you know you will be in for a real test. In the back of our minds was the fact that we had beaten them at home, and with the confidence of winning the grand slam, we had nothing to fear – but plenty to lose. If we were going to win a World Cup, we'd have to beat these sides, in their part of the world as it were, so the summer was a chance to put down another marker. In previous tours, Clive had rested or left people out of the team, but this time we arrived with a full-strength side, which was quite a bold move as Clive could have easily given people a rest after a long season. As a 'Cov Skin' would say, we were fully tooled up, and we wanted to continue the momentum we had gained over the past year.

Our warm-up game for this tour was against the New Zealand Māori in New Plymouth, a match we won 23-9. Most people felt that we were unconvincing and the media reports post-match were pretty negative, but it was a very difficult game, in poor conditions, so we did what we needed to do to win the game. By this stage, the world's media, especially the Australian media, had branded us as boring. We couldn't be called bottlers or nearly men anymore, as we kept winning, so they needed to call us by another name. To be fair to the New Zealand media, they were always reasonable with us, and they appreciated that winning was what it was all ultimately about. They stand loyally by their team and support them, which is something to be admired.

A couple of days before the New Zealand Test match, we were invited along to the film set of *The Lord of the Rings*, and met the cast and the director, Peter Jackson. Incredibly, Richard Hill is a second cousin of Peter. Following our visit we were called 'White Orcs' by the media and public. That trip helped to take the pressure off ahead of the Test match and relaxed everyone.

The New Zealand game was in Wellington, in the Cake Tin, in what can only be described as appalling conditions, as the wind and rain drove across the ground. We lost Daws from the grand slam-winning team because of an injury and he was replaced by Kyran Bracken, with Andy Gomarsall on the bench. It was always going to be a battle, physically and mentally, and then with the weather as well, it felt like a war. Little did we know that in the second half we would make things even harder for ourselves.

We felt in control of the game in the first half, in terms of territory, and we all felt confident we could push on, but a late Carlos Spencer penalty levelled the scores at 6-6 at the break. Jonny nudged us back ahead 9-6 early in the second half before in the 46th minute, referee Stuart Dickinson lost patience with the number of penalties in the game and I was sin-binned as the next offender for playing the ball on the ground. The All Blacks stormed forward with the man advantage and seemed certain to score a try, but indecision and our 'hit the beach' warrior-like defence held them up. Just 120 seconds passed between my yellow card and another – this time it was Lol, who was penalised for killing the ball from the side. It was carnage out there and we were down to 13 men, and were only three points ahead. They were ready to grind us down, and even when they won a penalty five metres from the line, they opted for a scrum rather than taking an easy three points. Scrum after scrum went by as they tried to force their way past, but our boys hung on. I imagine there would have been a few more 'hit the beach' shouts and probably some choice language too, during those ten minutes or so. Rodney So'oialo, their number eight, went for a quick tap and stretched for the line. The crowd cheered and it looked as if they may have breached us but the TMO (Television Match Official) showed that Rodney had made a double movement, and therefore it was no try.

Clive and his coaching staff had helped us to prepare for this kind of situation though, as we had trained in situations where the defending side were a man down, admittedly, not two men down, but the principle was there, so the guys were mentally ready for the situation they were facing. Looking back, New Zealand got their tactics wrong. They wanted to drive our scrum over the line and hurt us, but they took us on in one of our areas of strength, even though we only had 13 men on the field. They could have kicked some points, and got themselves ahead, but they wanted to visibly push us back and humiliate us, which was a mistake. They lost sight of what mattered; the result, not what the game looked like.

Me and Lol eventually came back on to help bolster the side and get us back to 15 v 15 and incredibly, we not only held on during that time with two players less, we actually won that period 3-0. That really says something about the side's mental strength. Johno was asked after the game by the media, what was going through his mind during those ten minutes. He replied, 'My spine'. The level of pressure on the team during that time was unbelievable.

Despite a late try from the home side, Jonny's boot and the sheer determination of everyone helped us to a famous victory. We won 15-13, which was England's first win in New Zealand in over 30 years. You just knew at the time what that result meant to us, and what it would mean for years to come. It was a hammer blow to anyone who doubted us. We were number one in the world, and we'd beaten the All Blacks on their own turf, with 13 men. Sure, it wasn't pretty, but you didn't win World Cups for artistry, you won them by getting through seven games and beating the best. After that achievement in Wellington, we were called 'White Orcs on Steroids!' which we loved. Clive used this opportunity to talk us up in the press after the game, and this was definitely a statement of intent from us.

With that huge result, following the great display in Ireland, we flew to Australia and the way we felt at the time we could have probably flown ourselves there. Our confidence was sky-high. The Aussie media were ready for us though, and they tucked in to us, but they were just supporting their side and trying to get in our heads. I wasn't an avid reader of articles about our team, and I genuinely used to laugh about it as I thought it was all in jest. You know your own strengths and weaknesses and any of the media stuff was just good fun in my eyes and helped to build up the hype ahead of a big game.

The Test against Australia was held in Melbourne at the Telstra Stadium, now known as Stadium Australia. The conditions were dry and it was very different to the game in Wellington. I guess that people would normally say that wet conditions suit English rugby, but we were no average England side. We were different, and we always fancied ourselves to outscore sides, in terms of points, and also tries. All the pre-match talk was of us wanting the roof open and for it to rain. We were confident in any conditions, but to be honest, the more perfect the conditions the better for us. We wanted to show exactly what we could do and leave no reason for anyone to have any excuses. You could see that in the way we started, as we came out of the blocks like a steam train. We scored a try in the fifth minute, after sweeping their defence back, wave after wave of attacks, and Will Greenwood got us over the line for a great start.

We extended our lead on the half-hour mark, through a try from 'Tins', as we showed great hands in difficult circumstances, under pressure and we were really on top. If you ever get the chance to watch this game back, it's worth doing, as our performance was top class, one of the best I was part of during my time wearing the white shirt. We went in 12-3 ahead at the break and we continued that dominance in the second half. Ben Cohen scored our third try with just over 15 minutes to go, as he raced through the Wallabies' defence and ripped them apart. We went 24-9 ahead, and a late Wendell Sailor try gave the home side some consolation, but they knew they had been outplayed throughout the whole game. We won 24-15 and that was England's first win against Australia on their soil, a real achievement. It was also our tenth win on the bounce against southern hemisphere sides, which is unheard of. I think that at this stage, we felt like we were getting to a position where we believed we were the best side in the world, believed that we could beat anyone, and most importantly, believed that we could win the World Cup. During the past year or so, we'd beaten sides home and away, so I guess, bar the French, who'd beaten us in the 2002 Six Nations, we could claim to be able to beat the best.

Despite that confidence, Clive played the media game very coyly post-match, and installed Australia as the favourites and the team to beat, as they would be the hosts for the 2003 World Cup and he stated that they knew how to peak at the right time for a major tournament. I don't remember a specific conversation with him about it at the time, but you can be certain that he didn't believe what he was saying. We'd just destroyed Australia and we believed we could beat them again, but Clive was always thinking one step ahead, and at this stage in time I think he wanted to ease the pressure on us and ensure there was no sign of complacency in the camp.

Two months later, we were back on the field again for the first of three World Cup warm-up matches, all in the northern hemisphere. First up was Wales at the Millennium Stadium, where Clive named a young, experimental line-up, and I was one of many to be rested. Jason Leonard skippered the side, and we scored five tries through Moodos, Luger, Worsley, Stuart Abbott and Dorian West, with no reply, for a 43-9 victory. That was our 14th Test win on the bounce, whereas Wales were on the ropes, having suffered 11 straight defeats.

A week later, the squad travelled to Marseille to face France. Clive again named an experimental side, seeing the bigger picture that it was important for the peripheral players to gain big-match experience. France, on the other hand, named their strongest XV. Dorian West skippered the side and Tins went over for the first try, but a Nicolas Brusque reply and the kicking of Frederic Michalak saw France squeeze home 17-16, and in the process end our unbeaten run. The whole squad was devastated as we wanted to go unbeaten right through until the end of the World Cup, and also break the record held by New Zealand and South Africa at the time of 17 consecutive Test wins. Michalak's injury-time kick was enough for them and we'd missed our chances to be out of sight, so it was a lesson for us. Looking back, I would say that France defeat was the best thing that could have happened to us ahead of the World Cup. We were flying at the time and this was a reminder to keep ourselves grounded and realise that in knockout rugby, just one kick, or one mistake, could be enough to send you home empty-handed. In all honesty, we were never an arrogant bunch anyway, and the peer pressure from the group would keep each guy in line, but the defeat was still just what we needed, in order to reach the ultimate prize.

Before games, Clive, as part of the preparation in the training camp, would gather the leadership group together, to ensure that every area of the team was happy with their duties and ready to play. Defensively, it was myself and Mike Tindall, for the line-out it was Ben Kay, the scrum was Phil Vickery and Steve Thompson, in attack it was Jonny and Will Greenwood. If we ever said we had a problem, or we weren't content, then Clive would look to our respective coach, Phil Larder in my case, and ask why we weren't ready. There was a fluid chain of responsibility and it ensured that no one was ever left wondering what to do, or who to ask for help. Clive would always turn to us to ask whether we were prepared, and that trust had developed over seven years. It was something that most players weren't used to in their careers. I had worked with some great coaches over time, but the meticulous level of detail that Clive and his staff went in to was really something else that you had to see to believe. What also helped us was that Clive wasn't afraid to make mistakes. He would always put his money where his mouth was, and that allowed us as a group to never really experience fear in what we said, suggested, or what we did out on the field of play. That environment allowed us to express ourselves, and it was a complete breath of fresh air for me to work closely with someone as talented as Phil Larder. Our key goals, which I mentioned earlier, were set not by one man in the team, but by the players collectively, and then adopted by Phil and then by Clive. We were empowered and motivated. I mean, our black book we had individually was so thick in size, and the detail was incredible. It wasn't handed to us, we'd created it together with our ideas, and that became our ethos and our blueprint to work from.

Alongside the warm-up games was our pre-World Cup training camp, at Pennyhill Park, which was, without any doubt, the most intense experience of my rugby life. Unfortunately, because of the calf injury I sustained against Wales in the Six Nations, I wasn't able to contribute as much as I would have liked, which was a huge disappointment to me. Often, I had to train alone, as my injury had to be monitored and managed throughout, to ensure there were no setbacks. Don't get me wrong, the training still meant that I went through some near-death experiences! This was the final blast for everyone before the World Cup started and if things weren't already serious, then they certainly were now. There were a few training prizes given out during that camp, to reward achievement and effort, and one of them was awarded to me by Dave Reddin. It was nice that I'd got it, but it was not just for that week, it was for my overall contribution, and it didn't quite feel right that I'd been given it. I guess it was just to encourage me back to full fitness, and the coaching staff definitely felt my frustrations during this period. I wasn't the only one who was being managed during this time, but the public perhaps doesn't get to see the behind-the-scenes work that goes in to making you the player, and the team, that you are at a major tournament. If I'd have overdone it during that training camp, or been played in all of those warm-up games, my final chance of World Cup glory could have slipped through my fingers. Clive and his staff made sure, due to their meticulous approach, that it simply wouldn't happen.

Our final warm-up match, ahead of the World Cup, was a rematch against the French, just a week after the defeat, but this time it was at Twickenham. It was a send-off for us before the long trip to Australia and the final World Cup squad was to be named the day after the game, so there was still real hunger in the camp to impress Clive and his staff. For some people it was their last chance, and we knew that five men would be heartbroken and would miss out.

Lol missed out on all of the warm-up matches, through injury, but the team for the final game was the strongest of the three. Martin Corry joined Hilly and me in the back row, Johno was back as captain, and we had the likes of Moodos, Daws and Josh Lewsey on the bench. The French were a little weaker than in Marseille and we took full advantage to absolutely smash them, gain revenge for the previous defeat, and end on a real high. Ben Cohen helped himself to two tries, Lewsey, Robbo and Balshaw all grabbed one each and we came home 45-14, with Wilko and Paul Grayson adding points from the boot. Johno and Wilko were taken off at 38-3 by Clive, and frustratingly we allowed Aurelien Rougerie to score a last-gasp try for the visitors, which took the shine off a little.

I remember Clive being asked after the game about the decision to play against the likes of Wales and France as the warm-up opposition. There was always a chance that both would be our opposition during the knockout stages of the competition, once the draw was made, and I'm sure that helped us in our preparation, as we knew both teams inside out. As I've said previously though, we had beaten everyone by this stage, so there really was nothing left for us to fear.

Clive named the World Cup squad the day after the final warm-up game, with five players missing out on the trip to Australia from the provisional squad, all of whom had played their part in the years leading up to the tournament. It must have been gut-wrenching for Clive and his staff, and I can only imagine how distraught I would have been, had I received the call that no one wanted. Thirty of us were privileged to make it, and as I said, five missed out in the end, but then there was a summer training camp group of 52, so each of those played their part too. Someone always had to miss out, and most notably, Graham Rowntree, who is now a coach in the current England set-up and a good friend, who played in four out of the five 2003 Six Nations games, was one of them. Wig played in that defeat to France in the warm-up matches, and he was a world-class player, but I guess that the staff went for Trevor Woodman instead. Simon Shaw missed out, but did later join up with the squad during the tournament due to an injury to Danny Grewcock, and Austin Healey, who had struggled with a knee injury, also didn't make the cut. He had worked very hard with Bill Knowles, an injury specialist, and was desperately unlucky to not make the trip, but I think Austin, while incredibly versatile across the back line, suffered from the fact that there was probably a better specialist player in each of those positions. Austin, as anyone and everyone knows, could and perhaps should have been a little more humble during his career, but you need characters in the game and he was certainly a character. I am sure he missed out due to Andy Gomarsall being a specialist number nine, and we'll never know what impact Austin could have made in 2003. I'm sure he'll tell you if you ask him though!

James Simpson-Daniel was another not to make the cut. The likes of Luger, Balshaw, Cohen and Lewsey who came from nowhere, and Jason Robinson, meant it was difficult for James to get past those guys. Ollie Smith, a real talent, was the final one of the five, and he'd had injury problems too.

With Charlie Hodgson and Alex King injured ahead of the squad announcement, that created extra space at fly-half, and Mike Catt made the trip. I'm a big believer in things happening for a reason, and circumstances dictated that Catty was needed in Australia. I recall that even he was surprised that he got the nod, but his experience and his ability was to prove absolutely vital for us, and hopefully will do for the current crop in 2015, through his role as England assistant coach.

I was gutted for Wig though. He was a mate and I'd played with him for Leicester, England and the British & Irish Lions. You'd never want to say you were in the squad for sure, but he'd played so well, especially in the win over New Zealand, when me and Lol were off the field and he held them off in the scrum on our line. That win was so crucial to everything we did, and probably signalled a change in people's thinking in the rugby world. For Wig to not make it showed the strength in the team and the squad as a whole. Hopefully now that Graham is part of the England set-up, he can use his experiences to help the current guys achieve World Cup success.

So this was it. Surely my final crack at winning the World Cup. It felt as if my whole career, all those battles and all the success and the heartache had built to this. Australia, and the final piece of our jigsaw.

6

Dad's Army

AS we boarded the flight to Australia for the World Cup, there was genuine excitement among the whole squad. On the flight over I had some time to reflect and I knew that, most likely, this would be my last World Cup. At the age of 34, although I would never normally say never, I knew that at 38 years old I would probably be too old for the 2007 World Cup. I had been privileged to play for the Leicester Tigers and England, winning everything possible, apart from the main prize – the William Webb Ellis Trophy. That, for me, would be the final piece in the jigsaw.

We carried with us the tag of favourites, although the All Blacks were highly fancied, as were the hosts, Australia. We were ranked number one in the world and I know that personally, I felt that we were unbeatable. I looked around the aircraft on the flight over, and I knew that we had the right characters to stay strong during a tournament, and our record over the past year or so meant that we had no reason not to be confident. That confidence was creditable as well. We had beaten everyone leading up to this tournament, so there was never even a hint of arrogance about us, despite that having been levied against us many times. I felt that if we could maintain our discipline, our togetherness and stick to our adaptable playing philosophy, then we would become world champions.

When we arrived in Perth, we were faced with the Australian media. As I have said already, I love them, as they are always 100 per cent behind their team, which doesn't always seem to be the case with the UK media in regard to our sports teams, particularly in England. Our media will always look for negatives in performance, or quite often in off-field issues, rather than showing support to the team and urging the public to get behind the players. We had won games in the past, and also in this tournament, where we were criticised for our performance, but ultimately we must have been doing something right as we were winning. We were faced with the same old story though; England are too old, too slow and too boring. Then the Australian media claimed that the RFU had more money and resources than other unions. Any opportunity they had to get under our skin, they would take it and get tucked in to us.

We were drawn in Pool C, along with Samoa, Georgia, Uruguay and our main rivals for top position, South Africa. We began with ten days in Perth, preparing for our first game, against Georgia. I think we all agreed that it was a good fixture with which to begin the tournament, as opposed to facing either South Africa or Samoa first up. We had a chance to acclimatise to the tournament and to get everyone firing, before the games that would determine qualification. There is always a risk of being caught cold in the first match, but in some senses, and with no disrespect intended to Georgia, we were able to ease in to the competition. To be honest, we had done all of the hard work in the training camp, back at Pennyhill Park, so those ten days ahead of Georgia was just to get us sharp, and to avoid anything unnecessary happening pre-tournament.

As expected, we took Georgia apart with a very comfortable 84-6 victory, in typically English conditions, with the rain absolutely teeming down. I think we adapted to the weather without discussing it, as we had prepared for this, and we had extensive experience of poor weather. For what it's worth, I scored the fourth try of our 12 in this game, which secured the bonus point, and Jonny kicked all seven of his kicks. It was a case of job done, and there was nothing to be gained really from a match that we were expected to win, and win well, but it wasn't an easy game. In fact I've never played in an easy international game, there is always a test, even if you thrash a side, they will still present both a physical and mental battle for you to overcome.

Will Greenwood and Ben Cohen both grabbed two tries, but for Will's second try the number two was important in another way, as he was tackled strongly as he went over the line and had his testicles grabbed by the Georgian defender. On his way back to the halfway line, after finding his breath, Will popped his hand down his shorts, and then raised two fingers in the air. The commentators at the time said he was signalling his second try to the crowd, but actually he was letting his wife, Caroline, know that his two balls were still intact! Tins, Daws, Thommo, Lol, Robbo, Luges and Ronnie all grabbed a try each to complete the dozen, and I was delighted that we didn't concede any tries, just a couple of penalties.

Mark 'Ronnie' Regan had to have it explained to him on more than one occasion why he was called 'Ronnie', when his name was Mark. When he was informed that it was because of the former President of the United States of America, he simply replied, 'Who's that babs?' Quite clearly, a sandwich short of a picnic. We could have quite easily named a weaker side for this game, but I agreed with Clive and his staff, as by naming our strongest side, we were able to make a statement.

We wanted to put Georgia to the sword, and metaphorically we put our foot on their throat, to show the rest of the pool that we were ruthless. Unfortunately, as Georgia were a very strong and physical side, we suffered injuries to Daws and Hilly, which meant they missed out on the next game, against our main rivals South Africa, and were replaced by Kyran Bracken and Lewis Moody. I think we always knew that the squad, as a whole, would play a part in the tournament though, and we had great options in terms of replacements, as competition was so strong. We didn't quite have that in the 1999 World Cup, but this time around, we had the real luxury of strength in depth, and also more experience, which proved critical.

The South Africa game was always going to be an interesting one. Roll back the clock to Corne Krige's comment to me of 'see you in Perth' and we knew exactly what we were facing. It was a big game. We didn't talk about it like that though; we all knew that we had to win the next game, whoever it was against, and that was the mentality that we had to maintain throughout the tournament if we were going to go all the way. At the final team training session, when ideally you would want closed doors and privacy, so you can practice and hone final moves and set pieces, we were absolutely inundated with media, and three helicopters were hovering over the pitch. We had security, but the media were swarming everywhere. Obviously, we tried not to let it affect us, but you couldn't help but notice the circus. It wasn't what we thought it was at the time either. We were sure that the media were trying to get an idea of what we were planning for the South Africa game, but actually they were all there to try and steal a glimpse of Prince Harry, as the rumour had it that he was going to attend our final pre-match training session.

Both Prince Harry and Prince William were, and still are, huge supporters of English rugby, attending games and coming in to the dressing room from time to time post-match, but they would never have interrupted our preparations.

My daughter Olivia was born on 27 September 1999, and two weeks after that, we faced New Zealand in Pool B of the Rugby World Cup of that year. Olivia attended our match on 9 October, having only been out of hospital for a couple of days. Jayne Woodward, Clive's wife, headed up a party of wives and girlfriends who had lunch in Richmond before the game and they travelled on the coach to Twickenham with Prince William. Jayne turned to my wife Ali, and said, 'We've got a very important person, who needs to get off the coach first.' With Prince William on the coach, people moved out of his way, but then Jayne introduced, 'Olivia Back.' Prince William waited and let Olivia, Ali and my sister-in-law, Linda go first, and helped them off the bus. That was a nice touch. All of the wives and girlfriends were invited in to the President's Box and then Olivia came down to the dressing room afterwards, so not a bad first game for her, even though we lost 30-16 to the All Blacks. That was the key game of the pool, four years previous, and defeat meant we faced a play-off game against Fiji in midweek, which we won, and then a quarter-final in Paris against South Africa, where Jannie De Beer's record-breaking five drop-kicks in the game broke our hearts. This time around, we needed to win the key pool match, to not only qualify for the quarter-finals, but to make our potential route to the final easier.

If we could beat South Africa, then barring something dramatic happening, we would qualify as pool winners. Keeping in mind Corne Krige's statement, and the brutality of our last game against them, we also heard rumours coming out of their training camp that they were dressing up bags with England shirts and numbers before tackling them. Ridiculous, I know, but all of this stoked us up, so why they chose to leak that information to the media, I'll never know.

At half-time we were level at 6-6 and the game was hugely physical once again, which is exactly what we expected from them, so it was no real surprise, despite Krige's ironic pre-match claim in the media that Johno was one of the dirtiest captains in world rugby. Will Greenwood's second-half try opened the game up for us, after fantastic work from Moodos in charging down a right-footed kick to the left-side touchline, a skill that no one in world rugby could match him on, and he would always back himself to get there.

We all practised that skill, and people would perhaps presume that a charge-down is just down to chance, but it was a tactic to target hitting someone's foot, rather than aiming for space around the player, and that way you would at least be able to create upset, in a legal way, for your opponent. Moodos was always going to be our best bet, as he was as mad as a box of frogs! You could see players rushing their kicks if Moodos was around. We cruised home with a 25-6 win, and again, didn't concede any tries, so we were happy from a defensive perspective. That was also our fifth win on the bounce against South Africa; something which gave us all immense pride as the games between us were always pretty tasty. At half-time, despite being level, we didn't panic, and we ultimately deserved to win, and establish an advantage in the group.

The next day, the Australian media hit back at us with, 'Is that all you've got?' in reference to us only scoring one try and kicking most of our points. It made me laugh, as not only had we completely nullified South Africa, and beaten them, we had found a way to overcome a side who were persistently using illegal methods to prevent us from playing a more free-flowing and attractive game. We were left to just take the points on offer, and if they were from the boot of Jonny, then we were quite happy to say thank you and rack up the points on the board. Jonny converted Will's try, along with four penalties and two drop goals. We were all quite content with the win, however, as much as the Aussies tried to mock us and get in to our heads.

After two games in Perth, we then flew to Melbourne for our next match against the dangerous Samoans. We checked in to the Sheraton Towers, where we had stayed previously in the summer, when we beat Australia. Clive and his team always tried to create familiarity in the group with where we were staying, almost like creating a second home. For example, whenever we returned to Pennyhill Park, our training base back in Surrey, we would stay not just in the same hotel, but in the exact same room, again to create the feeling of a second home for us.

I have already said that each game in world rugby is difficult, but the Samoans were a particularly physical side, who had a much higher tackling technique than most nations. They try and create that mental and physical pressure on a side, and outmuscle their opposition, but we were battle-hardened to that type of approach, and we were a physically strong side ourselves, so we weren't prepared to be bullied. After all, we'd faced the brutality of South Africa and come through the test twice recently. Having said that, Samoa came out of the blocks and scored a fantastic try from a sweeping move, finished off by Semo Sititi and for the first 20 minutes or so, they were extremely good, and we were clearly on the back foot. They were 10-0 up after five minutes, and we had to take the approach of keeping the ball in the forwards a little longer, and try to grind them down, using our superior fitness and stamina. We scored a pushover try and battled our way back in to the game, but Samoa were playing the rugby of their lives, lifting their game like so many nations did when they played against England.

At half-time we were 16-13 behind and there was a real calmness in the dressing room, no shouting or swearing, just methodically aired views to put right our wrongs. Our protocol at half-time was to go to your space in the room, take deep breaths and rehydrate, which would help to calm you and your thoughts. We'd be quiet for the first two minutes and compose ourselves. Then we'd have a discussion, where the leaders within the team were asked by Clive to give comment, before forwards and backs would break off and talk in smaller numbers about specific roles and things we needed to rectify. Then we would all come together again as a group, for some key messages, before returning to the field. On that day, we had made a lot of errors, and had struggled to keep hold of the ball. We needed to make Samoa work harder to get the ball back from us, and in the process, this would help to tire them out, which would allow us to dominate the end of the game. That half-time discussion was crucial, as our plan was exactly how the second half turned out. Even with just 17 minutes remaining, Samoa led 22-20, but there was no panic among the group.

In a normal World Cup support staff, you would take 12 people with you, but Clive took 18 members of staff to Australia with us. Although he achieved huge support from the RFU in many areas, such as paving the way for us to have our own rooms, instead of sharing as we had two or three years earlier, the RFU wouldn't cover the costs for the additional staff that Clive wanted there with us. They paid for a few, but not for everyone. One of those not covered was Richard Smith QC, our legal adviser, and I suppose there would be a few eyebrows raised at why a QC would be needed for a Rugby World Cup campaign. Well, this was why we needed him. At the end of the Samoa game, there was a blood injury to Tins, who went off to receive treatment, with Dan Luger his replacement. Dan was sent on by Dave Reddin, under Clive's instructions, and made a tackle during the time that we had 16 men on the pitch, and clearly there was an error made, for which Clive and everyone associated with England, including the RFU, directly apologised. Samoa showed maturity in the situation and didn't complain at all, but to complicate matters, there was an altercation and words were exchanged between fourth official Steve Walsh and our performance coach Dave Reddin.

I guess at worst, we could have been disqualified from the competition, or potentially deducted points, and that appeared to be what the Aussie media were calling for, along with Toutai Kefu, who missed out on the Wallaby squad for the tournament, and chucked his opinion in, 'The bottom line is that rules are rules. England defied a tournament official. That is the key issue here. They should be deducted the points they got from the game and the points handed to Samoa.' At the end of the day, sense prevailed, and we accepted a fine of £10,000 and Dave was banned for two weeks, although he was cleared of any wrongdoing by a Rugby World Cup disciplinary panel. Allegedly, Dave had water squirted in his face by Steve Walsh during everything that went on, and Steve was subsequently banned for three days for inappropriate behaviour, meaning he missed out on officiating in the France vs United States of America game. It really didn't affect the game, and was nothing but a storm in a teacup, but Richard Smith's support in ensuring that our punishment was no greater, once again showed just how well Clive had prepared us. He left no stone unturned, and by having Richard there, he covered all eventualities, however unlikely they were. I grabbed a try, and Phil Vickery added a late one, and we were home 35-22, and had qualified for the quarter-finals, with a game left to play.

Next up, on Sunday 2 November, were Uruguay who, like Georgia, were expected to be easy fodder for us. We needed to win the game in order to secure top spot in the group, as South Africa had beaten Samoa comfortably on the Saturday, and hopefully face an easier path to the final, although we knew that any path would be a serious challenge for us. Clive used the opportunity to give some players game time, while resting a few of us, to ensure we weren't fatigued going in to the quarter-finals. With no disrespect to Uruguay, we could afford to do that and still win the game, and when we played at full strength against Georgia in the opening game, we picked up injuries to Hilly and Daws. Now we were approaching the knockout stages, every decision held even greater importance. I was one of the players rested, and the plan was for us to all head to the Gold Coast for some rest and relaxation. Unfortunately, owing to the court case regarding the incident at the end of the Samoa game, all of the media followed us there, so it wasn't the most private of times for the squad. We were meant to have some downtime with our families, away from the limelight, but the media were all in the same hotel as us. It was quite a change for our families to have members of the media at the next table at breakfast, but we were getting used to the scrutiny we were under, and that was the nature of the challenge we were facing and also a strong sign of the increasing popularity of the sport as a whole. During the downtime, the management were flying back and forth to get the court case resolved. Thankfully, as chance would have it, being rested for the Uruguay game was a blessing in disguise, as circumstances would dictate that I wouldn't have been able to play anyway.

Martin Corry was named in the side, having flown home to be at the side of his wife Tara for the birth of their daughter Eve. Cozza was back and ready to play against Uruguay despite the long journey. Will Greenwood was in a similar situation during this tournament. Will and his wife Caro had tragically lost their first-born, Freddie, at birth, and Will returned home to be with his wife as she was in labour expecting their next child. Will missed the Samoa and

Uruguay games, and returned for the knockout stages as a father, which was wonderful news for him. The importance of family at this time could perhaps be forgotten when you are trying to win a World Cup, but family must always come first, and I know that was Clive's mantra, and he was always supportive of his players if they needed to be with their loved ones. It was just another example of the family bond he had cultivated within the group, which was a complete change to the way things used to be when on England duty.

My wife Ali arrived in Australia on the Wednesday before the Uruguay game, with her sister Linda, our four-year-old daughter Olivia, and our one-year-old son Finley. Olivia was ill before they flew to Australia, and she was cleared to fly by the doctor, but unfortunately deteriorated during the flight. When they arrived at their hotel, it wasn't ready, and Olivia was getting worse. I'll let Ali pick up this part of the story, as she remembers it much better than I do.

'My sister and I found out a week before we were due to fly out to the World Cup that our mum had been diagnosed with cancer and it was already a difficult decision as to whether to go or not, with Olivia being four, and Fin having just turned one. Obviously England had hoped to do well, but it was difficult to know how long to be there for, so we planned to be there for the last three weeks of the tournament. My mum was in hospital the whole time we were away, but Neil's mum and dad, Vanessa and Keith, visited her every day and they were fantastic.

'Olivia took ill two days before we flew out, just with a routine cough and a cold. We checked with the doctor on the morning of the flight and he said she would be fine. As Fin was under two years old, he was able to sit on my lap, but he was quite a big lad so there was no way I was going to do that for a 24-hour flight. So to take Fin, we had to have a car seat with us as well. We had luggage for the four of us, as my sister was with us, and a pushchair and medication too. Fin fell asleep and Olivia was quiet, so Linda and I had a glass of champagne and began to think that this wouldn't be so bad. We stopped off in Singapore to change flights, and we had to lug everything with us, without any help. By this stage, Olivia was deteriorating quickly, and my sister just filled out the landing cards for us as I was preoccupied. As we arrived in to Australia, we had sniffer dogs around our bags and we could have got in trouble for not declaring having baby food in our luggage, and also for Linda just ticking everything on the card, rather than me signing my own.

'We arrived in the early hours and couldn't check in to our room, so I rang Neil and got a taxi to his room, and the team doctor, Simon Kemp, checked Olivia out. He wasn't completely happy, so Neil and I accompanied Olivia to the hospital and we stayed overnight with her. We didn't know what was wrong with her and I was worried as it was suspected she could have meningitis, due to a rash she had. Then it dawned on me that we had been in the team hotel, so I was concerned that whatever Olivia had could have spread to the players. In the end, it was thankfully just a virus, and her body had reacted poorly to the flight as well, so she was very ill for the first week of our time in Australia. I remember people looking at her at the start of the next week, as she didn't look well, and she won't thank me for saying that now, but we were so relieved that she was recovering.'

The range of emotions that go through your mind at that stage is incredible. The last thing on my mind was being in a World Cup. I just wanted to be with Olivia and the rest of my family, and do anything I could to help my daughter. Linda took Fin back to their hotel, which to be honest, was horrible and stayed there for a while, until they could come over to our hotel, so we could be together in the same building. I probably shouldn't be saying this, but on our days off I was in the same room as my family regardless. There was no way I was having my family stay somewhere like that. It was a hotel that was booked for all of the wives and girlfriends, with a tour operator they were advised to go with, and it was awful. I spent the next day lying on my bed, with Olivia at my side, and eventually two or three days later, Olivia recovered, to our great relief. In hindsight, I regret that we put our small children through the travel, but understandably I wanted all of my family there with me for the tournament.

I could see in Ali's eyes when she arrived that it hadn't been a great flight, and that Olivia really wasn't well. Ali was, and always has been, so supportive of my career, of everything I do, and she waited until after the World Cup to tell me what a journey from hell that had been! She didn't want to put any extra pressure on me ahead of the final games. I still trained whenever I was scheduled to train during the time that Olivia was ill, so luckily I didn't have to take a break from training, as I would have obviously wanted to be by her side. It was an emotional period for us all, and we were just grateful that Olivia was well again and that Ali, Linda and Fin could finally settle in. Ali picks up the story again, from her perspective.

'I'll never forget how good Clive and his wife Jayne were to us during this period. In fact they had changed everything about the way we were all treated. Before Clive was in charge, after matches we would have dinner as wives and girlfriends on our own table, separated from the players, and he integrated everything and completely changed the culture. By the time of the 2003 World Cup, we were a settled group of people together, suffering with the players through the grand slam heartache, and I think that helped to develop a real understanding and togetherness. The biggest advice I could give to the current and future rugby wives and girlfriends is to ensure that they have their own lives and don't sit at home all day waiting for their man to come home. It's important to be independent and I'm glad that I have been like that, and have created a consistent routine for our children.'

The Uruguay game was an absolute rout, which was exactly what it should have been. We won 111-13, scoring 17 tries, way too many for me to list them all here! Josh Lewsey scored five himself though, equalling Rory Underwood's record for England, set against Fiji at Twickenham in 1989. I know I always go on about it, and it was even more frustrating as I watched from the stands, but we conceded one try, which showed a sign of weakness, however small it was. Everyone was delighted that we had scored over 100 points and 17 tries, but all I could think about was conceding that one try, that lapse in concentration and slight lack of mentality. I was annoyed that we had allowed that to happen, but maybe some of my annoyance was because I was unable to do anything about it.

People were probably wondering why I was unhappy, but being off the field, plus Olivia's illness and us conceding a sloppy try was more than enough to put me in a mood. Joe Worsley was sin-binned late on for a high tackle, which was needless, and he was then disciplined further for waving to the crowd as he left the field. At the time, I just felt that he should have got off the pitch. It was a minor incident, but in fairness to Joe, I don't think he did it in any way other than to thank the supporters, but Joe wasn't the sharpest tool in the box, like Ronnie! I'd been sin-binned along with Lol back in the summer against New Zealand, and all I felt was that I had let everyone down, so I'm sure that was just Joe's way of dealing with the disappointment. Another slight mark against the game was Iain Balshaw, who was in great form, being stretchered off with a sprained ankle, but Clive was confident of him being fit for the rest of the tournament.

We had secured top spot in the pool, and that meant a quarter-final against Wales, so we would remain in Brisbane, although we did switch hotels to the Hilton and the media moved too. They'd been with us at the Gold Coast, with us at the Sheraton, and then with us again. We were in a goldfish bowl. With our families with us, there was simply no privacy, but we had a good relationship with people in the media, so it was as we expected. I guess it was just a bit claustrophobic and it was part of the pressure of dealing with a World Cup environment.

Wales had lost to New Zealand in their final pool game, 53-37, but had really impressed in the process. The only time we'd previously faced Wales in a World Cup was in the first tournament in 1987, and they had come out on top 16-3 in Auckland. We were determined to make sure this wasn't the end of our journey. Clive maintained that if we beat South Africa in the pool stage, we would all back ourselves to at least reach the final, but actually doing it is a different matter and we knew that the Welsh would raise their game. They were the underdogs, but they had shown promise against the All Blacks, and they had quality players like Colin Charvis, Stephen Jones and Shane Williams among others. In some ways, they had nothing to lose against us and everything to gain.

In the first half we were terrible, but credit to Wales, they were superb and they came at us with everything they had. I returned to the side, as did the other regulars and we were pretty much at full strength, just with Hilly and Lewsey missing through injury. Robbo was at full-back for this one and Daws was back in after his injury, replacing Andy Gomarsall who had done well against Uruguay. I felt that there was a noticeable difference among the group going in to this game. Perhaps we were weighed down a little by something? I'm certain that we were all quite 'leggy' in the first half, as we had trained very hard between the Uruguay game and this one. This was without doubt the worst

40 minutes in Clive's reign with England, apart from the infamous 1998 'Tour of Hell'. We were simply awful. We had saved our worst performance, for the most important time to date, and we were just 40 minutes away from being sent home. We had beaten Wales in the Six Nations, quite comfortably, and also in the World Cup warm-up match, so we knew we had the measure of them, but we desperately needed to regroup at half-time. In all the times I've played alongside Johno, for Tigers, England and the Lions, this half-time was the best of his career. We were two tries to nothing down, and losing 10-3, and frankly it could have been a lot worse, as they had missed their two conversions. Johno had a way of saying the right things, without saying too much. He spoke about how hard we had all worked, and how it was too soon for us to go home. He refocused our minds and galvanised us all. We knew exactly what we needed to do to avoid an early exit. This was where everything that Clive had developed, with his support staff, through the leadership group, came together.

Clive, along with Andy Robinson and his coaches, also demonstrated a perfect example of T-CUP (Thinking Correctly Under Pressure), by making a crucial change, bringing Mike Catt on at 12 for Dan Luger, with Tins moving on to the wing. That move allowed Jonny some breathing space and Catty's kicking ability allowed us to dictate the way the second half was played. We played the next 40 minutes in the Welsh half. I think that Catty's skillsets and decision-making took the pressure off Jonny and gave us extra options. He'd obviously watched the game in the first half and was able to see where we were going wrong and he was an experienced pro, perfect for this kind of game. During the second half, Jason Leonard also came on for Trevor Woodman, and Stuart Abbott was on for Shaggy. Then Bracko replaced Daws. We showed what a strong squad we had, how composed we could be and how much fitter and stronger we were than other sides. Robbo then ripped through the Welsh defence, with a blistering display of pace, and set up Will for our only try, before he departed, which Jonny converted to level us up at 10-10. From being completely outplayed in the first half, we were level, and now had the momentum to go on and win the game. Martin Williams grabbed a third try for the Welsh, after Jonny had kicked a further three penalties, to tighten the score up at 19-17, then Jonny grabbed another two penalties and a late drop goal to finish. We had won 28-17, but in truth, the game was probably a lot closer than that.

I think that the Wales game was a great example of how we self-medicated. Throughout Clive's time in charge we'd suffered disappointment, normally in the form of failing at the final hurdle in our grand slam attempts, but we'd always learned from our mistakes and eventually we would put things right. In the Wales game, we were facing elimination and embarrassment, having hugely underperformed, but in that dressing room at half-time, almost like clockwork, each man in the room played their part in fixing our problems. No one ranted or raved, it was methodical and composed. We were energetic and loud, but it was thoughtful, not just an emotional outburst. It would have been easy for us to have argued with each other, and apportioned blame for that first half, with tempers frayed, but instead we worked as one slick machine, and we won that second half 25-7. If we needed another reminder of how tough this tournament was going to be, then Wales had certainly provided it. Wales were incredible at the start of the game. Over history, in the same way you think of the French, Wales have tremendous flair and are always capable of beating any side in the world. They have such a passion for the game, which is entrenched in to the history of their proud nation, and no matter what team they name, the Welsh will always have talented players, it is just a case of them being able to apply that talent as a team. We had to force them to play from deep and make mistakes, but the Welsh forced us to do that in the first half. Thankfully, we were through to the semi-finals. It wasn't pretty, and I remember hearing a few boos when Jonny kicked that late drop goal, probably from the locals, but that didn't bother us one bit. We were here to do a job, and we had taken one big step nearer to realising our dreams.

Following this game, I think that everyone outside of the English and Australian sides expected it to be a France vs New Zealand final. We faced France in the semi-final and the hosts faced New Zealand. Arguably, it was the two best sides of the northern hemisphere and the two best sides of the southern hemisphere against each other. I think as a result of our scares against Samoa and Wales, we were suddenly unfancied against the French. It was as if people had forgotten that we had won all five of our games at the tournament, were ranked number one in the world and had won 21 out of our last 22 matches. The one we lost was by a single point, with a weakened side. We all laughed and really enjoyed that suddenly, because the French had demolished the Irish 43-21 in the quarter-finals, they were the side in form and they were going to beat us. Clive and Eddie Jones, the Australian boss, must have been rubbing their hands.

I know that Clive had enjoyed playing down our chances back in the summer when we beat Australia in Melbourne, and this played right in to our hands. We hadn't won each game with flair and free-flowing rugby, but that was tournament rugby, it was about winning. We'd learned that in 1999 against Wales at Wembley, when if we had taken the points available from a late penalty, instead of going for a try, we would have had a grand slam for our efforts. We weren't prepared to make the same mistake again, and the wins over Samoa and Wales may not have been the prettiest, but they were wins nonetheless. In the tournament to date we had scored 12 tries against Georgia, one against South Africa, four against Samoa, 17 against Uruguay and one against Wales, so it wasn't as if we had suddenly become a defensive or negative side. Add to this our emphatic grand slam win over Ireland with five tries and the three we scored against Australia in the summer, and I think this helps to put everything in to context and emphasises that we were an attacking side at heart. We knew where we were as a group. I was able to look around the room and knew that in any conditions, we could beat anyone, and we had a strong collective belief, regardless of the difficulties we had faced at the tournament.

Despite the criticism, I didn't avoid reading the press personally. I wouldn't read everything, but I was aware of it. I just smiled about the criticism, and in some cases, used it as a motivation. We knew that historically, the French had raised their game for World Cup rugby, and that they were a dangerous side. They had beaten us in round three of the 2002 Six Nations, on their way to the grand slam, and had also beaten our weakened side in Marseille by a point during the warm-up games for this tournament. They also hated us with a passion, as many countries seemed to, to be honest! For them, this was the biggest game imaginable, but we focused on the fact that it was just another game to play and another job for us to do.

The weather was poor again for the semi-final, but I didn't really feel that way at the time. I always compared playing rugby to being similar to learning to drive. At first you would think about everything you did, like when you've just passed your driving test, but eventually it all becomes second nature and you are in the zone. It wasn't until after the semi-final, when I read the papers and saw all the quotes from the French about the influence of the heavy rain, that I really thought about it. We were ready to adapt to any situation; weather, injuries, opposition tactics or form, whatever it was, we were prepared. If you have to deal with heavy rain, then it's the same for both sides. Again, we would have rather played in perfect conditions, as we did in the warm-up game at Twickenham when we thrashed them. As I've said before, we learned the lessons of the 2000 grand slam failure at Murrayfield, and I was sick of hearing about how the English loved wet conditions. We wanted perfect conditions so we could show exactly what we could do.

Hilly returned to the side after his absence through injury, and Clive kept with Catty, after his superb second-half display against the Welsh. Catty's nous and particularly his kicking game would also offer some protection to Jonny, as French star Serge Betsen was always likely to try and target and unsettle him, as he had done in the 2002 Six Nations defeat in Paris. Josh Lewsey also came back in as we freshened things up. I'd say, looking back, that this was probably our best performance of the tournament. Although Betsen scored an early try for the French, which was converted by Michalak, we didn't allow them to score a single point after that. We scored 21 unanswered points, all from Jonny's boot, to win 24-7. He kicked five penalties and notably, especially given what was to come in the final, three drop goals. The French had a very good back row unit but Hilly, Lol and myself outplayed them in every area on the day.

Clive knew that Jonny would be targeted, so having Catty around was the perfect tactic, and we had learned from 2002's disappointment. The French seemed to lose the game mentally, as well as losing on points. Christophe Dominici, the French winger, was sin-binned for a cynical trip on Robbo, and then hobbled off as if he was an 'injured footballer' on 22 minutes, by which time it was clear for all to see that they didn't fancy the conditions and didn't want the win as much as we did. We led 12-7 at half-time and then, on 52 minutes,

Betsen tried to take Jonny out, as he had done a year ago, and hit him very late, and was justifiably sin-binned. The tactic had backfired as they had lost arguably their dangerman, and our dangerman used the opportunity to kick us another three points closer to the final. It was practically over as a contest from there. Betsen's face carried his battle scars and he was a formidable direct opponent of mine. I see quite a lot of him at games, and he is a good lad, a nice guy, but we had a strong rivalry on the pitch. Playing against someone like Serge was the pinnacle of the sport and I relished that opportunity to pit myself against the best. As he left the field that day, so too did French hopes, and Serge showed his emotions. He was hurting. He'd tried to hurt us, but he was losing to the old enemy and he was in pain. I remembered the pain of 2002, when he was magnificent and I was on my knees, visualising another grand slam failure. This time it was our turn to watch them suffer.

I just couldn't get over how much the rain had affected them. They were 7-3 ahead after nine minutes, but even that couldn't inspire them. There were examples in that game where the French were looking at the rain, looking at their hands and looking towards the heavens. They were gone, and we all knew it. Tins came on late to replace Catty, who had provided a crucial role in the quarter- and semi-final respectively. Michalak was taken off, having missed four kicks from five, and they had lost it. As the whistle went we were delighted to have reached the World Cup Final, but I remember us treating it for what it was; a job half done. We shook hands with the French and left the field. I remember the day previous, we had found out that Australia had beaten New Zealand 22-10, and as we were travelling on a coach, we watched the highlights and we all mentioned how much the Aussies had celebrated at the final whistle. It was as if they had just played their final, and emptied their tank. They walked off as if they had won the World Cup. Maybe it was a release for them? Perhaps the pressure of playing the All Blacks and hosting a World Cup meant they were relieved? I don't know. We didn't make that mistake a day later. We had plenty left to give for the final, and it was a good job we did as that turned out to be an epic.

It is worth remembering that Jason Leonard came on briefly for Phil Vickery in the semi-final, for a blood injury, to set a record as the most capped international in rugby history, and he remains the most capped English player to this day. 'Leopard' was one of the guys who still remained from the amateur era. Looking back at his career, I'll never forget his first interview with the food nutritionist as we began to move in to the professional era. The nutritionist asked us all to keep a record of what we ate and drank in a week so they could help us to improve our diet. If we didn't know the nutritional values of what we ate, we were asked to bring the labels off the packaging with us. Leopard brought two black bin liners full of wrappers and packaging. He hadn't eaten all of that, but just wanted to wind her up. Looking shocked, she also asked him how many units of alcohol he would drink in an average week. Leopard replied, 'Twenty-eight pints!' and the nutritionist looked as if she was about to faint, as she felt she was dealing with an alcoholic. Jason explained that he would have 25 pints on a Saturday night out after a game, and then three more to wash down his Sunday lunch! Clearly he had to change his lifestyle eventually, as we all did to some extent, but it showed the kind of guy he was. He was, and still is, a great guy to have around.

I remember our work with the SBS (Special Boat Service), ahead of the 1999 World Cup, where they analysed us in terms of leadership and mental toughness. I was with Jase and Danny Grewcock, and we were seen to have strong leadership skills. Jase was tactile, with great emotional intelligence, and was a really sociable guy, as the 28 pints over a weekend would illustrate! He was a key member of our squad, and when you think back to the neck injury he suffered early in his career, his achievement is even more remarkable. He is the RFU president during the 2015 Rugby World Cup, which is another deserved accolade for him. I know he'll have to perform at over 120 club dinners during that period, so I really do fear for him and his health!

Before the final against Australia, there was huge scrutiny and focus on the game and on both sides. It was same old, same old in the build-up. We were called 'Grumpy Old Men', 'Dad's Army' and the *Sydney Daily Telegraph* quoted, 'The *Daily Telegraph* reported yesterday that the England rugby side was boring. This is incorrect. In fact the entire country is boring!' They had to try and have one last go, and tuck in to us, but it just made us all laugh again. Johno said that he felt we were going to win this game, regardless of what happened, and I think that reflected how we all felt pre-match. As a captain, I played with Johno for England, the Tigers and for the British & Irish Lions, and he would lead the teams out as captains do, and then turn around to the team and shout a few motivational expletives at his colleagues. Just before we entered the playing arena, I was often just behind him, and found myself raising an arm towards him, not because I thought he would hit me, but just to prevent his spit from landing on my face, as he barked his commands. However, for the final, he walked out and stopped as usual, turned and looked at us all and said nothing. There was just silence and a glare. I thought that was strange and out of character.

When we got back to Leicester the next week, we spoke about it, and he said that he had looked every player in the eyes, and knew we were ready. It was the best bit of leadership I'd ever witnessed. Lots of captains, managers and leaders feel that they have to say a lot to get their message across. He said nothing and sent a stronger message than ever to us all. When I go out to visit schools, or speak at events now, I use that as an example, and in society we seem to say so much and expect our leaders to inspire us, but this was as inspirational as it got for me. The point being that sometimes only a few words or nothing at all can have a far greater impact. Will Greenwood said that Johno would be the first guy in the trenches, but that because of the respect he commanded, you would all be pushing him out of the way to go over first. You couldn't buy that loyalty; it was created over many years, brilliantly, by Clive, the players, and the inspirational team he had gathered.

Clive brought Tins back in for Catty, having told Catty and Will Greenwood, in a room privately, that Tins would start and one of them wouldn't. It didn't surprise me to hear that Catty, being smart enough to know his own body and the bigger picture, said that he would be better on the bench and Will should start. Remember, this is a World Cup Final, the biggest game in rugby, and the maturity Catty showed there again backed up the environment that Clive and his staff had cultivated. I would say that it also showed what a team player Catty was, but in truth we all were, and it didn't surprise me at all to hear what he had said. As I've mentioned, Mike is now part of the England coaching team and his experience of playing in four World Cups, and his attitude, could prove invaluable.

We conceded our seventh and final try of the tournament as Lote Tuqiri out-jumped Robbo, with a massive height advantage, to put them ahead after a huge crossfield kick from Stephen Larkham. Strangely, after the success of that kick, they didn't use that tactic again. Jonny kicked two penalties to put us 6-5 ahead and then Benny Kay spilt the ball as he was destined to score a try. I found myself as scrum half, passed to Daws as first receiver and I think everyone expected Daws to dummy and score, but instead he passed to Benny, who probably didn't expect it. If he'd have fallen over with the ball he would have scored. The reaction of the players was incredible though. The shouts of 'next job' rang around, which was a team call to condition us mentally, not to dwell on errors and let them impact on future performance, along with a couple of pats on the back and we got on with it. Fast-forward to the end of the game and he composed himself to make a great call in the crucial line-out that led to Jonny's drop goal. If he hadn't have composed himself after that first-half error we might not have been here today, talking about this. Having said that, if we'd have lost, then I guess we would have all tucked in to him after the game, as we did, but thankfully with big smiles on our faces!

Jonny looked injured at 6-5 but got back up to put us 9-5 ahead and then two minutes before half-time, Lol, as he so often did, found Jonny, who passed to Robbo and his quick feet danced him over the line for a try. Robbo celebrated by punching the ball in towards the crowd and we were 14-5 ahead at the break. We had dominated the first half and really should have had more points on the board and gone on to win more comfortably. If anyone had have said that we wouldn't score another point in the second half, at that stage, I would have thought they were out of their mind. That is elite sport though.

Australia slowly fought back and kept in touch with us and we were left to rue our missed chances. Greenwood burst through when we were 14-11 ahead and was tripped up with a football-style tackle. We ended up losing that second half 9-0, mainly due to penalties given away at the scrum. I felt that Phil Vickery had one of his best games in an England shirt, particularly at the scrum, but the referee, Andre Watson, didn't see it that way and was penalising him. Catty came on for Tins and with two minutes remaining, we were 17-14 ahead, defending a scrum in our 22, and Johno turned to the ref and said, 'You've got to penalise three,' referring to their number three, Al Baxter. The ref responded to Johno, 'I'll pen what I see,' and then duly penalised us, and Elton Flatley's kick sailed over the posts, took the game in to extra time, and temporarily snatched victory away from us.

We knew we had the ability and the fitness to beat them, so we weren't worried, and going to extra time was another sign of the character we had in the group. Clive used his experience, bringing Leopard on, and told him to sort out the scrum. Leopard pretty much said to the ref that he wasn't going to go up, down, forwards or backwards and wasn't going to scrummage. He did nothing but his job, and ensured that he wasn't penalised, which nullified the advantage the Aussies were gaining from the referees' decisions. It was strange that we weren't penalised again at the scrum.

It must have been very difficult for Clive and his staff at this time, as they came on with instructions and reminders, giving us information on what we needed to do, when all that mattered was looking each other in the eye and knowing the job we had to do. Clive trusted the players so he knew to leave it to us all. And the rest, as they say, is history.

I asked Ali for her memories of the final, sat in the stand, watching the drama unfold; at least I thought she was watching!

'At the final, I think it really hit me how much this all meant. Myself and Claire West were the only partners who took their children to the games, which were played late at night, and we were just sat in the stand. I wanted my sister there with us to share in this, and I knew that this was the only chance for us to be at a World Cup Final with Neil playing, so I felt that we should all be there together. I remember Fin crying his eyes out as the game had gone in to extra time and he was very tired, so as Jonny kicked the winning drop goal, I was in the loo with Fin! I came out of the toilet and everyone was going crazy, jumping up and down. We headed down from the back of the stand, to the side of the pitch, somehow, with our England shirts on and our faces painted, and we were waving towards Neil. For him, not knowing where we were, it must have been like searching for a needle in a haystack, but he found us somehow. Neil leant over to hold Olivia, while Fin simply didn't know what was happening. Olivia doesn't really remember Martin Johnson asking her to go and collect the World Cup with him, but it was an incredible and unforgettable night.

'With the phone network down, and the pouring rain, Linda was fantastic and took the children back to the hotel. Matt Poole, God love him, missed all the celebrations, just to make sure that they got back to the hotel okay, as we had an official celebration to attend. I remember being relieved to return to some form of normality after all of the celebrations, but our mum passed away around the Christmas that year, so we experienced all the range of emotions possible in those few weeks.'

The next day, the *Sydney Morning Herald*, with tongue firmly in cheek, brought down the curtain on the 2003 World Cup, issuing a full-page apology to us, a sample of which is below:

'We would like to admit the following: You were not too old (although we hoped you would be when the game went to extra time).

'You were not too slow. You scored as many tries as we did. You kicked no more penalty goals than we did. You ran the ball as much as we did. You entertained as much as we did.

'You played with class, toughness and grace. You were bloody superior.

'You are better singers than we are (and just quietly, Swing Low, Sweet Chariot is growing on us, as is Jonny without an 'h').'

Having fallen at the final hurdle on so many occasions, 2003 was the year that everything came together for us; number one in the world, the grand slam, Six Nations Championship, triple crown and the World Cup in the same 12 months was incredible, but nothing more than we deserved. No one could have predicted what lay ahead for us individually, and collectively, but I was determined to enjoy it. A 'Cov Skin', who was laughed at for saying he would play for England in the classroom at 11 years old, and was too small according to some, was a world champion. What choice did I have but to take it all in and enjoy it?

7

Changes

THE evening after the night before, so to speak, with most of us suffering from sore heads, we had one last engagement in Australia; the International Rugby Board World Cup dinner to close the tournament. The squad gathered from all corners of Sydney after our celebrations and I guess, somewhat reluctantly, got on to the bus and headed for the event. We were all exhausted by this stage and our minds were focused on returning home to our families, and to some rest and relaxation.

Throughout the dinner, video footage of the 1999 World Cup Final was shown, when Australia beat France 35-12 at the Millennium Stadium in Cardiff. I remember wondering if we would be shown four years later at the 2007 dinner, or if this was just to deliberately remind us of an Australian success? Anyway, Jonny was named Player of the Tournament, Clive the Coach of the Tournament and we were the Team of the Tournament. Despite that, it was a surreal night as everything was built around Australia, and judging by the footage shown and the speeches made you would have thought that they had won the tournament! We all smiled through the evening and enjoyed a few more drinks, before leaving and preparing for our long journey back to the UK.

Our aircraft home was renamed and rebranded 'Sweet Chariot', which was a nice touch. Our flight was 24 hours long and we stopped off to refuel in Singapore. We had a few supporters on the flight too, which was fun and I think they enjoyed travelling home with the players, the staff and of course, the trophy itself. I don't think I sat down on the first leg to Singapore, as I was stood on the staircase between the upper and lower deck, just drinking. To a man, we all celebrated and there was a renewed energy around the place as we all looked forward to getting home. On a flight that long, with the drinking that was happening, it was a blur as to what time of day it was and where you were. When we landed back at Heathrow, it was early Tuesday morning and I don't think any of us were even remotely prepared for the reaction we received.

At around 4am, we walked through the normal security checks, and smelling like a stag party on the way home from a boozy weekend in Prague, we were met by a group of police officers, who asked us politely to go out of the internal exits and through to arrivals in smaller groups of three. We thought they were joking, or that we needed security because we were the England rugby team. We said we would be fine and didn't need that kind of attention, but they explained that there was quite a presence of people outside the doors. It was only when we walked through that we all realised why. It was unbelievable. At 4am on a Tuesday, Heathrow Airport was packed, and cars had parked on traffic islands and kerbsides for miles from the airport. Over 10,000 people came out to welcome us home and I guess it was then that having lived in a bubble for the past few weeks, we realised what our achievement meant to everyone. There were St George flags everywhere, smiling and painted faces, and more than one banner saying 'Jonny, will you marry me?' which he got quite a bit of stick for from the rest of the lads. Jonny laughed, but I think he was embarrassed by it all. I think some of the lads felt a bit embarrassed about the whole thing, as we weren't used to that kind of reception, but we'd worked hard to win the World Cup, and I was proud to be walking through holding the trophy. I suppose some of the taller guys should have carried it, to keep it safe and out of the reach of people, but I had a tight grip on it as the fans reached over the barriers to touch it.

I was very aware at this time that we needed to soak everything up and enjoy it. I knew it was all over for me in terms of World Cups and I'd been very privileged to play for teams that had won every trophy you could win as a northern hemisphere player. During those immediate few days after the tournament, I wondered whether I would ever wear the England jersey again, but very quickly there would be a beer, or a journalist's microphone, not necessarily in that order, placed under your nose and you'd think about something else. It was an emotional time for everyone, and extremely difficult to put in to words. What do you do when you've achieved the greatest honour in your professional career? There is an empty void at that time, a bit of a downer in a strange way, but you have to celebrate the success and push the questions and uncertainty to the back of your mind. Steve Thompson obviously felt that winning the World Cup wasn't enough, as on the morning after the World Cup, he took his partner, Fiona, down to the beach and dropped down on to one knee and proposed. Fiona said yes, so it must have been even more of an emotional time for them.

I had fought so hard to get where I did for England, and I was desperate for the final not to be my last game. All those years of being deemed too small, or not good enough by England coaches, had meant I grabbed every opportunity I could under Clive's leadership. I didn't want to let go just yet. Anyway, of all those times I'd turned down a drink during my career, this was a time to say yes, and just be together with the team and enjoy the moment, as I guess we knew in our heart of hearts that we wouldn't all be together like this, a united team, as a family again.

As we left the airport, on the team coach, I vividly remember seeing fans stood on top of a police car, with the bonnet and the roof dented, and the police were stood next to them allowing them to do it. It was so packed that they couldn't have done anything about it anyway. We made our way back to Pennyhill Park, our training base for all those years leading up to the World Cup, to share our celebrations with the support team there, who had contributed so much to helping us become the team we were. We all had a huge full English breakfast together, and you knew that this was the end of it. There were a lot of goodbyes and big hugs, and even though we'd all meet up again in the coming weeks and months for formal engagements, this was the day I remember as the goodbye to that team.

I had made quite a few good friends at Pennyhill Park Hotel and Country Club, and I took the time to go and speak to each of them that day. Michael Wright, who was the guest relations manager there, used to invite me in for a coffee, and we'd often watch CCTV footage of people's movements through the hotel hallways to while away the early hours. There's another book I could write on that and the items left in the lost property room alone. Then there was the young valet, who would park customers' cars for them. I normally parked my own car and carried my own bags, but on one occasion I was running late for a team meeting, and had to screech up to the front of the building and let him park my car. I dashed in to the building and then realised I had left my black book, which contained our plays and team rules, on the front seat, so I raced back, and to my horror heard screeches of tyres burning through the car park. I left my black book, forgot about it and ran over to the meeting just on time. I spoke to Michael later, and got him to show me the CCTV footage, and all you could see was my new, sponsored car's headlights and red brake lights, which I'd just picked up and driven down, having handbrake turns performed on it in the car park! After that, I don't think the young lad was allowed to park people's cars, and thankfully it wasn't my own personal car. He kept his job, which I was pleased about, and we named him 'Schumacher' after that. When I told him I'd seen the footage, his face went bright red with embarrassment. There were some great people there, and we were pleased to spend time with them and thank them for all their support and hard work over the years.

Once I'd left Pennyhill Park and made my way home to Leicestershire, I arrived back at the house to be greeted by a huge banner that the neighbours had made, and hung outside their house, and a banner made by Ali and the kids, congratulating me. It was a lovely touch and was a very humbling moment for me. I remember in the coming days doing some mundane activities, like going to the local supermarket and having little grannies stopping me to say well done. Immediately, wherever you went, you were recognised by more people than normal. There was a huge focus on the sport and collectively, we had made a big impression on the public and helped to put rugby in to the public's hearts and minds. I think that was partly due to our attitude and character over the last few years, as much as our performances and results.

I found myself reliving the last few years, but there was no real time to rest as I needed to get back to Leicester and help out. Deano had done all he could while we were away at the World Cup, but the club was in a bit of a rut, so the World

Cup lads came in to training on the Wednesday. There were seven of us; Johno, me, Moodos, Cozza, Nobby, Benny and Whitey. We were asked to play against Bath on the Saturday, just a week after winning the World Cup, and unfortunately it wasn't enough to turn form around and we narrowly lost 13-12. The reception we received was incredible though, with the whole ground giving us a standing ovation. Benny started at five, Cozza at six, me, Johno and Nobby were on the bench, Moodos started at seven and Whitey at three. It was incredible that we were all involved so soon after, but we were club men at the end of the day and we wanted to do our best for Tigers and get back in to a form of routine and normality after all the hysteria of the past few days and weeks. I was so grateful to the fans for their response. Without Tigers and the people around me, I would never have been able to play for England, to play in a World Cup Final and to hold the Webb Ellis Trophy in my hands. I wanted to thank every single person and it hurt me to see Tigers struggling at this time, as they'd had five defeats on the bounce, but that was rugby, and there were always going to be sacrifices in pursuit of your objectives. Tigers had experienced the heart of the team being ripped out, in order to support England's World Cup bid and it had left the squad weaker. They'd also suffered injuries while we were away as well, so Deano had a threadbare squad, and a team which was clearly low on confidence. In total, he was missing 12 international players during the tournament, nearly a whole side, so it was always going to be a tough year for Tigers.

Two weeks after the World Cup Final and just a week on from the Bath game, we were back down to London for an open-top bus parade through the city. I honestly don't think that any of us, especially those who had played in rugby's amateur era, ever expected to be involved in something like this. We'd all seen football clubs parade league titles and cups through their cities, with thousands of people turning out, but we never thought it would happen with rugby. We met at the Intercontinental Hotel, on Park Lane, on Monday 8 December, and O2 had sponsored two double-decker buses, named 'Sweet Chariot', with images on the side of us winning the World Cup. Being a Tigers player, we had been invited in the past on open-top bus parades through Leicester, to celebrate league and cup wins. We would leave Welford Road and head through the streets of Leicester, towards the Town Hall Square, in the city centre. We would get on the bus excited, and then as we passed along the route, there would be the odd person who would give you a wave and that would be it, until we reached the Town Hall, when it would be packed with around 5,000 or so people there waving flags and scarfs. We thought this would be a similar experience, and keeping in mind that it was December, we just didn't think people would turn out.

It was a cold day, so we had all brought overcoats with us to stay warm, but Clive asked us to wear our number ones, a smart light grey suit with a small embroidered white rose on the left chest and a red rose buttonhole just above it. Some of the girls, sorry, I mean the backs, wore a vest underneath to keep warm. We are human after all but there was no place for the overcoats. As we climbed on to the buses, and made our way towards Trafalgar Square, winding down Oxford Street and Regent Street, and then finally down Pall Mall East, we were greeted by a sea of supporters. It was estimated that over a million people turned out to see us that day. If we were shocked by the reception at Heathrow, then this nearly put some of us on our back. We just couldn't believe it. As was becoming the norm at that time, there were quite a few drinks available for us all on the buses. Huge slabs of beer were there, which some members of the party tucked in to. I wasn't the biggest of drinkers, and I was back in to club mode anyway, plus we had a team meal to come at lunchtime, a visit to Buckingham Palace and then 10 Downing Street, for receptions with the Queen and the Prime Minister respectively.

There were an incredible number of journalists and cameras there, and it was quite an overwhelming experience really, with so many eyes on you. People were looking out of their office windows, waving to us and it was as if London had just come to a complete standstill for us. We headed to Trafalgar Square, where the Mayor of London, Ken Livingstone, awarded us all the Freedom of the City, and I'm still not quite sure what that entitles you to do, but it was a nice honour nonetheless. I'm certain it doesn't let you off parking charges anyway.

The story of the day though has been embellished over the years for after-dinner speeches, but it's worth retelling here. I wasn't going to share the character's name, as what happens on tour stays on tour I thought, but then realised that the guilty parties were already publicly named in Moodos's book. The players were on one bus and the management staff were on the other. Halfway through the journey, Jason Leonard, who had already tucked in to more than half a slab of beer, needed to go to the toilet. He went downstairs and realised that there was no toilet. He made his way back up the stairs and was bemoaning the lack of facilities. One of us suggested that he discreetly pee in to a can, but in his wisdom, he selected a champagne bottle, which obviously only has a small hole at the top. He was a front-rower and you can't be smart if you play there! Remember, the television cameras, microphone booms and media were all around us, but he crouched down and got away with it. Just before he finished, someone knocked him as we turned a corner and a fair portion of urine was spilt on to the light grey trouser leg of Lewis Moody. Lewis, with pee on him, hung his trouser leg over the side of the bus to dry in the wind, and even though the trousers eventually dried, you could still just about see the dehydrated tide line.

We returned to the hotel, ate lunch and then headed with our wives and girlfriends to the Palace, to meet the Queen. It was a really grand affair, with lots of dignitaries and VIPs and we were looked after well, with china cups of tea and cut sandwiches. Suddenly, I think we all started to wonder what we needed to do or say. I mean, it's not every day that you do something like that. We were taken off in to a private room, with huge oak doors and brass doorknobs, with a master of ceremonies explaining how to greet the Queen and the general protocol for the event. We were told that in the first instance you would say 'Your Majesty' and then if she speaks to you again, you say 'Ma'am'. Men were told to bow when meeting her, women would curtsy, and Louise Ramsey was the only one with us who was female. Dorian West spoke up, and Nobby as he is known, is from Ibstock in Leicestershire, and announced, 'I'm not doing that, I pay her wages,' which left us all praying that he didn't cause a scene. We were all a bit nervous to be honest and the doors smashed open and through came the Queen. I remember Clive saying that his mind went blank when he had to introduce the players and staff to the Queen, and as he walked along the group of us, lined up in an arc shape, he got to referee Tony Spreadbury and turned to Her Majesty and introduced him as 'Spredders'. With that many names I think he got away with it.

The Queen's corgis came bounding through in to the room, ahead of Her Majesty and made a beeline for Moodos, or more accurately, for Leopard's urine, leaving Lewis to lightly kick them away. The rumours that the Queen told him to 'kick his balls' in reference to one of the corgis and then when Moodos did it, she replied 'his balls are in my bag' are categorically not true. See, I said this story had been embellished over the years. We were all giggling like naughty schoolboys throughout the whole scene though. The Queen spoke to Jonny, Johno and Clive, and also to Mike Tindall, who was almost part of the family at that time, as she had seen him shinning down the drainpipes from Zara's room, but she only said a brief greeting to the rest of us. We were on tenterhooks waiting for her to reach Nobby as she made her way around the arc we had formed. As the Queen receives your hand, she politely returns your hand back to you, indicating that she is ready to move on to meet the next person. Everyone is looking at Nobby, and the pressure finally got to him as he bowed and curtsied at the same time, which left us all rolling about laughing again. After threatening not to follow protocol, he melted under the circumstances. The corgis were then sniffing around Moodos, which you can see in some of the photos from the day. Another likely embellished story concerned Mark 'Ronnie' Regan. When he was offered a drink, a maid said to him 'Earl Grey' and he replied, 'No, I'm Mark Regan.' You couldn't make it up.

I'm sure that the Queen was briefed before meeting us all on what to expect, and she seemed to know what to say and was pretty knowledgeable. We should have probably asked her whether she had watched the World Cup but it wasn't a surprise that she stood and spoke to Jonny for a while, as at that time he must have been one of the most recognisable faces in the world, let alone rugby. She is an iconic lady, with a strong personality, but again, the whole event seemed almost like a blur to me. It was surreal to be stood in the same room as her, at Buckingham Palace. I was just a 'Cov Skin' who played a bit of rugby and here I was mixing with the Royal Family.

After we said our goodbyes, we were whisked off to 10 Downing Street by invitation from the Prime Minister at the time, Tony Blair. His wife Cherie was there, and she was very lively and seemed a little hyper, so I was left wondering whether we were the only ones who had been on the bubbly that day. Again, it was another iconic venue to visit, part of a whirlwind of a day for us all. We had walked down the street and through the famous black door, and the house goes back such a long way. It was a lot larger than I expected, a little like the Tardis in *Doctor Who*. There were a few handshakes and a few drinks and everyone behaved themselves, so we didn't do the sport of rugby any harm at 10 Downing Street.

Inevitably there was a hangover from the World Cup and I think that at this time, we were so far out of our routine we were almost unrecognisable to ourselves. There had to be a trade-off, and we knew we had to make our appearances at these events, and we were grateful to be honoured and celebrated by everyone, but it felt like we were being paraded as celebrities rather than sportsmen at times. I enjoyed the experience around this time, but there was a little relief when it was all over and we could get back to the day job. All the drinking, travelling and late night appearances, away from home and from the training pitch, certainly had an impact on us all. I remember Clive getting everyone together around a month later, in the New Year, and saying that we needed to refocus and put a cap on things.

Perhaps the final one of the events I remember was our invite to ITV's *An Audience with the England Team*, hosted by Chris Tarrant. My wife Ali surprised me at the end of the show, as my daughter Olivia carried the World Cup on to the stage, while holding her mum's hand. It evoked memories of the day itself, when Johno asked Olivia if she wanted to collect the World Cup with him. Ali had bought her a posh, expensive dress, but what made me laugh was when Ali was interviewed on the show, she put on her 'phone voice', which was an upper-class accent. Ali said afterwards that the production crew had got in to her head by reminding her to speak clearly and pronounce her words properly. When she looks back on it she just cringes, but for me it just reminds me of when she worked for AXA Equity and Law, and she was speaking to clients on the phone, only this time it was in front of millions of people at home. We still have the video of the show at home, but Ali can't face watching it again.

In the New Year, Johno announced his retirement. I remember thinking back to before the World Cup Final, when Clive had stated that he didn't want anybody talking about retirement until after the tournament. The French captain and scrum half, Fabien Galthié, had announced that he would retire after the 2003 World Cup, which we felt was a mistake as it would be a distraction and the tournament would almost become a send-off party for him. Clive had said there was no way he would let that happen to us. There were a number of players who would have been considering retirement, but we kept it professional and then people decided upon their futures after the tournament had finished. There was also an England XV vs Barbarians game just before the New Year, which England won, but was another distraction from club rugby I guess.

My personal reason for not retiring straight after the World Cup was that I didn't want to let go, after having worked so hard to be part of it all. I thought back to the 'Tour of Hell' in 1998. I turned up ready to play and picked up my kit, and remember speaking to Jonny's parents as he'd just been brought in to the squad, and I told them how much I was looking forward to playing alongside him. I assured them that we would look after him as he was only 18 years old. The next thing I knew, Clive had pulled me aside and said I wouldn't be going on the tour and that it would be explained publicly that injury would be the reason for me not travelling to Australia, New Zealand and South Africa. I knew that I had to trust Clive's reasoning, as he wanted me to have the summer off to train and recuperate. I remember training at David Lloyd's gym in Leicestershire during the 76-0 defeat to Australia, and the match commentator explained my absence due to injury. I was doing a cardio session at the time, and some bloke turned to me and said, 'I thought you were injured?' I thought to myself, why hadn't I forced the issue to be there and support my team-mates? In some ways it was a good thing to not be involved in that tour, given the results and the criticism, but that didn't stop me wanting to be there with the guys, helping them. They conceded 11 tries that day, something that will have lived with them all for a while, as did the thrashings against New Zealand and South Africa.

The point I am making is that you never want to turn down or give away a cap for England. I'd represented my country at schoolboy level in 1987, making my debut against Australia at Twickenham, through to my final game, as it turned out, in the World Cup Final against Australia. I didn't want to walk away. I was also aware that a number of others were ready to retire, so with experience leaving the squad, I wanted to support Clive and the staff with my nurturing and coaching instinct to help keep the standards high. I knew that the next generation were coming through and there were some exciting players around, who I was certain I could help.

Clive was going to be the coach going forward for England, and he'd stood by me in the past, and I wanted to stand by him now too. I knew that with all due respect to Scotland and Italy in the opening Six Nations matches of 2004, I wouldn't be picked, so Clive and his staff could look at other options and bring through younger players and allow them to experience international rugby. England won both games comfortably and then I was named as a replacement for the third game, against Ireland at Twickenham. Sadly I wasn't used and spent the 80 minutes sat on the bench as we were beaten 13-19, our first defeat since becoming world champions, and our first since the warm-up game with France before the tournament. I watched the game, feeling that I could have contributed at

THE DEATH OF RUGBY

the contact area, where we were being turned over and weren't retaining possession. I felt I could have made an impact and it was frustrating to just watch from the sidelines. I walked on to the pitch after the game and looked around at the empty seats. If I wasn't going to be used in a game like this, then it didn't seem as if I would be used again. That was my goodbye, in my mind. I didn't say anything to anyone at the time, but I knew it was the end. It might seem like a hasty decision, but it really wasn't, and I wasn't emotional about it either. I totally understood why I wasn't involved and I respected the decision taken by Clive and his staff. I guess I felt that time had moved on and it was time for me to move on. As I walked away down the tunnel, I remembered the 11-year-old me, being asked to stand up in the classroom and announce that my ambition was to play rugby for England and own a Porsche. I was laughed at, and slumped back in to my chair, but I could stand on the Twickenham pitch that day and know that I'd achieved at least one of my childhood aims. And the Porsche would come in good time as well.

It was a natural progression at that time for England to evolve. People may look back and say that the team was changing quickly, but that was always going to happen as we had players who were retiring, and as I've said, Clive was keen to blood some younger players as we needed to build towards the next World Cup in 2007. I was selected for the next game, at home to Wales, but when the call came in, I explained that I was retiring from international rugby. I don't really remember making an announcement as such, but I explained that I felt I needed to be there for the Tigers and for my family too. I looked ahead at the England summer tour of Australia and New Zealand and it just made sense to call it a day there and then. It wasn't easy to do, as I'd worked so hard to play at that level, but I guess it was just the right time to say enough is enough, and let someone else wear the

SCHOOLBOY DREAM: As a kid, all I wanted to do was play rugby for England and drive a Porsche. I didn't have the Porsche at this stage, but I went one better on the field, captaining England in Johno's absence as we claimed the 2001 Cook Cup, 21-15 against world champions Australia at Twickenham. Left to right; Austin Healey, me, Phil Vickery (behind me), Dan Luger, Dorian West, Ben Kay and Kyran Bracken.
© PA Images

BACK AS CAPTAIN: Leading out my country on four occasions as captain was a real honour, and here, at the Stadio Flamino in Rome, I got to do it for the final time whilst earning my 50th cap in a 45-9 victory in the final game of the 2002 Six Nations Championship. © PA Images

TIME FOR A TREBLE: Celebrating the dramatic 34-30 2001 Heineken Cup Final win over Stade Francais, my favourite game, and completing the treble in the process, with Will Johnson left, and Paul Gustard, centre, who is currently the defence and forwards coach of Aviva Premiership champions, Saracens. © PA Images

FOUR MORE YEARS: Holding aloft the 2002 Premiership title, saw us record a remarkable four league titles in four years; a reward for hard work and incredible team spirit. What an era that was for the club.
© PA Images

MY FRIEND, MY MENTOR: Dean Richards, the man who I joined Leicester Tigers to play alongside, and the man I would have run through brick walls for. An inspirational player, coach and man, and one of the biggest influences on my career. © PA Images

THE HAND OF BACK: Moments after my infamous 'Hand of Back' incident, the whistle blows and we have retained the Heineken Cup, with a 15-9 win over Munster, at the Millennium Stadium. I can't hide my delight! © Getty Images

WE SHALL NOT BE MOVED: Johno explains, in no uncertain terms, that the England side will not be moving, as we line up for the 2003 Grand Slam showdown with Ireland, in Dublin. Irish President, Mary McAleese subsequently had to walk across the grass to greet the teams, but the whole thing was totally blown out of proportion. © Getty Images

KINGS OF THE NORTH: The 2003 Grand Slam, Six Nations Championship and Triple Crown is all ours, after years of heartbreak, as we seal our position as the best side in the Northern Hemisphere, with the World Cup to come. Not for the first time, my shirt is off and the celebrations are well and truly on!
© Getty Images

WE'VE GOT THE BOTTLE: Celebrating the 2003 Grand Slam in Dublin was a huge moment for us, as we'd been written off as bottlers and nearly men. Now we were ready to take on the world.
© Andrew Fosker/ Seconds Left Images

THUMBS UP: My daughter Olivia poses for the world's media on Manly Beach, Sydney, as we enjoy some family time before the World Cup Final.
© Eddie Keogh/ Seconds Left Images

LOOKING GOOD: A blood-splattered face and shirt shows just what it took to get past the brutal South African side of 2003, as we negotiated Pool C and claimed top spot.
© Eddie Keogh/Seconds Left Images

LUGES ON THE FLUMES: My England colleague Dan Luger and I enjoy some downtime at a waterpark during the 2003 World Cup. I hope my wife, Ali, can remember my body in this state when we are grey and old!
© Eddie Keogh/Seconds Left Images

THE CAMERA NEVER LIES: I show devastating pace and a clean pair of heels to Imanol Harinordoquy, as we leave the French down and out in our 24-7 2003 World Cup semi-final win, one of our best team performances and a great back row display. © PA Images

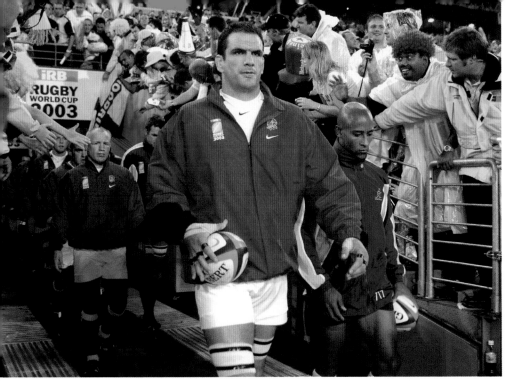

LEADER OF MEN: Johno didn't need to say a word in the tunnel on Saturday 22 November 2003. He took one look at us all and knew we were ready for the biggest game of our careers; the World Cup Final. © Eddie Keogh/Seconds Left Images

THE BACK ROW BOYS: From left to right; Me, Lawrence Dallaglio and Richard Hill, with the Webb Ellis Cup in the dressing room after the 20-17 victory over Australia in the 2003 World Cup Final. The three of us became extremely close during our playing days and remain good friends to this day. © PA Images

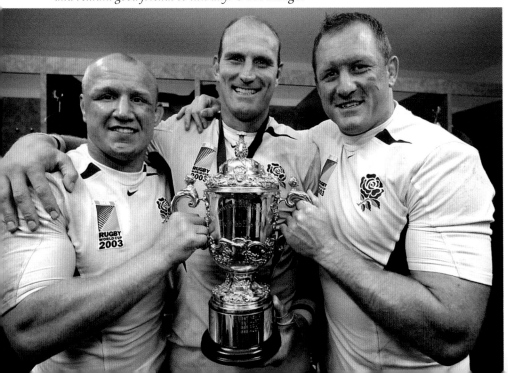

HANDS UP IF YOU'RE A WORLD CUP WINNER: Johno, Phil Vickery and Steve Thompson celebrate the ultimate triumph with me and Olivia.
© Eddie Keogh/ Seconds Left Images

VICTORY: The England squad and our invaluable management and backroom staff celebrate as one as we complete the final piece of the jigsaw; the Webb Ellis Cup.
© Eddie Keogh/ Seconds Left Images

THE MAGNIFICENT SEVEN: From left to right; Lewis Moody, me, Martin Corry, Dorian West, Ben Kay, Martin Johnson and Julian White, all Tigers and all World Cup winners.
© PA Images

THE STREETS ARE OURS: It seemed like the whole country came out for our open-top bus parade through London; it was an incredible day, part of a whirlwind few months as we adjusted to being World Cup winners and 'celebrities', something I was never really that comfortable with. © Andrew Fosker/Seconds Left Images

HIGH TIDE: The World Cup winning squad meet Her Majesty the Queen at Buckingham Palace, whilst Lewis Moody and his pungent trousers attract interest from her corgis. © PA Images

THE FINAL PIECE IN THE JIGSAW: My smile tells it all, as I hold aloft the Rugby World Cup, the trophy that had eluded us all until 2003, on our open-top bus parade through the London streets, lined with thousands of England supporters; a day we will all never forget. © PA Images

THINKING CORRECTLY UNDER PRESSURE: Our coach, Clive Woodward, masterminded an unrivalled culture in English rugby and cultivated a fantastic management team, backroom staff and group of players. We were ranked number one in the world, Grand Slam winners and here, he holds the 2003 World Cup. Just over a month later he was knighted by Her Majesty the Queen. © PA Images

FROM 'COV SKIN' TO MBE: Who would have thought it? I may have an MBE, but I'll always be the boy from Cov. The day was incredible, and I got to share it with my lovely wife, Ali, pictured, and my mother and father. © PA Images

FINAL TRY: I cross the line for my final try as a rugby player, coming for the British & Irish Lions against Manawatu in a 109-6 victory. © Andrew Fosker/Seconds Left Images

DAN THE MAN: Jonny Wilkinson joins me in trying to bring the mercurial talent of Dan Carter to a halt, but we can't prevent the All Blacks winning the first Test of the 2005 Lions tour, 21-3. © Andrew Fosker/Seconds Left Images

EXIT STRATEGY: Sir Clive Woodward, right, leaves the hastily organised press conference with media consultant, Alastair Campbell, left, after our first Test defeat to New Zealand on the Lions tour of 2005. I found Alastair to be fine as a bloke, but we clashed over his interference in team matters. © PA Images

CATCH ME IF YOU CAN: I cross the line at Welford Road in my final game, having shown my pace to leave Matt Dawson trailing in my wake. Sorry Daws! © Andrew Fosker/ Seconds Left Images

FAREWELL, OLD FRIEND: My final game at Welford Road as a player, a 45-10 victory over Wasps, was also Johno's final game at the ground where we enjoyed so much success together. Don't we look sweet! © Andrew Fosker/Seconds Left Images

TIME TO HANG UP OUR BOOTS: Peter Wheeler (far left), and Peter Tom (second right), present me, John Wells (centre) and Johno with our pegs from the Welford Road home dressing room in recognition of respective service to the club. © Andrew Fosker/ Seconds Left Images

THREE'S A CROWD: Richard Cockerill, left, and I look on, with head coach Marcelo Loffreda, centre. The Argentine struggled to settle in the role, and despite being a nice guy, his appointment with hindsight was a mistake. © PA Images

THE KEY TO SUCCESS: Pre-match with director of rugby and good friend from my Leicester Tigers days, Andy Key, in our second season at Leeds Carnegie, as we prepare to face London Irish. We survived that season, but our collective efforts were sadly always in vain, due to the club's lack of meaningful ambition. © PA Images

HEAVE: The Leeds Carnegie players working hard, as they did throughout my time as head coach at the club, but sadly we were let down by a lack of genuine ambition off the field. © Tom Dwyer/Seconds Left Images

A PICTURE PAINTS A THOUSAND WORDS: The crowds turn out to watch Rugby Lions and we storm to the top of the division; as our 'owner', Michael Aland (standing centre, front) enjoys a beer and cigar. Need I say more? © Jack Somerset

TELLING STORIES: Michael David Aland (holding microphone), was the man who David Owen entrusted with ownership of Rugby Lions. Following that fateful season, players and staff were left with broken hearts, deprived of 12 months of their lives, with many still recovering to this day. Hopefully we'll never see this in rugby again. © Jack Somerset

LIONS AT THE DOUBLE: Rugby Lions, made up mainly of development players, complete the double for the club and celebrate winning the Warwickshire Cup 10-9 against Sutton Coldfield, bringing to an end a rollercoaster season of on-field success and off-field turmoil. © Jack Somerset

TOGETHER: This picture illustrates just how unified the players and staff were at Rugby Lions, despite the deceit and strain we faced during the 2011/12 season. This book is for each and every one of you boys. © Jack Somerset

FACING THE CAMERAS: Michael Bradley, centre, and Billy McGinty, right, and I face the media a month after I joined the Edinburgh Rugby coaching set-up as forwards coach. I enjoyed my time in Scotland but left with the sense of a job half done. © PA Images

ME AND MY BETTER HALF: Arriving for the ten-year reunion of the England World Cup winning squad, at Battersea Evolution, London, with my beautiful wife, Ali. I simply couldn't have achieved half of what I did in the game without her by my side.
© PA Images

MY FAMILY: From left to right; me, my daughter Olivia, son Finley, and my wife, Ali. I've been told on many occasions that the kids have inherited Ali's good looks, but she has given them so much more than that. I'm very proud of my children; Olivia represents England Hockey U16s and Finley goes in to his fifth season with Nottingham Forest's Football Academy. They mean the world to me.
© Neil Back

jersey. I've said before, that I don't really regret any decisions that I've taken, and I stayed available for England for the right reasons and ended things for the right reasons too, which is something I am proud of.

Only a few months later, in early September, Clive left, announcing his resignation from the role less than a year after our World Cup success. The Six Nations had ended in defeat in France, which meant England had won three matches and lost two, finishing third behind Ireland in second and grand slam winners France. Clive had the Lions tour in 2005 to prepare for, and his eventual move in to football with Southampton, but it was pretty clear that things had moved on much quicker than we all expected after the success in Australia. He was clearly upset with the RFU and he was the kind of person that wanted to see change happen immediately, which is one of the many reasons he was so successful with us. I think he had grown tired of the battles and felt that he had lost control after we won the World Cup. It was a very sad departure, and it all happened so soon after the greatest day in English rugby history.

Tigers, post-World Cup, was another story of unexpected change. I had been named as captain for that season, to allow Johno to concentrate on his role as England skipper, and we had more than one eye on the 2003 World Cup, meaning many of us wouldn't be around for Tigers duty in the early part of the season. Josh Kronfeld was to lead the side in our absence, and what a player he was. At this time in history, we had so many leaders throughout the team, that whether you were captain or not, everyone knew what was expected, and there were others around like Dorian West, Cozza and Moodos who all captained England at one stage, so we were not short on experience.

When we returned from the World Cup, the club was low, and we lost narrowly to Bath within a week of England's success and then went down 14-0 away to Northampton Saints. We were depleted with injuries and the hangover of people coming back from Australia and we had made a poor start in the Heineken Cup, losing 26-15 away to Stade Francais and suffering an awful 33-0 defeat at Ulster, with a 34-3 home win over Newport Gwent Dragons sandwiched in between. The Ulster result was a freak really and was our worst loss in four years. Back then there were 21 players in a squad, and after just ten minutes we lost both of our centres, Daryl Gibson, the experienced New Zealander, and Ollie Smith, who was a very smart player, to injury. The following week we won 49-7 back at Welford Road, with only four changes to the 21-man squad. It was a unique position to be in, losing two centres, and we conceded four tries, at a tough place to play in atrocious conditions. We also played poorly, and I don't want to take anything away from Ulster's achievement, but there was a lot against us that day. The fact that we pumped them a week later showed to all that it was circumstances that dictated that shocking defeat.

Johno announced his retirement from international rugby just after the return game against Ulster, and just 16 days later, we were all shocked by another announcement; Deano was leaving the Tigers. People were putting two and two together at the time and getting five. Some commented that Johno would be taking over from Deano and also that we knew about the decision and were involved in some way. I can categorically state, here and now, that Johno and I had nothing to do with Deano's departure.

Deano was dismissed by the board of directors after the 26-13 home defeat to Stade Francais, which ended our participation in the Heineken Cup at the group stages. Clearly we were struggling on the field. I was called by the board and invited to Peter Tom's house to discuss the future of the club. It was my 14th year there and I was invited as a senior player and of course, I wanted to help where possible. I didn't think anything of it, other than wanting to help to turn things around. Johno and I arrived in separate cars, and as we arrived at Peter's house, John Wells, who had just arrived, was stood on the doorstep. As I walked in through the front door I asked where Deano was, and was told that he wasn't coming. Then it struck me; something was wrong and Deano had gone. The board sat us all down and told us that Deano was leaving. We didn't discuss the decision, we were informed. I mean, I didn't even know who was going to be at the meeting, so there was no way I knew anything about Deano. I was captain of the club, but obviously I didn't have any say on who was in charge.

Once the penny had dropped, I guess I felt naïve about the situation, but I was powerless to do anything about it. I was shocked and surprised that Deano was leaving and the meeting was a blur as I couldn't quite believe what was happening in front of my eyes. I knew we weren't doing well in the league, and we were out of Europe, but this was Dean Richards; the man who I'd joined the club to play alongside and who had done so much on the field as a player and off the field as a head coach and director of rugby, to make Leicester Tigers the great club it is. It felt sudden and harsh to me. It was stated at the time that Deano had resigned, but I am sure that he was asked to leave. The board claimed that the decision was based on results of the past couple of seasons, but I have always felt there was more to it than that.

Peter Tom and Peter Wheeler matter-of-factly explained that John Wells would be taking over from Deano as head coach and I was asked to take on a player-defensive coach role, with Johno asked to take over as captain from me, given that I would be on the coaching side as well. I can remember driving the few miles back home, thinking about the brutality of modern rugby. When Ian 'Dosser' Smith retired, it was

Deano, who was England's number eight, who brought me to Leicester and I had always looked up to him. Back in 1990, I played two games in three days, firstly for England under-21s and then in a non-capped international for England against Italy, with Deano and John Wells in the back row. It was a dream to work with these guys, so to lose Deano in these circumstances was just sad. I'd not just lost a head coach, I'd lost a friend, and I'd lost my mentor. I remember thinking back at the time to Deano driving me down for my England debut in 1994, and the times I'd roomed with him for the Senior Midlands side. We'd been out for a few scoops of beer, and I think we were playing against South Africa. I had long blonde hair back then, as did his wife Nicky, so when Deano climbed in to bed and put his arm around me, I had to remind him that I wasn't his Mrs with a quick elbow to the chops! I also remembered a journey down for my second Test for England, against Ireland, with Deano, and him asking me to go for a few beers the night before the game, which showed just how much times had changed from the amateur era. Some of the lads had six or seven pints of Guinness and I nursed the one all night, but Deano had always taken me under his wing, and I'll forever owe him a great deal.

I accepted the offer from the board to step in to the player-coach role as I wanted to help the club I loved. I was hardly going to say no, Deano had already gone and there was going to be no turning back. I think that for a time, the whole affair changed my relationship with Deano, which was really sad. I was interviewed on television about him around three months later, and gave an in-depth account of what he meant to me and his legacy at the Tigers. I was asked in that interview how Tigers were coping without him and I replied honestly, 'Well, we're doing all right and we haven't lost in the last 12 games.' We'd won ten and drawn two since he left. The interview was aired, just with the quote above as a standalone statement, and taken completely out of context. I saw him at a dinner, not too long after, and said hello, and he replied rather sternly and dismissively, 'We'll talk later,' and I could understand that. Deano was hurt, but he was an ex-copper, and over the next couple of months he did his own investigation and discovered the truth of what happened and knew that I had played no part in his departure. I have always maintained that we would have turned the corner, in the way we did, if Deano was there too, I have no doubts about that.

I think it's interesting to read what the board said at the time, through chairman Peter Tom, 'Unfortunately there has been a steady decline in the team's performance over the past two seasons. The board felt that this decline could only be checked by significant changes within the playing structure. Dean did not find these changes acceptable.'

What did that mean? The recruitment, the playing style, even the coaching? I felt that they must have had an issue with Deano, but I can only speculate. I have to be honest though and say that I didn't think the Tigers board supported us enough, as senior players, when accusations were made regarding our involvement in his departure. The whole saga was left as ambiguous, so the media and then the public could draw their own conclusions, which left us a little unprotected. That is why I felt the need to clarify things in this book.

We managed to salvage something from a disappointing season. We finished fifth in the Premiership after winning 11, drawing three and losing eight in what was an inconsistent and fragmented year. It was the second consecutive season where we had underperformed. That meant we would have a last chance of qualifying for Europe, via the play-offs, and we took it with both hands, beating Harlequins 43-26 in the semi-final at Welford Road and then dismissing Sale 48-27 at Twickenham in the final. We'd failed to get out of the pool in Europe, but at least we'd managed to get back in to the competition next season, which was the absolute minimum expected of us.

I have to say that it was the strangest of years, in more ways than one. On the field, at international and club level, it was all about change, and off the field, we all had to adapt to our roles post-World Cup. So, when a letter landed on my porch floor, asking me if I would accept an MBE, I guess I shouldn't have been surprised, as anything and everything seemed to happen during those 12 months. I was proud to be asked, and to receive the honour. All of these awards in your life, to me, just signify teamwork, effort and dedication, and I think that the MBE was a way of acknowledging our achievement at the World Cup, for the nation to share. It was also for all the people who had contributed towards my career to enjoy. Clive was given a knighthood and Johno received a CBE, while the rest of the squad got an MBE. For me, it was an opportunity to invite my mum, dad and Ali to the ceremony, so it was as much for them as it was for me. I remember before the ceremony, enjoying lobster, chips and a glass of bubbly with my family, at The Ivy, which is a nice memory from that hectic year. I never imagined my 'Cov Skin' making two visits to Buckingham Palace in such a short space of time! It was just nice, as a small payback for my mum and dad, for the sacrifice they had both made for me over the years and it's a day that we all remember fondly.

8

Farewell

THE 2004/05 season was my first full season as a retired international, meaning I could concentrate fully on supporting the club, but I knew that it was likely to be my last as a player.

My role, as well as playing, was as part of the coaching staff, supporting head coach John Wells as defence coach. Pat Howard was backs coach and Richard Cockerill assisted John Wells with the forwards.

I was fully committed to making the most of that year, and looking back, I'm proud of the fact that I played 26 times, with another two appearances from the bench, showing that I was still able to make a contribution on the field, even if my future lay off it. In some ways, I enjoyed this season, as there was one focus; Leicester Tigers. There was no stress or distraction of international rugby, which had been such a big part of my career. Don't get me wrong, I had loved playing for England, but it was nice to be able to give my all, one last time, for the club that had done so much for me. Without the nine or ten England matches that season, in my 17th senior club season, the physical and mental strains of an overloaded year were kept at arm's length and I was as fit as a butcher's dog.

I was delighted to have the extra responsibility of helping out with coaching the defence, and by this stage I had a real hunger to develop my coaching skills and to learn more about this area of the game. I'd spent my whole life, whatever I'd done, trying to soak up everything, like a sponge, and I felt that being able to play while coaching was the perfect fit for me in the 2004/05 season. As a senior player, and as captain for a brief period, this was the natural progression for me. I'd been involved in decision-making previously, but now I would be involved in the selection process, and the added responsibility of analysing players and team performances, which I relished. Then I needed to come to terms with giving honest feedback to players, individually and collectively, who were my colleagues, but this was where I wanted to be, and I appreciated, myself, how regular feedback is critical for player, unit and team development.

For me, I stumbled in to playing rugby at a senior club. If Jim Robinson, the former Coventry forwards coach, hadn't left the club to join Nottingham and asked me to join him there, I'm not sure what I would have done, I can only speculate. Rugby wasn't a career back then, it was an amateur game and was something I enjoyed doing. I wanted to be the best I could, but I hadn't felt that it was necessarily my calling. I had played virtually every sport going through my sixth form years at The Woodlands School, Coventry, and continued to play cricket for Massey Ferguson, two or three times a week, to a competent standard, from age 16 through to 19, until I focused solely on rugby. However, that attitude drove me on throughout my playing career, and still does now in everything I do. As such, I looked after my body throughout my playing days and didn't suffer from too many injuries and not many long-terms ones at that. I think that my love of the game from the start, and my approach to it throughout, helped me to play on as long as I did, but even though I hadn't announced anything or told anyone, apart from Ali, I knew that my time was almost up. It was just a feeling I had. Perhaps I didn't want to outstay my welcome and it was time to let others take on the famous Tigers jersey, but I knew that my passion for coaching was growing and that it would be a smooth and enjoyable transition to the other side of the white line.

I'd begun talking to Kevin Bowring, the head of elite coach development of the RFU at Twickenham, about the transition from being the best player I could be to becoming the best coach I could be. Over the subsequent years, I developed a strong relationship with Kevin and he was the guy I could turn to for advice regarding my next step. I think the Rugby Players' Association have done a lot of good work to improve things for retiring players, and the support is certainly better now than it was back then, but I was grateful to have Kevin to speak to and learn from. Clubs are now working to link players throughout their careers to businesses, further education, and development opportunities. As a player, there should be a realisation that your next training session or your next match could be your last, and I think that enabled me to remain grounded and to work hard to earn whatever the prize was. Dean Richards and John Wells had done so much to help me, and like all good coaches, they worked closely with their players to demonstrate certain skills and aspects of the game, and I was a big part of that, and of the huge success that we'd had over the years. I was determined to contribute to the club, whatever the role was to be.

The 2004/05 season was a great one for us. It was the return of the real Leicester Tigers that we had known over the majority of my playing career and that was fitting for me, given that it was my last wearing the famous scarlet, green and white jersey. We had experienced a couple of below-par seasons by Tigers standards, and after the drama and sadness of Deano leaving, we needed to show what the club was really made of. Deano's shoes were massive shoes to fill and while he had left during the previous season, things were never going to change overnight at Tigers. We had a strong philosophy and culture at the club, regarding how things should be done, aligned to the high standards we set ourselves. Having said that, I felt that Pat Howard had a huge influence on me, and is up there with the best coaches I worked with during my career. Pat became an outstanding head coach; his knowledge of the game, and ability to set up a team to win was first-class, and he was an outstanding coach and person to work with. His record speaks for itself in terms of what he has achieved in the game. I also loved playing with Pat. He was a highly-skilful and creative inside centre, and we had a great working relationship on the field at Tigers. He would take the ball in, and wait until it was the right time to offload to me, and if that opportunity didn't arise, he would hold on to it and was never wasteful in possession.

We had some big names and big characters involved in the coaching staff at that time; John Wells, Cockers, Pat Howard and myself. There was a great level of leadership within the ranks at the time, led by our captain, Johno, and that helped us to recover quickly from Deano's sudden exit. The experience on and off the field transferred to the younger players and we were able to steady the ship. From within that coaching group, I was probably most surprised that Cockers went on to become a director of rugby at Premiership level. I could have seen him becoming an excellent forwards specialist coach, but he wouldn't have been a name you would have associated with the top job. Controversial or not, and nothing personal here as I'm just giving my honest opinion, Richard has benefitted hugely from having the right people around him, like Matt

O'Connor. Matt joined Heyneke Meyer's coaching team as backs coach in the 2008/09 season and although Heyneke left due to personal reasons, six months in to his three-year contract, Cockers and Matt led the Tigers to the Heineken Cup Final, losing to Leinster, and they won the Premiership. Matt was then promoted to head coach in 2010, with Cockers moving to the director of rugby role, and if you talk to many of the players or staff from that period it was the former who really ran the show until he left to join Leinster in 2013 and led them to the Pro12 title in his first year. Without Matt, Tigers have struggled slightly, as my good friend and genius footballer Geordan Murphy learns the ropes after retiring at the end of the 2013 season and becoming an assistant coach, taking up some of Matt's responsibilities and under Cockers's lead, the club appears to have gone back to type.

You just wonder how much influence Geordan has been afforded, because his brilliance hasn't come through on the field over the last two seasons. I'm sure that like I, the players and amazing Tigers fans will be hoping that the new head coach for 2015/16, Aaron Mauger, will help to put us back on track both on and off the field and particularly bring a much-needed change of thinking in our attacking philosophy and include Geordan in that process. In the regular league season we've only scored 37 tries, ten of which have come against the bottom club, London Welsh and have had 39 tries against, in 22 games, with a points difference of only +32. Relegated London Welsh, are the only team to have scored fewer tries. Compare this to Northampton, who have scored 75 tries and have a points difference of +221, and seventh-placed Wasps, who have scored 77 tries and have a points difference of +145. Incredibly, despite these statistics we made the play-offs, but against Bath in the semi-final our lack of attacking prowess was once again evident, and we were blown away, seven tries to one, in a 47-10 defeat.

Don't get me wrong, I want to give credit to the club for reaching the Premiership play-offs for an eleventh consecutive season, but in my view leading an elite rugby club is about so much more than that; it is about building relationships with your playing staff, local community, supporters, the media, local business, and understanding your environment and developing a vision for the club, while plotting a path to get there and achieve it. We seem to have edged forward, but other clubs have overtaken us and forged ahead. Leicester means so much to me, and I want to see us succeed and it hurts me to see us falling behind. I've given my views out of frustration more than anything, but I haven't explained them in depth until this book. Our lack of success in developing young players and retaining them, especially in the case of a talent like George Ford, plus the training facilities, recruitment policy and the loss of players, such as Geoff Parling to Exeter Chiefs, is coupled with a lack of success in the biggest club competition in the northern hemisphere, the European Cup. Since last reaching the final in 2009, we have failed to get out of the pool stages on three out of six occasions, which further illustrates this.

For the 2004/05 campaign, our Heineken Cup group was incredibly strong. This came off the back of having recently failed in Europe, so we were determined to put things right. We were drawn with Biarritz, London Wasps and Calvisano, beginning with a 37-6 win over the Italians. We lost in France to Biarritz, but then stormed back in to contention with consecutive wins over Wasps. Those two games were high-scoring and decided by just a few points. Wasps were very strong at the time, but we were almost possessed. We then lost 21-17 at home to Biarritz, who eventually won the group, so we were left waiting on the fate of others on the final day. Perpignan had to lose at Edinburgh and we needed to beat Calvisano in the final group game for us to squeeze in to the quarter-finals. Somehow it all happened for us, and we qualified as the lowest-ranked side, which meant we would face an away quarter-final against the top side from the pool stages, Leinster.

Leinster were unbeaten in Europe that season and were heavily fancied to beat us and progress. It was always dangerous to underestimate us, but in fairness to Leinster, they were one of a few sides who were more consistent than us at the time. Against all the odds, we won 29-13 and reached the semi-finals. It was a remarkable effort from us all. We would always have the ability to beat anyone, and that even goes for today. On Tigers' day they can compete with anyone, such is the stature of the club.

Having survived a 'group of death' as runners-up, and then beating the highly-fancied Leinster away, we were handed a home tie against Toulouse in the semi-finals. The game was played at Leicester City's ground, known then as the Walkers Stadium, which gave more supporters an opportunity to see the game and was the first-ever rugby match to take place there. At this time, there were ongoing discussions between Tigers and the football club about ground-sharing, but an agreement couldn't be reached and Tigers decided to redevelop Welford Road, which will have pleased the traditionalists of both clubs.

Recently I was asked by the media to comment on the decision to hold games at Leicester City's ground and not at Welford Road during the 2015 World Cup. I didn't want to comment at the time, as it is easy to upset people one way or another. However, I'll comment here and simply say that if Tigers had kept all of their big games in the past at Welford Road, then I would have argued with all my might to have the games staged there. Given the number of matches that were moved over to Leicester City, I don't think that anyone can blame the IRB for the decision. It also gives more people in the region an opportunity to watch World Cup rugby live. The ground doesn't have a rugby tradition, but it was clearly a no-brainer for me and there can be no real arguments.

As a player, home advantage is a factor, but for me, if you picked a pitch up and lifted it anywhere in the world, that's where you play the game of rugby and everything else is just a distraction. It didn't bother me that we played at a football stadium. I just wanted to play, and games didn't come much bigger than a European Cup semi-final against Toulouse. You often see in football, particularly in the FA Cup Final, for example, the pre-match tradition of players walking to the centre of the pitch while the stadium is filling up. They would be looking at all the things that would be a distraction from your performance, rather than focusing on what actually mattered.

We spent years at Tigers, and even more so with England, focusing on mental preparation and visualisation, performance and factoring out those distractions. That's not to take anything away from what supporters gave to the teams I played for and coached over the years. Of course, I'd rather have 80,000 fans screaming for us, than against us, but personally I always tried to train and play to the same high standards whether no one was watching, or there was a huge crowd. The same could be said for weather conditions. In my mind's eye, when I picture a ground, I always see the pitch, the blades of grass, what's in the dew on a single blade. I could stand on a pitch now and visualise a play, the running lines and my line of support, not the stadium or the surroundings. During a match you have an awareness of your supporters, particularly during a break in play, but if you are focused correctly then it's at the back of your mind. Post-match is the time to celebrate and acknowledge the supporters.

Going back to the Toulouse game, they scored three tries on the day, but we gifted them two of them. We kicked badly, missing penalties to touch, and despite there being a few forward passes in there, history shows that we lost and we were out. I wanted to win every game in my career, and always approached each match in that frame of mind, but this was a game I really wanted to win as I knew it would be my last chance of glory in Europe. We lost 27-19 against one of the top sides in Europe and it was frustrating more than anything, especially for me as the defence coach, but either way we were out.

As sad as that exit was for us, it came only a couple of weeks after an awful day for the sport of rugby, and for young Tigers prop Matt Hampson. Matt was a great prospect at Tigers and at the age of just 20, he was preparing for an England under-21 Six Nations match in a training session at Franklin's Gardens, Northampton, when a scrum collapsed and damaged his spine. In just a matter of seconds, doing something he loved, his life was completely changed and he was paralysed from the neck down. Tony Spreadbury, who we had worked with at the 2003 World Cup, was present at the training session, and as a trained paramedic he was able to clear Matt's airway and keep him alive until the ambulance arrived.

Just as Johno and I were weeks away from saying goodbye to the game, Matt was denied the chance of what appeared to be a promising career. It was just so cruel. The fact that he is able to be such an inspirational person, ten years on from that incident, and do so much positive work through the Matt Hampson Foundation, helping others who have suffered similar injuries, is testament to him as a person. His ethos of 'Get Busy Living' is something to be admired, given what happened to him on Tuesday 15 March 2005, and is something we should all attempt to embrace in our own lives.

We exited that season's Powergen Cup 20-13 at home to Gloucester, but with all due respect to the competition, it was used by us as more of a development opportunity than a real priority for the club at first-team level. Johno and Graham Rowntree didn't play and I was on the bench and didn't get on. Two weeks later we played Gloucester away in the league and beat them 28-13 with a first-team line-up, so I think that showed the real quality we had for the games we gave greater priority. The match fell just after those impressive back-to-back wins over London Wasps in the Heineken Cup, which as I've said was a huge achievement given how well Wasps were playing around that time. On a personal note, I became the highest cumulative try scorer in league matches, with my 74th try, coming against Worcester, surpassing Jeremy Guscott in the process. So despite my age, I wasn't doing too bad!

We reached the end of the regular league season, knowing that a win against Wasps at home would be enough to finish top of the division and avoid the second- against third-place semi-final, with the side finishing top going straight to Twickenham to face the winner. The Wasps game, on 30 April 2005, was to be my last home fixture for Tigers, along with Johno, who was also retiring, and John Wells, who was set to move on to a coaching role within the RFU National Academy. Knowing that it was my last home match, strangely, I found myself looking around and trying to take it all in pre-match, even though I'd made that journey thousands of times to the stadium. Johno led us out and the response we received from our colleagues and of course from the great Tigers supporters was really special. I tend not to be too emotional or dramatic about life, as I've said, but that day really choked me up.

The game also means a lot to me for another reason; I scored my 125th try for the club, our fourth of the day, beating Matt Dawson down the wing and securing us a bonus point. Making reference to this was to prove that I didn't only score pushover tries at the back of our mighty pack, and that I was able to use my erm…pace from time to time! We went on to score five tries that day and smashed Wasps 45-10. It was an incredible day and the perfect way to say goodbye to Welford Road as a player. Wellsy, Johno and myself walked around the pitch and waved to the crowd, and we received a standing ovation in return. There was also a nice touch by Lol, who brought his Wasps side back out on to the pitch to acknowledge our contribution to an amazing club with the best supporters in the world.

Wasps went on to beat third-placed Sale Sharks 43-22 a week later to set up a rematch against us at Twickenham, to decide the Zurich Premiership. We had a two-week break between the win over Wasps in the league and the play-off final, whereas they'd had the Sale clash, which you could argue kept them battle hardened and match sharp.

Going in to the game, I suppose given that Johno and myself were retiring, and Wellsy was moving on, we could have all been forgiven for thinking that the script was written for us to finish by lifting the trophy and ending our time at Tigers with glory. But that's simply not how elite rugby works. I always tried to approach every match the same. I know that this was my final game for Tigers, at Twickenham, but I was hardly going to change my approach and my habits of a lifetime. Sadly though, our habits of winning when it mattered deserted us on the day and Wasps comfortably beat us 39-14.

I know in my heart that my impending retirement didn't affect me, and didn't change the way I felt on the day, and I doubt it affected anyone else either. We just had a bad day, that's all. Credit to Wasps as they learned from the previous four matches between the two sides that season and they adapted to the game and did what was needed to beat us. Mark van Gisbergen scored 26 points, including a try, three conversions and five penalties, and all we could muster was a try and three penalties. We were well beaten and it wasn't the way we'd hoped to finish.

There was another incident that cast a shadow over the game, and the weeks to follow, involving yours truly. My England colleague and opponent on the day, Joe Worsley, could play anywhere across the back row at six, seven or eight, and on this day he was picked at seven. He played off the tail of a full eight-man line-out and in the first half, at a line-out, they were going to play it off the top, down to nine and pass to their ten. Your role, as a seven at the back of the line-out, is to exert pressure and tackle the opposing ten. Joe, trying to prevent me from making the tackle, ran a blocking line. If I'd have ran that blocking line, which is essentially cheating as it's an illegal move, I'd have had an arm up to protect myself. Joe didn't put his arm up, and I removed the threat, so to speak, and struck him in the face, so that I could make the tackle. Building up to the game, I had a slight calf strain, so I had been doing a lot of conditioning on the 'grinder' and for the previous few weeks, most of my anaerobic fitness consisted of boxing, so I was in decent shape. My action was autonomous, and I sat him down with a right to the chin, but tackled the ten, which was my job. My view was that Joe was stopping me from doing what I was trying to do, and I didn't have a nasty side to my character, I was just determined not to be stopped. I wasn't a player who stood up and had fights with people, as I just wanted to play rugby, but he was in my way and I wasn't going to stand for it.

I had to go to a disciplinary hearing soon after the final; only the second time in my career I was sat before a panel, with the only other time being for the push on referee Steve Lander, eight years in to my career, which I think showed that despite the position I played in, and even after 17 years in the game as a player I didn't have a particularly bad disciplinary record. It was just a shame that it happened in my final game for Tigers. There was no penalty awarded on the day for my incident but it was dealt with retrospectively. I was proud of my record over the years, having built relationships with officials, while understanding the rules of the game and the limits I could push myself to. I never wanted to let my colleagues down by giving away penalties. I attended the hearing, with judge Jeff Blackett and former Wasps player Jeff Probyn part of a three-man panel. I was accompanied by representatives from Leicester Tigers and the panel showed video footage of the line-out and me striking Joe. I asked them to show the next five seconds, which confused them, as they claimed that nothing of note happened afterwards, but they eventually showed the footage, where I tackle the Wasps player. I tried to explain that Joe ran a blocking line on me, but they responded by saying that it didn't negate my actions. I also asked for leniency given my record over the years, which they took in to account and handed me a four-week ban from the game. There was no arguing against it, but I just wanted to explain that it wasn't premeditated and I wasn't a dirty player. It was just a reaction to a situation, and while it may have been over the top, there was a clear reason as to why I had done it.

Going back to the game itself, I remember reading in Lewis Moody's book, *Mad Dog – An Englishman: My Life in Rugby*, his thoughts about the emotional send-off for John Wells, myself and Johno and I could understand why it was a big deal to him. We were the furniture at Welford Road, particularly Johno with his outstanding leadership and presence at the club. When Lawrence Dallaglio talked about how all he'd heard about was us in the build-up to the game, it was little wonder when you added up our collective contributions. It was certainly something to talk about for the media and the general public. We hadn't lost to Wasps in four games that season, and having smashed them a couple of weeks earlier, there was a great rivalry there. However, if we weren't leaving and retiring, then the chat would have all been about the game itself. A year earlier, I'd looked around the Twickenham field, in to the stands, and knew it was going to be my last time in an England shirt. Now I was doing the same thing, and saying goodbye to playing for Leicester Tigers. It was an incredibly emotional moment, on an emotional and ultimately disappointing day. I'm not someone who has regrets as such though. I had to be happy with my lot. We won a lot more than we lost over my career and I felt very privileged to have been a part of some very special teams over the years. There were highs and lows throughout my time with Tigers, and this defeat, however frustrating for us all, was just something to take on the chin and learn from.

On 11 April, around a month before the Zurich Premiership Final, the British & Irish Lions squad for the tour of New Zealand was announced, and despite having retired from playing for England a year previous, Clive invited me to be part of the 44-man group. People may have been surprised, but I never gave up hope of achieving anything in rugby. I only retired from playing for England because it felt right to do so. When Clive's call came through to invite me to be a Lion for a third tour, I was honoured, and I was delighted. I felt that I was still in good shape, had played regularly that season for Tigers, was match fit, very sharp and let's face it, had come within one game of finishing my club career with a further Premiership title.

I understood why people retired, whether it be through injury, fatigue, or age catching up on them, but I still enjoyed the game and still had a passion for playing. I'd said after the World Cup that I would never retire from playing for England, but come the Six Nations, I started to think clearly about the future and about people other than myself, like my family, and came to the right decision. Being named on the Lions tour was the perfect way to bow out of my playing career, and an opportunity to get one last chance on the international stage, an arena I'd worked so hard to reach in the first place. In a Lions tour you need players who are playing well, who are winners, but who are also good tourists. I felt I could tick those boxes, as I was in good form for Tigers, and I'd performed well and enjoyed the experience of my previous two tours. I had also been part of the England side who had beaten New Zealand the previous two times I'd played them, so I felt I could add something to the squad. I've been asked whether I was surprised to be named, but I honestly wasn't. Clive knew he could rely on me and I couldn't wait to wear the famous red jersey, and help to make history. Given my four-week ban, I was frustrated, but I just needed to work hard, be patient and I would hopefully get my chance.

9

Once, Twice, Three Times A Lion

HAVING retired from club rugby after the defeat to Wasps, I was excited and extremely proud to have one more chance to play at the highest level and wear the British & Irish Lions jersey for a third tour. As I've already said, retiring from international rugby was very difficult, but it was the right thing to do at the right time, so to be given another chance like this was incredible and one I was determined to enjoy and make the most of.

As far as I was concerned, I didn't feel I'd lost any of my skill or speed of thought; and as for being away from the international scene, well I saw that as a bonus in terms of managing my training and playing schedule, which I feel was justified given that I made a strong contribution to Tigers reaching the Premiership Final. I was playing regularly and I was fit, with the added determination of wanting to go out with a bang.

Being banned for my punch on Joe was heartbreaking, as I really feared that my chance with the Lions could be taken away from me. My immediate thought was that I could have been withdrawn and denied the chance to represent one of the best teams in the world. Fortunately, Clive and his staff supported me, and I remained as a part of the touring party. I was given the role of 'waterboy' for the warm-up match against Argentina at the Millennium Stadium on 23 May 2005, before we left for New Zealand. I really enjoyed being involved and being part of the build-up but the Argentines were a little upset that I was involved at all, given my ban, and felt that my participation by bringing drinks on to the pitch wasn't fair as I was passing coaching instructions on to the field. Rightly or wrongly, I was doing exactly that. I'd got the coaching bug and as an experienced player, I was trying to motivate my colleagues and perhaps mention little pointers I'd noticed from the sidelines; nothing official through the management staff, just my views on how the game was going.

I still feared that the ban would leave me conceding ground to a competitor as well. I always attempted to throw myself 100 per cent in to everything I did, and I still do to this day. I hate it when people say that they are going to give 110 per cent or 120 per cent; it's just not possible and it's ridiculous to even say it. I don't actually believe that you can quite get to 100 per cent in elite sport all of the time, for every second of every game, but you've got to aspire to reach it and get as close as possible. Therefore, I was already behind as Martyn Williams, who had won the grand slam with Wales that year, would have a chance to show his worth on the tour before I would. Martyn had played well throughout the past year or so and I'd given him ground, which I had to try and make up in training. I did everything I could to support the team, apart from enter the field of play. It was frustrating, but I had to live with my actions in the Premiership Final and that punch.

Clive had received a lot of criticism for his squad selection for the 2005 tour. He picked 44 players to travel to the other side of the world to face the All Blacks, with 20 of them English, 11 Irish, ten Welsh and three token Scots. Sorry, I'm only teasing there. I guess that Clive was always going to pick the best squad he could, but if there was a close call between players for the same position, the coach is going to go with the player that he knows and trusts. I'm sure Warren Gatland would have gone through the same process for the 2013 Lions tour of Australia, but the difference being he didn't have to justify his selections as they won, and we didn't. Me and Lol were both picked, despite being retired from international rugby. I thought that selection for a tour would be based on factors such as who was a good tourist, who had the skills and experience required, and who had shown that they could already do it against New Zealand. We'd both done that already, so that was probably the thinking behind it. Also, to defend Clive on this tour, New Zealand is traditionally the most difficult opponent, so comparing this tour to the previous two against South Africa and Australia would be unfair.

One of Clive's strengths as a coach, and as a person, is his ability to try things. He is never afraid to fail and then to learn lessons from his mistakes. During our time working together, there were a number of initiatives or methods he tried which worked, and then there were things he did which didn't work, but he was always willing to test the boundaries and look for innovative ways to improve our performance and motivate the squad. One example I remember, going back to the build-up to the 2003 World Cup with England, was his idea to bring an Israeli fighter pilot over, with all the relevant hardware and software, to reproduce the experience of flying a fighter jet on a simulator. Some of the younger lads within the group really enjoyed it, but the seasoned members of the group weren't so keen, like Johno, who held the joystick, had a quick wobble and dropped it down on the table. Clive was prepared to have a go, and then acknowledge that it didn't work with the group and this exercise was never revisited. When I think back, we lost only four matches in my final four years as an England player, and those were the games where we learned the most about ourselves, and ensured we didn't make the same mistakes again.

Going back to the Lions tour, it was the largest squad picked in history and there was also a larger management staff than usual who toured with us. There were essentially two management teams, which was a break from tradition by Clive. I feel that while there were some quality coaches out there, there were mixed messages on the tour and that may have come from the fact that we didn't all travel together to each game. Clive was keen to cut down on the travel and only have those needed going to each game, rather than dragging everyone along to here, there and everywhere. The methodology was right and everything he did made perfect sense, but I guess, with hindsight, the tour was a little too clinical and lacked the emotion required for the Lions. At least that's how I felt if I was to think back and stack this against the feeling I had from the previous two tours. With the Lions, you need to get the players from the four nations together and develop a bond almost immediately.

Firstly, as Clive's touring party did, you get the kit given to you and all players loved their 'stash', with the Lions badge on it, and then there's an ice-breaker, and you are all together. That togetherness was perhaps lacking a little, as Clive then followed his tried and tested methods from our time with England, and decided to allocate the players their own rooms, rather than rooming with someone else from within the squad and a different nation. I think that didn't help with us getting to know each other, and remember, we were guys who were kicking lumps out of each other not that long ago, either for clubs or country. With England, the separate rooms thing worked brilliantly, as we all knew each other so well anyway that we were perhaps grateful for a bit of quiet in our own room. I guess it was just too cold and clinical, when you need to integrate players and coaches quickly. I can see why we did it, but I just felt like it didn't work for us, despite the good intentions.

Once we got on to the field, except me of course, we won our first two matches quite comfortably against Bay of Plenty Steamers, 34-20, and Taranaki, 36-14, so the tour was off to a decent start and people were acclimatising and getting valuable game time. In the third game though, things went wrong for us as we came up against a strong New Zealand Māori side, who recorded their first win over the Lions, 19-13. They were a very competitive and unified side, whereas we were still trying to gel and hone our playing philosophy, and ultimately we paid for that. That was the last game of my ban, so I was able to start in a 23-6 win over Wellington, before the team beat Otago 30-19 and Southland 26-16 and we were back on track, although we weren't particularly convincing against sides that we were expected to beat with ease. Not playing in that final warm-up match meant that my chances of playing in the first Test were much stronger.

The first Test was held at the Jade Stadium in Christchurch, and I was selected to play, which was without doubt one of the proudest moments of my rugby career. I wasn't aware of it then, but by walking over the white paint on 25 June 2005, I became the oldest Lion to play in a Test match at the age of 36 years and 174 days. I was immensely proud to wear the shirt, and age is just a number, as all that ever mattered to me was whether I was good enough. I felt I had been picked on merit after a good season with Tigers, but I guess that in hindsight, it was a nice achievement so I could see why it was mentioned in the media.

Just two minutes in to the game and our tour captain, Brian O'Driscoll, in great form at the time for Leinster and Ireland and undoubtedly a world-class player, was tackled by

Tana Umaga and Keven Mealamu. Brian was lifted up and dumped on to the ground, resulting in him dislocating his shoulder. It was a bad tackle, no doubt about it. There was clearly a lot of adrenaline pumping at the time, at the start of a Lions series, and it was a really unfortunate moment. Brian played 141 Test matches in his career and was a real giant of the game, an incredible talent and a great guy too, but I'm not certain that he was targeted as such. I think that in the heat of the moment, the All Blacks guys would have left their mark on any player, and Brian just happened to be the one in the firing line at that time. It was an awful start for us in every way possible.

Post-match there was a great deal of analysis of the incident and a lot of uproar, most of which I feel was created by the presence of Alastair Campbell, the former Labour Party director of communications during the Tony Blair era. Alastair was brought along by Clive to handle the media on the tour, as part of the extended management team. I feel that the decision to take Alastair on the tour backfired massively, as the members of the rugby media were a very knowledgeable group of people who were not about to allow a spin doctor, with his profile and history, to pull the wool over their eyes. I believe that having Alastair there was an insurance policy against the PR disaster of the 2001 tour of Australia, when Matt Dawson's diary of the tour and the difficulties in the camp were published as part of an agreed insight in to his trip, on the day of the first Test. Matt was fined £5,000 and ordered to apologise to everyone, while nearly being sent home in disgrace. Sadly Alastair's presence did nothing in 2005 to ease the scrutiny, it simply added flames to the fire. He made a big issue of the O'Driscoll injury, replaying the footage with Clive to the media, but ultimately we had lost 21-3, were 1-0 down in the series and this was just turning the tour into a travelling circus. Then there was the Gavin

Henson incident, and the alleged staging of a photo of him looking cordial with Clive, with Gavin later claiming that the staged photos were taken without his knowledge. I don't know exactly what happened there, but either way I felt that we had lost the ethos of what a Lions tour was about; the camaraderie, having the odd beer together, the spirit of the amateur era and being able to chat to a rugby journalist knowing that everything would be kept private. Now it was all so cold and clinical.

I could understand completely why Clive brought Alastair on the tour. He was big on having experts in their field, and that approach had served us well for England. I want to make it clear that I have nothing against Alastair either. I found him to be a decent guy, who was quite sociable and you could go and talk to him if you wanted to, so there was no issue there. I just felt that you didn't need a high-profile spin doctor on a Lions tour. It was the wrong fit and we just needed a media liaison person there, from within the rugby world, to help manage the relationship with the media. An example of Alastair being out of place was after the first-Test defeat, when he was invited by Clive to speak to the players ahead of the second Test. He had spoken to Clive and the management staff about his own experiences of the feeling when something is going wrong, and the need to turn it around before it's too late. Clive urged him to speak to us and he did, but his references to the war in Kosovo in the late 1990s and also our lack of heart, and our lack of passion, and lack of effort, didn't wash well with us as a group. Maybe if the words had come from Clive, Ian McGeechan, Andy Robinson or Eddie O'Sullivan, as respected rugby coaches, perhaps we would have taken the words on board, but we didn't know or trust Alastair.

What I do know, is that I never played in a side which didn't show those character traits that he questioned, especially not on a Lions tour. I took umbrage at his comments and challenged him directly. I made sure that I made my points, very clearly, in the lift, face-to-face, when I knew there was nowhere to go. I told him in no uncertain terms that he should never say those words again, and I was seething. He listened to me and seemed taken aback, maybe at the velocity at which my reaction to his speech was delivered. In business or sport, no matter what level you are at, you need everyone to be pulling together and I felt that we were moving in different directions as a squad.

Having lost the first Test we needed a reaction. Following Brian O'Driscoll's injury, Danny Grewcock was cited for biting Keven Mealamu and banned for two months, plus Richard Hill was injured, among others, so there was a real feeling that we were not knitting together at the time we needed to most. Seven players replaced injured players on the tour, taking the grand total to 51 players who were involved in some way, at some time, on the trip. I was picked to play in the next midweek game, against Manawatu, which meant I was unlikely to be picked for the second Test match. My strengths as a player were my defensive organisation, continuity, support play and leadership support, and if I'm honest, at times in my career I had felt like I'd only done okay but been named man of the match. That was rugby. I felt I played okay in the first Test, but we'd been well beaten so I expected there to be changes. I knew it wasn't a man of the match performance, but I'd hoped to get another chance. Anyway, we beat Manawatu 109-6 and I managed to score a try, in what turned out to be my last competitive game as a rugby player. I then did my duty and supported the team for the second Test.

I felt that Clive succumbed a little to media pressure, making 11 changes to the squad from the first Test, and included many of the Welsh players who had done so well earlier in the year to win the grand slam. It was a huge number of changes from one week to the next, which was a little surprising, and I felt that there was a lot of pressure on him to act. Unfortunately, even with the introduction of the Welsh lads, we lost 48-18, which was a heavier defeat, including the worst points against total conceded by the Lions against the All Blacks. We were at a real low at this point, and being 2-0 down going in to a third Test is a horrible situation for everyone. We beat Auckland 17-13 in the midweek game, before returning to Eden Park a few days later for the third and final Test of the tour. The All Blacks completed the rout and a 3-0 series win with a 38-19 victory over us and we were sent back home with nothing, and with our tail firmly between our legs. When you look back at the tour, even from the first Test, you can see the faults and the warning signs. We had ten losses of our own ball from set pieces; the cornerstone of any good side, which I think showed the lack of understanding among us and the general lack of togetherness.

In 1993 I was picked as a standby reserve for the Lions tour of New Zealand, but as there were no injuries I wasn't required. In 1997, we didn't play brilliant rugby, but we won the series 2-1. In 2001, in six halves of rugby, we won four of them and only lost two, yet lost the series 2-1. We played much better rugby in 2001 than four years earlier, but that's elite sport and the fine lines between winning and losing. I guess to compare my previous two Lions experiences to the 2005 tour is difficult, but put simply, that tour was just too calculated. I know that since then, Lions tours have returned to the one coaching team, rather than two coaching the midweek and Test teams, which is the right way to do it as it helps to create a strong squad togetherness and avoids the feeling of a separated camp. I want to be fair to Clive though and express that he and his staff had solid reasons for all of their decisions. Sometimes a team is just better than you, and New Zealand were the best in the world at that time, as they so often are. Maybe they would have won 3-0 regardless of the management staff decisions on and off the field, and any argument over why Clive didn't pick more Welsh players was put to bed once we were stuffed out of sight in the second Test. I think that subsequent Lions tours have learned from the decisions that didn't quite work in that environment, which is at least one big positive to take from the trip.

As for the future of those tours, the Lions is simply unique. There is no other way of explaining it, I hope it never dies, and I'm sure it won't. Playing and wearing the famous jersey is, in my view, the highest accolade you can receive as a rugby player from Britain and Ireland. Once you have played internationally for one of the four countries – England, Ireland, Scotland and Wales – then this is the greatest honour. There is clearly a growing demand on players now, with more fixtures, both domestically, in Europe and internationally, and matched with concerns over injuries and fatigue, and particularly concussion, which at the time of writing is prevalent in the game, meaning it would be easy for the authorities to question the role of the Lions in the rugby calendar.

In the 2013 tour, for example, there was a questionable warm-up match arranged against the Barbarians in Hong Kong, which was obviously just a commercially motivated decision and was played in high humidity, which could have had a detrimental effect on the players. They also played against squad teams on the tour, as sides were facing their regular league matches at the weekend, meaning they would put out a weaker side against the Lions, so the organisation and scheduling left a lot to be desired. Saying that, despite the poorer warm-up games and the commercialisation of the tour, 2013 was a huge success with the Lions winning 2-1 and gaining new supporters in the process. It will be interesting to see how the 2017 tour of New Zealand is handled, and then when the current agreement runs out, how the future of Lions tours are handled. I could see the Lions touring America, Canada and Argentina at some stage, as the appeal of the team and the popularity of the whole concept continues to grow.

I'll leave the final words on the Lions to Sir Ian McGeechan, who was head coach of four tours, including our success in 1997, while coaching the midweek side in the doomed 2005 trip. His words before the second Test in 1997 in Durban against South Africa sum up, with great understanding and genuine emotion, what the Lions meant to him, and in the process capture what the Lions really meant to me, 'I've given a lot of things up. I love my rugby, I love my family and when you come to a day like this you know why you do it. It's a privilege because we are something special. You will meet each other in the street in 30 years' time and there will just be a look and you'll know just how special some days in your life are.'

After the tour of New Zealand, and a brief family holiday, it was time to return to the excitement of beginning my full-time role as a coach with Leicester Tigers. With my playing boots metaphorically hung up I felt a real comfort and genuine optimism from my role in helping to develop the next generation of players for the club, while retaining my involvement in the game of rugby. Essentially, I became the club's assistant coach full-time, with my main focus on being the defence coach across the whole of the club, at every level, while assisting the forwards coach Cockers, and offering support to Pat Howard as head coach.

I was very keen to develop as a coach as quickly as possible, in terms of my personal development and I spoke to Kevin Bowring about furthering my education. I'd already done quite a bit of coaching as a player-coach, along with my playing career, which meant I didn't have to do levels one, two or three, so I moved straight to undertake my Level 4 RFU Coaching Award that year. In order to do that, I had to be coaching a side regularly, so I also took on the role of head coach of the Tigers Academy. We were essentially a 'mini Tigers', with a mirrored set-up from the first team, including a dedicated management, support and medical team, along with our own development fixtures. Players such as Ben Youngs and Dan Cole came through from that era, as did many other players who went on to play competitive professional rugby. The level of planning for the academy squad was as meticulous as for the first team, but the fixtures were not part of a league table, they were purely a platform to give players game time to witness progression and highlight areas for improvement, although we would always keep a keen eye on progress with results, while skill development was the main focus. I spent a lot of time working closely with younger players, getting to know them as characters. I would have loved to have worked with a 'me' when I was that age, so I was determined to give the academy lads as much of my time as I could, as I strongly believe that regular feedback is critical for player development.

It was a great opportunity for me to cut my teeth as a coach full-time while balancing all of the roles across all ages. I was also given the responsibility by Pat Howard to head up the 'A' team, along with his assistant backs coach, Andy Key. The 'A' team was used to develop and integrate young players, as well as reintegrate injured first-team players attempting to get back to fitness. In the first year, we reached the 'A' league final and played against Harlequins at Welford Road, with their director of rugby being none other than Dean Richards, who that day made his first return to Welford Road since his departure from the top job. We won the final and that was effectively my first piece of silverware, in my first season as a full-time coach, that was directly related to my role. I was proud of the set-up we had among all of the staff and players, and I was really enjoying my new roles. I was also able to stay pretty fit, as I was doing so much coaching and working with the younger players, and the bonus being I wasn't battered and bruised as I was each day as a player.

I suppose, looking back, my early coaching days came a little earlier than expected, when Deano departed the club, but even if that hadn't have happened I would have always gone in to coaching as it was a real passion. I'd always gone in to schools to help out and coach, through to unofficial coaching roles with England when Phil Larder wasn't there, so it was something I thrived on and was something that was planned as my next step in the game. I think that Kevin Bowring had identified me as a potential future coach as well, probably due to my strong relationship with Clive and Phil while with England, and also with my hunger to move in to this area. I'd also gone out of my way to broaden my experiences, by going and watching coaching methods within other sports, spending time at Coventry City and Leicester City Football Club, which I felt would help me to pick up good practice and transferrable habits and methods. I knew that one of the main differences between being a player and a coach was the analysis side of the game, as well as the fact that your day would carry on much longer, as you dealt with administration and community duties as well. I was prepared for that and enjoyed the variety of the work, while trying to develop new skills.

In my early days, I'd worked in insurance, so an office environment wasn't quite as alien to me as it would have been to some people, but we had a great backroom team to work with and a strong camaraderie off the field as well as on it, so it was a smooth transition for me.

In the first year, the 2005/06 season, the club needed a new captain, and Martin Corry was selected for the role. He was a quality player and had captained England so he was a strong choice. The club had a reasonable campaign but we just missed out in the league, finishing second to Sale in the regular season, before beating London Irish 40-8 in the play-off semi-final and then losing 45-20 to Sale at Twickenham in the Premiership Final. We also lost to Bath 15-12 in a dire Heineken Cup quarter-final at the Walkers Stadium. Tactically we were poor on the day, with Bath losing two players to the sin-bin, and we were unable to take advantage of the space out wide and instead tried to go route one. In March of that season, we were the only side in contention for three trophies, yet finished the campaign empty-handed.

In my second season, 2006/07, the Level 5 coaching qualification was scrapped in favour of the Elite Coaches Development course, which was essentially the same thing. Graham Rowntree finished his playing career and took on the academy role, as part of his development, which left me to focus on the 'A' team with Andy Key, along with my main role as the club's defence coach. I still helped Graham out with specific sessions for the academy players, making myself available to support him and them.

I vividly remember Pat sitting us all down at the start of that season and asking everyone what we needed to do to win all three trophies. He then set about ensuring we were as well equipped as we could be, in all areas, to succeed. Looking back, we were so close to achieving his ambitious aim, and it was a remarkable effort from everyone involved. Pat had previously left Leicester as a player and in his spell with French side Montferrand, he developed a strong relationship with Cockers as they had lived and worked together, and that bond continued when he returned to Tigers as backs coach and then as head coach after John Wells's departure. I really respect Pat as a person and as a coach, as I've already said, and in that second year, he led us to the domestic double, losing the Heineken Cup final to deny us the treble.

On 15 April 2007 we won our first silverware in five years against the Ospreys 41-35 to seal the EDF Energy Cup, and followed that by finishing second on points difference to Gloucester in the regular league season. We then beat Bristol 26-14 in the play-off semi-final and crushed Gloucester 44-16 in the Premiership Final. All that was left was the Heineken Cup, and standing in our way were our old foes, London Wasps. We'd already beaten Stade Francais 21-20 in the quarter-final at Welford Road, and then at the Walkers Stadium we ended our hoodoo by beating Llanelli Scarlets 33-17 in the semi-final. To maintain our assault on all fronts put a real strain on the squad, with extra games at a time of the season when fatigue and injuries would be most present. Wasps had that little extra spring in their step and beat us 25-9, but it was still a season to be very proud of. We'd shown real strength of character and only just fallen short. Among those achievements, I was very proud of us going to Munster and winning there 13-6 in the Heineken pool stages, which was their first home defeat in 27 matches, and was sweeter for me because of the great rivalry over recent years. It was a near-perfect year and we were all gutted that we didn't quite manage to complete Pat's aim of the treble.

Pat had announced in December 2006 that he was going to leave the club, and soon after his return to Australia he became the general manager of their high performance unit, and has gone on to other challenges since then in cricket. Pat was honourable with his announcement, ensuring that the club had as much notice as possible to recruit a quality replacement. Everyone was disappointed that he was leaving but respected his decision. I firmly believe that Pat would do well at anything he put his hand to, and we were certainly in a stronger position when he left, than when he joined.

At that time, I felt it was important to consider my own future. I spoke with Kevin Bowring and we discussed the possibility of me moving on to another opportunity, outside of the shadow of the Tigers. In those discussions with Kevin, the club and my family, I made the choice to stay for a third season as a full-time coach at Welford Road, as I wanted to work with and learn from the new head coach, Marcelo Loffreda. Marcelo was the head coach of Argentina, who he had led brilliantly in the build-up to the 2007 Rugby World Cup, and he would join Tigers after the tournament. The Pumas were a revelation, finishing third in the tournament, beating the hosts France in the first game and in the third-place play-off for their best performance at a World Cup. They were only halted by the tournament winners, South Africa, in the semi-finals.

Cockers was the caretaker boss for the start of the 2007/08 season, with support from Andy Key and myself, but to be honest, Pat had created such a strong squad and ethos that we were in a very good position while Marcelo was over in France. We had some new arrivals added to the squad as well that season; Marco Wentzel, who later joined me at Leeds, Mefin Davies, Ayoola Erinle and Benjamin Kayser, who were all signed by Cockers really, as Marcelo left it to the staff while he was finishing his role with Argentina. There was a real excitement that he would be able to build upon Pat's great work, but that soon disappeared. During his spell with Tigers, I can honestly say that I learnt more about what not to do, than how to do things. Don't get me wrong, he was a good bloke, whom I respected and fully supported, but he couldn't effectively communicate as he struggled with English, and once you looked into his coaching background it was clear that he didn't have the necessary experience to manage a professional club in England from week to week. He had limited experience in Argentina with amateur club sides and had done a marvellous job with their national side, but being a full-time boss with Leicester required much more. In some of our initial sessions, we had 35 players on the pitch huddled around, sometimes doing nothing, with Marcelo speaking in broken English and getting very frustrated with himself. There was no organisation, and it was completely different to the two years under Pat, where no stone was ever left unturned. Marcelo had proved to be good at organising and managing an international squad over a two-to-six-week period, who had been developed physically and mentally at professional club teams. If one of his international squad got injured, he would just bring in the next player. However, at a top Premiership club, over a full season of club and international fixtures, he was sadly so under-equipped and out of his depth, it was slightly embarrassing for him and those who had recruited him for the role.

When the dust had settled on Loffreda's time at Tigers, the stats didn't really tell the truth. He won 16 out of 26 games, and reached two finals in the process, in a seven-month spell. However, he had taken over a strong squad which had reached three finals the previous season, so in some ways any relative success was in spite of him and he was carried throughout that period. I could see pretty early on in Marcelo's reign that he was going to struggle and I felt sorry for him. I tried to work with him and assist him as much as I could, as it must have been a real culture shock for him. We all fought and supported Marcelo to the hilt, as we all wanted it to work for him and for the club, but sadly it simply wasn't going to. He left on good terms and there was no animosity between Marcelo and anyone. I guess that looking back, the board must have realised that they had made a mistake, selecting someone who had a good record, but just wasn't a good fit for Tigers and the professional environment of English top flight rugby. Seven months in to a three-year contract, the board let Marcelo go and for the second time in a year the club was looking for a head coach.

Once again, it was time for me to think about my own position at the club and my coaching future. I'd remained at

Tigers after Pat Howard's departure, in order to learn from Marcelo Loffreda, and it was ultimately a disappointing experience. Cockers and I both spoke to the board about the future in the close season, and they decided to begin a worldwide search for a high-profile head coach, but this time one with the relevant experience for the role. Looking at it on paper, we had reached five of the last six finals, so we were an attractive proposition for any coach in world rugby. The board elected to appoint the South African, Heyneke Meyer, and with no reflection on Heyneke, who is a quality coach, I just felt that as he had signed a three-year deal I wanted to test myself as a head coach elsewhere. I had a packed three years as a full-time coach and one and a half seasons in a player-coach role prior to that, so I was ready to take the next step. The board and my coaching mentor, Kevin Bowring, were supportive of me moving on for three years, with a view to me coming back to the club after gaining experience as a head coach in my own right.

I had looked at potential opportunities with Kevin Bowring the previous season and again this season, and the situation at Leeds Carnegie presented itself, as their head coach, as future England head coach Stuart Lancaster had left the club to join the RFU as their elite rugby director. I remember feeling sad as I left Tigers, but I told myself I would be back one day. Leeds was a great opportunity for my personal development, and everyone who was close to me, and whose opinion I valued, agreed with me. It was time to come out from the shadows of Welford Road, and go in to a completely different environment and challenge myself. Leeds had just been relegated to the Championship, so I knew I had a battle on my hands to turn around their mood and get the club back to the top flight. The apron strings had been cut, and I couldn't wait to get started.

10

Leeds

I GUESS the easy option in my career would have been to remain as a coach at Leicester Tigers, and while we'll never know, if I'd have stayed at Welford Road, I suppose I could still be there today. As I've said before though, I don't hold regrets over my decisions and after 18 years at the club, I wanted to try a new challenge and Leeds Carnegie was a great opportunity for me to do just that.

Knowing that the operational and subsequently the playing and recruitment budget wouldn't be as large as I'd experienced at Leicester, I needed someone with me who could help to provide value across all areas, on and off the field. Andy Key, or 'Kiwi' as he's known, agreed to join me at Leeds as director of rugby after 30 years at Tigers, and on the day we were unveiled at Headingley, Heyneke Meyer was unveiled at Welford Road as the new head coach of the Tigers. We left with the club's best wishes, after giving so much of our respective professional careers to Leicester.

Kiwi and I devised a three-year plan for the club, matching the length of our contracts. Leeds had just been relegated from the top flight so we knew there was work to do to galvanise the club. We presented our vision to the board, with the aim of a non-negotiable promotion at the first attempt, followed by consolidating our position in the top flight in year two and then in year three, our aim was simply to move forward, and establish the club as a regular top flight side. We illustrated it to the board as a Formula One car gradually moving up the starting grid, ahead of each Grand Prix meeting.

Kiwi assisted me as a backs coach, while casting his eye over the academy structure at the club, as we were acutely aware that we would need to develop players in-house due to not having a great spending capability at the club. Andy also had the remit to help engage with the local community and businesses, in order to help gain extra support both in terms of finance and also in terms of our attendances. Leeds Carnegie were traditionally positioned behind the likes of Leeds Rhinos Rugby League Club, Leeds United Football Club, and Yorkshire County Cricket Club, but we felt that if we could establish the club in the Premiership, then we could develop a strong fanbase as well. We shared responsibilities and worked together to get agreement from the board, which we did.

Andy had been the driving force behind the development of Tigers' superb academy, and matched with his business acumen, and organisational skills, we had a strong crossover of skills and knowledge, which we felt would allow us to work well together at Leeds. I was already friends with Kiwi at Leicester and I knew we would complement each other well. In the first six months of our time in Leeds, we shared and rented a flat together and worked six days a week, sometimes in to the early hours, just to try and ensure that we got off to a good start in our new roles. We made a lot of sacrifices in those early days, particularly in terms of family and social time, and our relationship was almost like a marriage, only we lived and worked together so had pretty much no time apart.

That placed a lot of pressure on our professional relationship and on our friendship, but we coped well with that and
we could see the bigger picture and the long-term benefits
of this initial challenge, as Kiwi explains, 'Backy and I lived
together for around the first six months of our time at Leeds,
and he was a really tidy boy. It was a bachelors' pad, without
the antics, just in the sense that it was quite minimal. It wasn't
so bad for me, as my family were a little older than Neil's,
and we created that intensity to ensure that we gave the club
and the project our all. Our families understood what we
needed to do in that initial period, but then we needed to
live separately for Neil and I's working relationship and our
friendship to continue. We adopted the mantra "You only get
one shot, do not miss your chance to blow, this opportunity
comes once in a lifetime" from Eminem's "Lose Yourself" and
following some persuasive discussions with the management,
the team adopted this song as their signature tune and used
it to enter the field with a clear reminder of the task in hand.

'It was a great experience living with Neil though. I'm a
process-driven person, like a finisher within business terms,
which can be a pain in the arse to some people, but the balance
was there between us both and Backy knew that he could trust
and rely upon me and vice-versa. Neil is methodical, he can be
intense, but he is a winner and it was a really rewarding period
both working and living with him. He was an outstanding
player, and he carried his determined nature in to his coaching
career, but was very accepting of others and was a real team
person throughout our time at the club.'

We decided, after those six months, to move in to
separate places, just to give us some breathing space from the
intensity, and also to allow our families to visit us in comfort
at weekends.

We were under no illusions about the task we faced
though. We followed two very good coaches in Phil Davies,

who spent a decade as the club's director of rugby, and Stuart Lancaster who was there for a couple of seasons directly before we joined the club. Both had experienced some success at Leeds, but hadn't necessarily been able to establish the club at the top table of English rugby, and we felt that with the knowledge we had, we would be able to make a difference and help the club to take that next step.

I think that, looking back to this time, you are almost in a bubble at Leicester and the way things are done. It is an elite environment, with extremely motivated people around you and a winning mentality flowed through the club for the majority of my time there. Then you cut the apron strings, move to a club like Leeds and try to bring that mentality to the place, but it's difficult to replicate and difficult to change a culture on and off the field. I wanted to make people realise that we could achieve anything if we worked for it, but there was a real struggle for the people off the field to share my view. I was grateful for all my experiences at Leicester, but nothing could really prepare me for the battle that we faced at Leeds over our three years there.

For the first two or three months, Andy and I spent time talking to everyone at the club; players, staff including our defence coach Simon Middleton, skills coach Daryl Powell, great friend and kitman David Matthews, and our supporters, to learn about what they felt had gone well, and wrong, in the previous season, so we could understand what we needed to do to get the club back on track. We gained a good feel for the club, as we didn't want to come in on day one and just tell people how to do things. We wanted to engage and then empower the group, in the hope that they would relish the added responsibility. It was important for us to share our three-year vision with the players and staff and work together to try and create an elite environment, like we had cultivated over the years at Tigers. The whole approach was geared towards developing an open atmosphere, in a similar sense to the way that Clive had encouraged everyone to speak their mind within the England camp. I didn't feel we could be successful if there was fear within the players, and I wanted them to rise up individually, and collectively, and dictate their own destiny.

The whole process felt like starting over again. Kiwi and I were really excited about the project. My real passions in life have always been family, rugby and cars, with the order dependent upon who I'm speaking to! At this time though, we had a real zest for our work. Yes, the days were long, but we were at the start of a journey that we were creating and we felt we were beginning to get a strong response from the players too, which acted as an endorsement of our methods. It was an incredible experience at Leeds for Kiwi and I, and I really felt like my own personal development as a coach came on leaps and bounds. Sadly, as I'll explain in more detail, there were broken promises and a lack of real support from the board, which if I'd have known about on day one, I wouldn't have signed on the dotted line.

Despite that, we made a perfect start on the field, winning our first 23 league matches on the bounce. The players were motivated and they all pulled together. We had all created a very positive working environment and the camaraderie was strong too. Generally, the group wanted to make it work as they were deciding upon the way we approached training and games. I loved watching players who were at Championship level, demonstrating the maturity of a Premiership player and it was a source of real pride to me and Kiwi during that first season.

Our first defeat came on 7 March 2009, 27-12 away to Doncaster Knights, and we lost the following week too, 27-24 against Bedford Blues. It was a real test of character for us, as it would have been easy for people to begin to question whether the wheels had come off, but we never doubted ourselves for a moment. Those two blips were our only defeats in a season where we stormed to the title, winning promotion to the Premiership with 28 wins from 30 games. It was an incredible effort from the players and the staff, and I was so proud of everyone. Exeter Chiefs, who finished second, were 14 points adrift from us, so we thoroughly deserved to return to the top flight at the first attempt.

In our first season in the Premiership I felt that we acquitted ourselves pretty well. Our crowds doubled from around 3,000 to 6,000 people, which showed that there was an appetite for rugby union in the area, and I could really see the makings of a decent side, although we were a long way off the top teams in the division. We lost both league games against Leicester Tigers, but I received a great reception on my return on 28 November 2009 when we were beaten 39-6. We came closer in the home match, a 14-9 defeat. It felt strange lining up against Tigers, but as I looked around Welford Road, I was proud to be leading my own side there, showing everyone that I could do it elsewhere and not just with Leicester. We did manage to beat them 28-17 in the LV= Cup, but we exited the competition at the pool stage.

So at the end of the year we had massively ticked our year's goal of consolidation in the Premiership. We finished on 36 points from 22 games, with seven wins, one draw and 14 defeats, and we did enough to survive, with Worcester Warriors relegated, Sale Sharks just surviving and us in tenth out of the 12 clubs in the top flight. It was at this point that we needed to build on our achievements. In terms of our three-year vision, the first two years had gone to plan, but it was year three where we would really learn of the board's intentions, or lack of them, as the case was.

In year three we had finished bottom of pool two of the LV= Cup, and lost both of our league games against the

Tigers. It was clear that we hadn't moved on and we'd already performed a minor miracle by competing at this level in the first place. My frustration was clear for all to see, as we were just short, but I was determined to keep going and try and see the job through and complete the aims we had set out at the start.

The final game of my time at Leeds demonstrated what winning was about. The top teams have quality players, and quality costs money. The Leeds board were not prepared to spend money and to take the club on to the level that we had agreed when we set out our three-year vision at the start of our time at the club. It was so disappointing to come so close to survival and to fail by the smallest of margins. We had maximised everything we could, out of the limited resources we had, but ultimately we fell short.

We had fought like hell to stay in the Premiership, and had kept our side of the bargain, but others simply didn't back us as they had signed off on three years ago, as Kiwi remembers, 'Unfortunately, we saw a heavy rugby league influence at the club, rather than a divorcing between the two sports, and those issues were still there when we left. The individuals at managerial and board level just couldn't and wouldn't change their way of thinking.

'After the success of getting promoted in our first season, followed by survival in the Premiership in our second season, I think that the delays in making decisions and the over-cautious approach at board level contributed to our downfall in year three. For example, we could have retained Seru Rabeni, but alas the club hesitated and we lost him. We both acknowledged that to promote long-term success for Leeds Carnegie would mean them working through a culture change. Staff and members appreciated our efforts in looking to change the club's thinking; however, we both knew that to achieve this would need the board to ultimately change as well. Unfortunately this was beyond us, despite all of our efforts.'

In February the board decided to dismiss Andy from the director of rugby role and not replace him, as part of a 'restructuring' that would see Gary Hetherington, the club's chief executive officer, take on some of Kiwi's responsibilities. I was invited to a press conference where I was told just prior to going in that Kiwi had been asked to leave. I was at the press conference but didn't speak as Gary addressed the media. I was shocked. We had worked together for over 20 years and I felt let down, just as much as I felt for Kiwi losing his job, which he picks up on here, 'It was very hurtful for me when I left the club, and I had to ask myself a lot of questions as to why it had happened. I attended a meeting, presuming it was about budgeting and planning ahead, especially as we could have been in either of the top two divisions. I was told that I was leaving as part of a restructuring, but it was a bit of a blur to me after I'd been told I was being released. The board had accepted that the club was going to be relegated, but there were months left of the season. I was a casualty of a relegation that hadn't happened yet. I subsequently met with Chris Gibson from the club, to try to understand the rationale behind the club's decision, but in playing it safe he told me that this was part of sport.

'I went along to watch the final game against Northampton when Backy and the guys came so close to keeping the club up, which was a strange experience, as I had been a part of the journey from the start, and I really felt for Neil and the lads when the final whistle was blown. Looking back, whatever had happened in terms of survival, the club was struggling to cope off the field, showing what an impossible job it was to complete the vision we had laid out at the beginning.'

We had been 11 points adrift at Christmas, we were still bottom of the league and had only won one league game all season and they decided to remove someone and not replace him. This is what we were facing. At that stage, I knew that time was up for me as well, but I was determined to finish the season, keep Leeds in the Premiership and complete the job that Kiwi and I had started.

Gary Hetherington was probably one of our strengths, while also being one of our greatest weaknesses during my three years at Leeds. He was a good person and a good CEO too, but if you cut him in half he would bleed rugby league blood, no doubt about it. Gary could never get his head around the fact that Kevin Sinfield, a top-class rugby league player, was earning roughly the same as an average rugby union player. We would identify players to join us, through our thorough recruitment process, but Gary wouldn't sanction the spend on their wages and we'd end up missing out to a rival club, who as a result would then be stronger than us on the field. The two markets were completely different and it was an archaic approach to have, but it was what we had to deal with unfortunately and it always left us with an uphill struggle to compete at the highest level. While writing this book, Kevin has decided to switch codes, from league to union, something that he discussed during our time at the club, as Kiwi picks up, 'It was incredible that Kevin was willing to join us, completely out of the blue he contacted us to state he was interested in playing for Leeds Carnegie and switch codes. Following our initial meeting and having heard his reasons for the change, we felt it only proper that we speak with the powers that be within the Rhinos to seek their blessing for the switch. Yet within a matter of days we had heard that Kevin would not be joining us. Our emotions had once again turned from sheer elation to that of disbelief! We can only imagine what Kevin would have brought to the club, on and off the field.'

We also shared training facilities and all off-field resources like marketing and public relations with Leeds Rhinos and across the board, preference was given to them. They had the better pitch to train on and also, when it came to the crunch, the marketing team, who were given no financial incentives throughout my time there, were always going to focus on the easier sell of the Rhinos as opposed to us. If there was a big game, what was the easier sell? The fully-funded and successful rugby league team or us? There was never any contest. The odds always seemed to be stacked against us.

I felt that Leeds had potential, but getting other people to see that was the real challenge. I was convinced that getting them back in to the Premiership would attract more interest, and the crowds did increase, but the lack of support meant that it was obvious that the board were prepared to just allow the club to drift. I wasn't.

We had ten matches left to secure our survival and we got to the last game, away against Northampton Saints, needing either to win, or to at least score four tries and stay within seven points of Saints, to secure a bonus point. We raced ahead with an incredible start, scoring three early converted tries and a penalty to lead 24-3 after just 18 minutes, but Northampton had some unbelievable talent on the bench and they were chasing a Premiership play-off spot, so they were never going to take it easy on us. The quality, which we were unable to buy, they were able to introduce from the bench. That was the difference and we just couldn't get that final try. We lost 31-24 and it was devastating for everyone. I am still proud to this day of the achievements we made during those three seasons and I'm still convinced that we left the club in a stronger position than they were when we joined. It was so clear for all to see that we just didn't have the support that our effort, and our planning had deserved.

When I look back, I am pretty certain that our total operating budget for a season, on and off the field, was less than some teams in the division were spending on just the playing budget. If we'd have had that little more investment, a couple of quality players, maybe a Kevin Sinfield, then we could have survived and then built on that success to perhaps challenge for a place in the European Cup, but the attitude was simply to exist and do everything on the cheap unfortunately. I remember, when we took over the reins from Stuart Lancaster, we tried to instil an attitude and behave like we were a Premiership club, even though we were in the Championship. Sadly, the board remained in the Championship in their approach, and there is only so much a coach can do. We had exhausted everything we could; every option and all those hours of blood, sweat and tears, and effectively we were relegated on that final day. Worcester still needed to secure promotion, as their ground was the only one that fitted the criteria for Premiership rugby, and they did, by which time I had resigned.

I had decided, before the final game, that regardless of the result and our status, I was going to leave Leeds. All the promises that had been broken, the departure of Andy without my involvement, and the struggles and strains we had all been through, meant it was time to move on. I wasn't prepared to give up any more than the three years I had already dedicated to Leeds. Of course, I was disappointed, but I have always been a realist. I knew in my heart that I had given it my all, and that it was time to let someone else have a go. I was ready to give time to a project that matched my ambition. My only concern was how I would break the news to David Matthews, our kit manager; he was the heart of the club and is still a good friend today as Ali, the kids and I had grown close to him and his family over our three years up in Leeds. That job done, little did I know, that my next move was going to be a case of out of the frying pan, and in to the furnace.

11

The Death Of Rugby

I WAS due to meet Leeds Carnegie's chief executive, Gary Hetherington on Wednesday 11 May 2011, but on the morning of Tuesday 10 May my resignation as head coach of Leeds Carnegie was announced to the media. Pretty much within minutes of that going out, I was called by Dean Richards, who wanted to talk to me about an opportunity at another club, Rugby Lions, which he thought would be worth me speaking to the club about. They were being rebranded as The Rugby Football Club (2011) Ltd, and had an ambitious plan to take the club, the birthplace of the sport, up through the divisions to the top table of English rugby.

At this stage, Deano was two years through his three-year ban from the game after the 'Bloodgate' incident with Harlequins and wasn't allowed to be employed within the game. He was acting in a consultancy capacity and explained the vision of the club and that after he had served his ban, he would then be involved at Rugby Lions as well, probably to run the off-field affairs, with me handling the coaching side.

Legion Sports, through my rugby agent David Ricketts, had received contact from London Wasps, who at the time were looking for a new director of rugby and had expressed an interest in me. David and I were looking at potential opportunities with a few clubs, but the dialogue was strong with Wasps and they sent me a couple of drafted contract offers, as they had narrowed their selection down to two candidates; me, and as it turned out, Dai Young. I'd had an initial meeting with Rugby Lions, with Deano present alongside the club's new owner, Michael Aland, before I went away for a short family holiday to contemplate the Wasps and Rugby proposals. Wasps had struggled and finished ninth in the Premiership in the previous season, way off the pace of the play-off places, and there were a few question marks about their finances at the time, so I did have some reservations about joining them and finding myself in a similar position to the one I'd just left behind at Leeds Carnegie. It felt very much like 'out of the frying pan, in to the fire'. Wasps were a much stronger club than Leeds traditionally, but regardless of the environment you create, you can only maximise the potential of the club with some stable financial support. I wanted to challenge at the top of the Premiership, or at least aspire to be there and be competitive, not battle against impossible odds at the bottom again.

The other point worth making here is that my decision wasn't about the money, as will become blatantly obvious later in this chapter. It was always about the project and the opportunity. Wasps were not as stable as they were in the past, or as they are now, and something kept bringing me back to the excitement of working for Rugby Lions and helping to take a club through the leagues, from scratch. That fresh challenge really appealed to me after the three frustrating years I'd had at Leeds. It was a huge decision for me to make and it really distracted and consumed me during that family break. For the past three years, I'd lived away from home at Leeds, and while living near to Wasps wouldn't have been too different for me, it was worth considering working in Rugby, which was much nearer to our home in Leicestershire.

I was motivated by the opportunity at Rugby Lions; to take a tier five club up through the divisions was exciting, and that, coupled with the other factors mentioned, was ultimately why I decided upon them. Wasps chose Dai Young as their director of rugby, and after the difficult first season, where they stayed up by just one point, Dai has done a good job there, helping the club to climb to mid-table, along with the off-field developments such as their recent relocation to Coventry and the expansion of their fanbase. They have a much more stable club there and a lot of that is to do with Dai and the good work he has done, for which he deserves great credit.

In the initial meetings with Rugby Lions, finances didn't appear to be an issue at all. Michael Aland explained the vision for the club, the plans for an all-seater stadium in the future and the fact that we would be investing in facilities and players, so the structure would be there for success. I was focused upon creating the right environment at the club, using my experiences from Leicester Tigers, England, my three tours with the British & Irish Lions and my three years at Leeds. I knew what it took to be successful, and I believed that with the people we had involved, we could replicate that success at a lower level. I didn't want to just buy in a team and get promotion that way. I wanted to assess the existing set-up and then build a team gradually, while connecting the club to the local community and developing a strong bond there. In year one, to get the side out of National League Three (Midlands), I didn't feel that we needed to sign a new squad, we just needed a few additions and we would be fine. Initially the aim was to build strong, reliable foundations and then we could gradually add players as we moved up through the leagues. We needed four promotions to reach the Premiership, but in those early days our focus was just on getting out of the division in the first season, so we didn't need big players on huge wages at that stage as it wouldn't have been sustainable, despite being linked with pretty much every big name I'd played with.

There was a certain amount of romance about joining the club. I remember discussions taking place, looking ahead to the 2015 Rugby World Cup, and aiming for the club to re-site and develop the museum within our new stadium in time for the visitors who would be coming to England and would want to learn more about the history of the game. I was shown plans and diagrams, which were drafted by a local architect, Malcolm Foulkes-Arnold, who played over 260 times for Leicester Tigers between 1979 and 1992. Sadly, Malcolm is still seriously out of pocket for the work his company did on behalf of Michael Aland, one of many people who were left in that position.

Obviously, a big factor in me being considered for The Rugby Football (2011) Ltd opportunity, and one of the main reasons I took the job, was the influence of Deano, as I trusted and respected him. We enjoyed a great friendship throughout our playing days and I hope that this book emphasises just how much the guy means to me and the positive role he played in my development as a player, a coach and a person. He saw me as the right person to kick-start things at the formerly-named Rugby Lions, but even he wasn't to know what was to follow.

The new owner, Michael Aland, had purchased the club from David Owen. I felt that the vision that was sold to me was almost too good to be true. If only I'd stuck to that initial thought, and not allowed myself to be persuaded to join. Deano was motivated by the opportunity, and Michael was a strong salesman, with a passion for the sport and for business. He had played for the club in the late 1980s, before moving to Canada, where he was based in Vancouver and owned the Rugby Construction Group. As I've touched upon, he was planning to build a 30,000 all-seater stadium, with a retractable roof, a hotel attached and of course the museum. It sounds laughable now, but when you are shown what you believe to be real plans, produced by a top local architect, with respected people from sport and business around the table, you begin to believe in it all and you don't want to miss out. I also felt that at the time, prior to Wasps' move, that there was a gap in the market for another Midlands club to attract and cultivate a supporter base. If we had climbed through the divisions, I think we would have gained great media interest and the crowds would have grown over time.

Michael convinced Deano to be involved in the background and that convinced me. Glen Thurgood, a highly talented and organised strength and conditioning coach, was already on board before I signed. He had done well in football working at Notts County and Northampton Town, and was excited by this opportunity in the same way that I was. We also had some other good coaches like Mark Ellis at the club, who had a lot of experience at that level, knowing the players, other teams and local schools.

Glen explains here how he joined the club, 'I had football contracts on the table, but went for an interview at Rugby Lions with Mike Aland, Dean Richards and Mark Ellis, and that was the first I knew of Deano's involvement. We met at the Hinckley roundabout and I was up against two other people for the role of head of athlete performance, and fortunately or unfortunately, whichever way you look at it, I got the job and accepted it.

'It was another week later when I realised what a serious role this was, having planned pre-season with Deano, I was then sat with him, Backy, Mike and Ben Gollings in a pub and everything pointed towards success. Deano spoke about the vision and that was enough of a pull for me. The aim was to get to the Premiership and with the likes of Backy involved, I was able to look in the mirror and say that this was real. A couple of weeks later, Andy Key joined, and it really did seem like a dream job, working alongside people I respected in the game.

'I'm an ex-athlete and a competitive individual who enjoys sport. I always strive to be a winner and I knew that everyone around me had the same attitude. I wouldn't say that rugby was more favourable, as I enjoy working in football, but the role is more demanding in rugby from a strength and conditioning perspective, and you have the opportunity to work closely with the director of rugby. I knew I was going to get a say in shaping the future of the club, which really appealed to me.'

I looked at the big picture and felt there was a lot of work to be done and it suddenly hit me that I'd dropped from Premiership rugby down to tier five, and with all due respect, junior level rugby. We committed to achieving promotion in the first year, and we managed to strengthen with the acquisition of Ben Gollings, the England rugby sevens star, as a player-coach. Ben scored the most points in sevens history and had played quite a bit of 15s as well, and we had a few others who had played at levels above Rugby Lions, which helped us to create that environment of excellence I was striving for from the off. In doing all of this, for clarity, I was given assurances over our budget at every step of the process.

Having worked with Andy Key at Leicester Tigers, and then for most of the past three years at Leeds, I felt that we needed him to come in and help with the community side of the club, as well as using his experience in developing the academy at Leicester Tigers, where he had done such an incredible job. Andy came in with the title of chief executive, so we had a first-class set-up, which I felt would see us through the next few seasons as we climbed the league.

I'll let Andy pick up the story here, with his initial recollections of Mike, 'Right from the word go, it was evident to us all that Mike had the gift of the gab and I know in those early meetings we had, either as a management team or presenting to future stakeholders, Mike presented a very powerful message for the future of The Rugby Lions. You only have to look back at the quality and amount of people he got involved to help promote and build his dream. However, history now tells us, that's all it was, just a dream and as a result he ensured that a lot of people were badly hurt.

'Promises after promises were made about the money coming from either Mike in person, by e-mail, or even by other members of his management team, who he brought in during the season, only to be let down time and time again. Everybody became massively despondent and by the end of November we all started to seriously question the integrity of the whole project. With no money coming in from Mike's bond the strain started to show both individually and for the families. Not everybody could turn to their savings or a supportive family member for help.

'It was explained to Mike on numerous occasions that this was not just a business he was dealing with; it was a community, a rugby club, with people whose lives revolved around it. The members and people of Rugby were all passionate about supporting Mike in his quest and I honestly don't think he truly understood the potential devastation he would cause, if his money and his project didn't materialise.'

I wanted us to be as professional as possible, right down to the kit we wore, and we were encouraged to do this by Michael in all areas. We had no reason to question finances as everything was approved by Michael before we signed off on it. Training took place twice a week, with games at the weekend, but obviously the handful of full-time players would come in for conditioning throughout the week and everyone contributed to the community programme, as we looked to represent the club in a positive manner and build good relationships.'

The first warning sign for me, when I began to question the legitimacy of the operation, was when our first payday passed without anyone receiving their wages. It wasn't acceptable and people were not happy with the situation but we were assured by Michael at a meeting that it was only a temporary problem and that the funds would reach us shortly. He was waiting for a multi-million pound bond to materialise, which would then provide the funding, not just for our wages, but for everything in terms of the development of the club. It wasn't just a meeting though, we saw e-mails from big financial organisations, which showed what we believed to be evidence of funds that were set to be transferred to the club imminently. Everything looked above board, as there was written evidence from reputable organisations stating that the money was set to be with the club soon.

I asked my wife Ali to contribute to this book, with her first impressions of Mike, and her recollections of that period in our lives, 'I met Michael Aland at Rugby Lions, after Neil had already met him a few times. We were on holiday in August in Portugal and Neil was supposed to have been paid at the end of July. Neil explained that Mike had experienced a bit of trouble and that we would all be paid once the money was transferred over. The whole thing set alarm bells ringing for us all, but Neil had seen documents which appeared to show that the money was there, and also had signed documents to say that if everything fell through, he would be paid, which were checked over by Neil's legal team and everything seemed fine. There was just something about Mike that I didn't like.

I didn't trust him because of the missed payments, and he seemed arrogant and shady.

'I could sense the guilt that Neil felt for bringing people to the club himself. At the time I was fully in support of Neil for lending money to people to help them pay their bills. I know he truly felt that he had to stay, to give everyone a better chance of getting their money. Michael certainly had the gift of the gab, and he told people what they wanted to hear. Michael brought in a guy called Steve Dunn, who gave the staff a presentation which showed that everything was fine, and helped to convince everyone that their money would be coming.

'What the team achieved that year was incredible, especially considering everything that happened. It was a horrendous time for us as a family though. I would really take it out on Neil and scream at him; I could have throttled him, as I could clearly see that Mike was not straightforward, but I didn't see the other side of things and the camaraderie of the team and the staff. Now I look back, I can see why he stayed, but it was awful. I struggle to see how those responsible have got away with what they did. There is no justice if Mike is able to still be out there, and is not held accountable for what he did. How can he get away with ruining so many people's lives?

'I think that this was the biggest lesson for Neil, as he always tries to find the best in people, and I think he found it quite hard to believe that someone would scam so many people. Personally, I think Neil became stronger under those circumstances and he showed real character for staying with everyone to see the job through.'

The next issue we found was while on a pre-season tour of Dorset, having not been paid, Mike called to say he would drive down to us to sort everything out. He turned up late, in a relative's clapped-out banger of a car, claiming he was delayed as he had been arrested for driving without the necessary insurance. These were hardly the actions of someone who owned a rugby club and was meant to have a successful background in business, and more importantly, the capital to make a success of Rugby Lions. I remember people thinking that we just had a character in charge, and I suppose we tried to laugh it off a little, but it was embarrassing and it was only going to get worse.

Glen Thurgood picks up the story here, 'I remember being down in Bournemouth during pre-season, when we had a meeting about our situation as a coaching staff. We'd arranged our training plan for the camp and all of the activities to keep people occupied and happy, and then all of a sudden we realised that our accommodation hadn't been paid. Mike drove down in his car to pay for the camp, but arrived another 24 hours later, having been arrested, as he was driving his nephew's car without insurance or a valid MOT. We weren't happy about it as a coaching group as it was embarrassing, but people tried to laugh it off as us having a bit of a "character" in charge. The reason we stayed for so long was because of the good people around us, and out of loyalty, but his actions constantly chipped away at our faith. There was another time when he claimed that money was being driven over by a Dutch lorry driver, who was then stopped at customs, so the money never made it to us. I've lost track of the amount of stories we were told.

'I'd like to think that we weren't stupid, but I guess we were at times. We held out to be paid for the second month, and then we were told that we would be paid in the third month and so on. As a management group, we were all told different things, slight variations on certain details, but we were always led to believe that the money would come.

'We had reached a point where we were so far in to the project that if you walked away you would have no chance of being paid; something Mike would remind you of constantly.

More important than that, as it was during a season, you would be unlikely to find a role elsewhere as everyone had their coaching staff in place if you left, and you also didn't want to be the one who missed out on being part of what seemed like an amazing opportunity, as crazy as that sounds now.'

I was prepared for the level of rugby I had stepped in to. A junior club that had functioned well for years, but was rough around the edges and was in need of investment. I wasn't prepared for being misled. I kept thinking to myself, chin up, and think of the future and where we are going to take this club, and told myself not to worry about the present and think that the vision is worth the initial sacrifice. I thought back to the days when I was a player, and I would train on Christmas Day, just to get an edge over my competitors who were sitting back drinking and stuffing their faces with turkey. I wasn't prepared for this project to fail through a lack of effort.

Sadly, a lot of our effort was spent on the off-field distractions. It was the toughest job that I have ever undertaken in my life. We were forever spinning plates, trying to keep people focused on their roles and the vision, while trying to win rugby matches, with the distraction of no one being paid always on my mind. Throughout the season, I and many others in the management team played the role of a parent, a carer, a social worker and a psychologist as the true horror of what was happening began to unfold. I was available to the players and staff 24/7, 365 days a year, no matter what time they needed me, which was my attitude throughout my career.

Normally during my playing and coaching days it was just regular rugby-related questions, but here at Rugby Lions, I was fielding calls, texts and e-mails at all times of the day and night, regarding people on relatively low incomes not having enough money to feed their families, or to pay their rent or mortgage. It was heartbreaking. I paid money, between £5,000 and £7,000 over the course of the year, out of my own account, just so those lads could continue to live and then play for us at the weekend. We all did this, like Glen with his performance staff, Kiwi put his hand in his pocket, and Nadio did the same for a club tour to Italy, when he paid for a meal for everyone, while Michael came up with another excuse for funds not being available, as the management and coaching team tried to help those less fortunate in the club. We were asking players and staff, those on the lower salaries, what they needed to survive on a week-to-week basis. The strain that put on people's relationships and on their own health was immeasurable.

Ultimately, people reading this will wonder why we stayed as long as we did. Well, put simply, we did it out of loyalty to each other, wanting to finish the season and obviously in some part, because we were being told throughout, with what looked like legitimate documentation, that we would be paid. Personally, I'd reached the end of my tether before Christmas. After months without pay and numerous broken promises from Mike, I felt that if we didn't get the November pay then we had no chance of getting paid at all. On Friday 25 November 2011, I met with Mike and demanded that the players and staff were paid. You could see in his face that he knew I was serious. I was absolutely fuming and I was sick of it all. I think he realised that he had to pull something out of the bag to keep things going. He said that the money would be coming from Lloyds Bank, and as such if anyone had a Lloyds account, then the money would clear that day, but others would have to wait a few days. Mike was crafty, and paid around £600 in total to the people who had Lloyds accounts, and players were sat there and were able to show others that they had been paid a small amount.

As it was the players who were earning a relatively small amount, it was a low-pressure move to make, but it was just enough to ensure that we put a side out the next day. Those who were told they would be paid on Monday never received the money. We played again on 3 December and 10 December before having three weeks off as there were no scheduled games over Christmas, but the players had decided that they wouldn't train again until they were paid. I met with Mike and explained the players' situation and that they needed to be paid and wouldn't train until they were paid. They would play in games still, as they were committed to going the season unbeaten and winning the league.

I decided to go in and called a meeting with some of the senior players; Leigh Hinton, Ben Gollings, Sam Raven, Andy Vilk and Peter Wackett, and I announced that I would have to leave on 2 January, and said that it was the end of the road for me. This was a key moment. The players and staff persuaded me to stay, as they felt they would have a better chance of getting the money they were owed with me around. I had to stay. I had convinced many of them to be part of this project, so I could hardly walk out on them now when they needed me most. They said that they had nowhere else to go. We were in the middle of the season and we were playing tier-five rugby, so people had dropped their level and they knew that clubs from above that level were unlikely to take them on. I said clearly to everyone that I felt we were having the piss taken out of us, and they all agreed. No one was naïve here, everyone knew what was happening in front of them. There was no getting away from the reality of the situation. I remember one of the senior players, Andy Vilk, giving an emotional and impassioned speech and I knew then that the right thing to do was stay and fight with everyone else, on and off the field. Then we beat Manchester 114-0 on Saturday 7 January, which I suppose didn't really do us any favours as the threat of not training had no effect, and we cruised to another win.

I made the decision then to stay until the end of the season and see the project through. I used the analogy of being the captain of a sinking ship, but wanting to stay and get the ship safely in to the port, before stepping off with my head held high, knowing that I had kept my side of the bargain. It looked at that stage as if we were going to get promoted, so I knew that we would have a tick against us for our success on the pitch, but financially I knew it would be a whole different level of battle to get any of the money we were owed, but at least we were in it together. No one split from the camp and people remained okay with each other and retained that great spirit. We were just sick of the unfulfilled promises from Mike, and from his cronies.

Understandably we wanted action, not just words, from someone who we had lost all respect for anyway, as Glen Thurgood explains further, 'I found Mike to be brash, confident and arrogant, but people who work in those kinds of roles usually were. I have friends in banking, and have known people who go to work and lose a lot of money on that day and not think too much of it. He was a chancer. At the end of the day, you would expect that the RFU wouldn't have allowed someone with so little substance to run a club, but they did.

'I used to take my performance staff for a coffee or a "Dun Cow Friday" lunch as we used to call it. Dun Cow was the name of the pub. I used to pay for it out of my own money, just so I could help to keep them happy. Mike found out about it once and said that he would pay the next time we went. I think you can guess what happened. I gave our physio, Tom, £2,500 of my own money to stop him from being evicted from his flat around Christmas, as I felt responsible. He is now a lecturer at Coventry University and only found out recently that the money was from me, and not from the club. I developed new partnerships, with companies and facilities, and got burnt as we ended up not paying the bills. Thankfully some of those people have stuck with me beyond Rugby Lions, despite their experience.

'On the field, it was honestly a great experience; you couldn't have asked for a better year. We didn't lose a single game, but if we had then I think that would have caused real problems and we may not have let it go on for as long as it did. The problem is that winning is addictive and all the problems we encountered during the week disappeared for those 80 minutes at the weekend. We lived for that time when everything was forgotten until the final whistle, before it all started again. It was an unbelievable achievement in my opinion, no matter what team or league, to go unbeaten is a great accomplishment. Arsenal may have been the invincibles in the Premier League, but they didn't have to put up with half of the stuff we did. I'm still certain this would make a great film; it has all the makings of a good script, big outlandish promises, brash businessmen, triumph during times of financial and emotional heartache, and an elusive boss!

'I used to pick Ben Gollings up for training so he could get there. My wife met Mike Aland at Ben's engagement party to Lauren, which was a little way in to the season, and she couldn't stand Mike and said on the way home that he wasn't a nice guy and she could see why we hadn't been paid. Thankfully, I've still kept my friendship with my best man and close friend Charlie, who I persuaded to move up from London to live with me and my wife, and who started working as a commercial guy at the club. Charlie wanted out of London at the time, so I felt it was a good opportunity for us both. My poor wife would be sat in the middle of it all, listening to us talking about the club and the two different sides that we would see, business and playing. He eventually moved in with Mike and lived with him in the accountant John Tarrant's house. I think that he learned a lot about Mike and got to understand him. He felt he was an egotistical maniac, who was reaching way above his intellect. I had seen Mike write things out on paper and while I'm no member of Mensa, I could see that he wasn't the sharpest. Do I wish I'd done anything different during that year? Yes, listen to my wife. It was embarrassing that I had allowed myself to get in that position.'

We had some good players, led by Ben Gollings, and, without wishing to seem arrogant, my presence was always going to motivate the opposition, so every team treated playing against us as a cup final. We established a playing philosophy that suited the players we had and we tried to replicate everything that would be done by a Premiership club. We were fitter than any of our opposition, we had individual skill development and training programmes, and we had analysis to provide the relevant data for individual, unit and team feedback, and a scouting set-up to rival any club. We had pre-match meals in a hotel, but didn't stay overnight, and we would pay for all of this through gate and bar receipts that we had helped to generate, and through a beg, steal and borrow approach, so that the club could make ends meet.

I suppose that anyone reading this book, wondering about this chapter and the title, will focus upon the statements and promises of Michael Aland and his associate Tim Murray, who was CEO of Libertas Capital Corporate Finance Limited at the time, and the role played by David Owen, the previous owner, in all of this, but I'll come to that later. However, it would be easy to forget that the backdrop to the scandalous off-field situation was the fact that we won 31 out of 31 matches that season, winning the league, gaining promotion, and winning the Warwickshire

Cup in the process. To go a whole season unbeaten at any level, in any sport, is remarkable, and it showed the level of professionalism we had created, that all of this was achieved despite the actions of Mike Aland and people having to work without any pay.

Our last game was the Warwickshire Cup Final against Sutton Coldfield. We treated the competition like the LV= Cup is treated in elite rugby, and we allowed Mark Ellis and Richard Gee, as assistant coaches, to run that team as they had done so well all year. We wanted to go the whole season unbeaten, and not fall at the final hurdle, but we stuck with the Rugby Crusaders, our development side, who had played throughout that competition. We won 10-9 and I honestly couldn't have been prouder. I remember watching the game from the grass verge at Broadstreet RFC, wondering whether I'd done the right thing, as it was such a tight game, one that we could have lost. I was obviously emotional, which is something that I knew would come at the end of a season that couldn't have gone better on the field, and for laying our foundations, but couldn't have gone worse off it.

In fact I'm still emotional today when I think back to what happened that year. Here, Andy Key explains how the season affected him and his family, 'Right from the outset, Mike had explained that the finances to bankroll this project would come from a bond that he, in conjunction with a finance company, had put together and once trading would provide the necessary funds. We all saw copies of the bond and transcripts depicting its worth and validity. Having said this, and looking back on the whole debacle, you seriously have to question whether Mike had done his due diligence. With no money turning up, the club needed to generate finances like any other rugby club would do. This money was used to pay certain overheads but mainly went to paying the players some of what was owed to them. None of the management, including myself, Glen and Backy, were ever paid a penny. In fact, all three of us at some time during the season used our own cards to support the club.

'Under the circumstances the achievements from the team were outstanding when you think about what we had to deal with. Were we naïve? Were we silly to continue? That's up to people to judge. What we did know is that collectively we had a club to run and although Mike was totally responsible for the ultimate outcome at the end of the season, we all fully understood survival for the club came first.

'My wife Jo and I are pretty resilient characters, but if it had not been for the support from family members financially, I know this situation would have had an even bigger impact on me earlier in the season. I guess I may not have been able to stay. I believed in the project and wanted to see it through. As such, my family supported me. The overriding outcome was we were left with a financial debt that was resolved by doing two things; selling our house in Leeds to pay my family back, while beginning a different challenge by taking on The Wheel and Compass Pub and Restaurant in Weston-by-Welland, just outside Market Harborough.

'We all learnt some hard lessons during our time at the club; however, I was concerned by the lack of support from the RFU. Come the end of the season, when everything was revealed, the RFU simply stated that the club was in breach of the financial regulations and was demoted. I ask, "What about the employees?" I would have thought as a club under the umbrella of the sport's governing body we would all have been protected in some form or another. I do hope, if nothing else happens, that the RFU appreciates that it is normally the people that get left behind in these circumstances that get hurt!

'It is now only us that can dream that one day Mike will stand up to his responsibilities and pay all of those that he owes. It is either this or that the story is properly investigated and that he is made to answer for his actions.'

I can't thank the players and staff enough for everything they did and everything they achieved during that fateful season. They won every game, they worked hard with professionalism throughout, and they coped with the pressure of financial factors that they should never have had to deal with, and I will never forget the year I spent with them and the honour of being their head coach. I often think about what they did, and what we achieved together with pride and sadness over the circumstances.

I heard that Mike was holding a meeting at the club on 21 June, after the season had finished, so I went along with my letter of resignation, prepared to hand it to Mike in person. Mike was talking about how the club would move forward, explaining to the supporters and members about the vision, despite not having paid people for nearly a year. He was ranting on stage, bad-mouthing me to everyone, calling me all the names under the sun, and I walked in to the room and stayed at the back. Once he had finished trashing me, I attracted his attention and asked him to sign my letter as receipt of my resignation, which was witnessed and signed by a supporter. That was the last time I spoke to Mike.

I guess that the Warwickshire Cup Final win and my departure was meant to be the end of the road, but this disgrace has carried on long after that. David Owen was the owner of Rugby Lions, before Michael bought the club from him. However, as that transaction never actually took place, David just took over ownership of the club for a second time, once Michael had left and the club had been demoted. I find it incredible that the people punished were the club and the supporters, who were demoted to tier nine, and obviously us as staff and players, who are owed thousands of pounds. Then there are the local businesses and suppliers, who offered their great support throughout the year, and were left with unpaid invoices. It was scandalous.

Glen Thurgood offers his view here, on who was at fault and what should happen, 'The main person to blame for what happened at Rugby Lions is, of course, Mike Aland. There are others involved too but I think, rather stupidly, they got sucked in.

'Mike played on the fact that he had a World Cup winner in Backy, the best sevens player in Ben Gollings, and good people around him, and I believe he wanted to use those facts to encourage investment from others, who were obviously impressed. He fooled everyone. I think he lost control and the worst thing about this was that he was allowed to get away with it. For example, if you want to buy a cup of coffee from a shop, you have to pay for it; you can't just say, "I'll pay for it at a later date." He was given guardianship of the club from day one. I think everyone got sucked in and to be honest it probably suited everyone involved to believe it.

'Towards the end of the season, Mike wanted to talk to us about the situation. I told him that he'd have to come and meet me, rather than me travelling to him. My wife put her foot down and said he can pay to travel as you've still not been paid, and you're not spending another penny on that rugby club. I lived in Market Harborough and I didn't want anyone to see me with him, as this is a rugby town. I drove out to the village of Tur Langton and sat down for lunch with him. He ordered two main courses, unsurprisingly, and I ordered one. He was still peddling the same old rubbish about his plans for the club, and when we got to the end of the meal he suddenly blurted out that he'd forgotten his wallet. I had no choice but to pay. I'd been done again and just put it on the card. He owed me the best part of a year's salary.

'Nadio Granata, a colleague from the club at the time, tells a story of how Mike went in to one of the pubs in Rugby, just after we'd won the league, celebrating, and wanted to buy a drink for everyone in the pub. The owner replied quite bluntly, and said, "If you can stick £30,000 behind the bar, I'll let you buy everyone a drink, if you can't then you can f**k off!" The whole pub erupted in laughter and Mike just walked out. I guess that landlord was a lot smarter than us. I was even offered a ten-year deal to sign by Mike, which wasn't worth the paper it was written on and was just given to me to keep me quiet. I didn't sign it, but I still have a copy of it.

'We were still being told that the money would come, long after the season had finished. I felt a responsibility to my wife, my backroom staff, the players and my friend Charlie Parker to get that money back for everyone, so I carried on trying. I consulted my solicitor who suggested that I put a personal guarantee contract to Mike; if he was going to find the money at least this would show he was willing. Nobody ever thought he would go bankrupt.

'I got up early and travelled to London on the train on my own to surprise Mike, who was meeting with Tim Murray. I pulled up a chair and on legal advice, I put a personal guarantee document on the table in front of Mike and said I wouldn't leave until he had signed it, which he did. He didn't even read it and I don't think he even cared. I stayed around afterwards and had some breakfast, which is the point when I met a Malaysian guy, who Mike introduced me to. Mike had told us before about this guy who was a rich financier, who could afford fast cars and watches, and would come in and buy the bond and then the money would be released to us. He couldn't speak any English, while Mike made jokes about the guy, who I could have sworn was just some random bloke Mike had just placed there, and he just nodded along and smiled. I hadn't got a clue what was going on and couldn't believe my eyes.

'I saw Mike for the final time on 11 November 2012 and I wanted to keep close to him, almost like keeping your friends close and your enemies closer. He had personally signed and guaranteed a five-year contract for me. I was informed that some people had been paid, but they were the lower contract players, as we only had a few full-time players at that level. I guess it was easier to appease a few people in one go, rather than paying one person higher up the chain. I took the view that I wouldn't be paid until all of my staff were paid, as I felt a responsibility to them as I brought them to Rugby Lions. It would kill me if any one of the players or staff felt that I'd been paid during that time. Telling this story is the end to this chapter in my life. This isn't a moral crusade or anything, it is just about trying to do what is right and to bring some closure to this for everyone.

'Put simply, the RFU should have done their due diligence properly. They sent people up to see the club and speak to Mike on two separate occasions, but they left and were fine with how things were being run. Read in to that what you will. I was constantly on e-mail and on the phone trying to find a way to resolve this and get our money back. I was reliably informed by a senior figure that there probably wasn't an appetite for getting involved with this case and that's the point when I thought, "You know what, it's time to move on." I couldn't understand why nobody stepped in to help us. Instead the club was demoted. How does that help anyone? Yet Mike was allowed to walk away with no punishment. Unfortunately, we were all contracted to The Rugby Football Club (2011) Ltd and once that was wound up, that was it, but surely there is a responsibility for the current owner, who "sold" the club to Mike, yet technically still owned the club throughout the time we were there? We were let down by those people and by the sport's governing body.

'Do I think we will ever be paid? No chance. I think it's past the financial side now and I hope that everyone involved who did a great job during their time at the club has moved on like myself. Now for me, it's about telling this story so that this is never allowed to happen again. Mike Aland should be blacklisted and never allowed to do this to anyone again, and hopefully lessons have been learnt from everyone involved.

'When Backy left at the end of the season, Mike called a meeting of the club's players and then also another meeting for members and supporters in the bar downstairs. Mike called Backy a c**t and blamed him for being fractious and divisive, and I knew we were totally screwed, as he wasn't talking about the guy we had been working with all season, the guy who had led the club to the league and cup double. I wanted to go up there and smack him one. I turned to Ella [Mark Ellis] and said that we needed to stay there and try to see if we could recoup what was owed to everyone. At the second meeting, Mike was stood outside having a cigarette, with a glass of wine in his hand and seemed upbeat, so it looked promising, as if there was money finally available. Strange, but we still rather stupidly had hope. He walked up on stage and announced Ella as the new director of rugby of the club. It was the first that Ella knew of it!

'After all of this, I went down to London with Ella. We decided to stay with the whole thing until November, as we'd known each other for a while and we were good friends, and said that we should stick close in the hope we could resolve this for everyone. We never had any intention of working for him again; why would we? As soon as we got an inkling that he had some money, we would act on everyone's behalf and inform the relevant people. We were invited down to Libertas to meet with Mike and Tim Murray in the boardroom. Tim was the owner of Libertas and harboured Mike there. The more I look back, the more I feel stupid about all of this, but we knew that if we walked away we had no chance of anything, which Mike always threatened us with as well. I sought legal advice, and I was urged to stay involved. I stayed on the back of them all. Mike even sent me a Goldman Sachs ticket photo on e-mail, which showed that the "money was coming". It was an endless stream of information that was probably just lifted off the internet, just to try and appease us.

'When I went down to Libertas in November with Ella, Mike sat across from us in their boardroom and told us that the deal was done, the money would be with us and we would all be paid. We'd finally got the result we wanted. Then Tim Murray walked in, took a seat, and looked quite chilled as he sat peeling a tangerine, with his feet up on the table. It was all so relaxed, which was a change from what it was normally like when Mike was in the room. Ella and I went off for a coffee and it was quite emotional. Mike wanted to take us out for dinner, which had never happened before, and after getting stung the last time I wasn't so sure it was a good idea. Anyway, we went for it and ordered foie gras and Champagne. Mike went to the toilet and I took a picture of Ella eating his meal. He looked up and I said, "We're going to remember this night whichever way it turns out!" We couldn't quite believe it was happening, and now experienced in the world of Mike, we quickly devised a plan so that if we felt we were going to get stuck with the bill, again, one of us would use a code word and we would make our excuses to go to the loo a few minutes apart and then bolt it out the back door. It was a strange night and to top it off he actually paid, which was the only time he ever paid for anything for us. I guess we should have ordered two mains!

'We went on for a couple more beers before we got the train. I'm not the best drinker as my close friends will testify too, so by the time I got to London St Pancras station I was a little worse for wear. I fell asleep on the train and nearly missed my station. It was an emotional release that night. We probably got carried away but both felt that we had finally reached the end and got the solution that we set out to achieve. My wife was a bit disappointed with me coming home drunk, understandably, and I know what I was doing at that time by staying involved with Mike and his cronies was not great, but I wanted to be able to turn around to everyone and say, "Look, myself and Ella stuck with it, and here's your money, now we can all move on with our lives." I used to think about that a lot but not so much now. I have moved on. Of course my life is different now to what it would have been, and I think we all missed out on what could have been a fantastic journey, in fact I think the rugby world has missed out too.

'I felt very isolated after the final visit in November. My wife banned talk of it in the house, which again I understood. She felt that I was going to make myself ill, and I thank her for doing that and trying to move me on. I realised just what I'd put her through. I wanted the money to make amends for what I'd put people through, not so much for myself. I didn't want to be ringing up Backy every five minutes either. I spoke to the insolvency company, but they explained that there was nothing that could be done and as the company had gone bankrupt that was it. I kept discussing plans with Ella, just to look as if we would carry on with our jobs, so that we could get the money, but I would never have worked another day for Mike. I knew that if we fell out with him, we'd have no chance; we only had to look at how he loved Backy, and then hated him.

'At the end of November, I was trying to contact Tim Murray, and then I received an e-mail from Mike stating that Backy and Ben Gollings had started legal proceedings against him. Then I received e-mails from Mike saying to me that I was free to go to the media if I wanted. In January

I wrote to the BBC's *Panorama* show to try and gain interest from them in the story. I received an automated response, that was it. I spoke to Mike and Tim on the phone, and I've kept hold of every text exchanged between myself and Mike. I demanded to know from Mike where the money was and stated that I'd been told I would be paid on numerous dates, all of which had passed. I pushed him on that one matter; if he couldn't just pay me to get me off his back, then I knew we would get nothing. He just screamed at me, told me to f**k off, and was laughing loudly with Tim Murray, and before I could speak he slammed the phone down on me. That was the last contact I had with him.

'In my view, Mike should be locked away for what he did to us all. He let us all down and simply didn't do what he said he would. I guess what it comes down to is that no one wants to accept responsibility for what happened. It wasn't our fault; we did our job and won the league and cup, and upheld the traditions of the sport, all while our lives were falling down around us.

'There is one person that I really need to thank and that is my wife, Carrie. She stood by me throughout this difficult period, allowed my friend Charlie Parker to live with us during this time and had to listen to endless conversations, often very one-sided, about all the goings-on at the club. It put a real strain on us, as it would anyone, but very few people knew it, only a handful of our close friends. I wanted to do something special with my career and Carrie knew that and supported me throughout no matter what. I am not sure I would have coped without her. To this day, and until this book comes out, my parents and in-laws don't know that I wasn't paid throughout that whole year. It's the last thing you want people to know.

'I now own a gym in Market Harborough called the Training Shed, which is a training and education facility, and treatment clinic. Phil Littlewood, my business partner, has belief in me and I in him, and that is really what counts; good people working together to achieve a common goal. Of course I miss Saturdays and I miss working with the players and coaches within a club, but it would be a big decision to go back in to sport in that way after the experiences I've had. I sleep much better than I did when I was at Rugby Lions.'

People deserve some answers and I hope that this book will help to provide them, and also bring some justice to this issue.

Firstly, I'd like to know how Mike Aland has not been investigated by the police and RFU for what he did, promising money and signing contracts, before leaving good people without salaries for ten months, ruining lives and relationships in the process.

I want to know how David Owen is allowed to own Rugby Lions again, after he let Mike run the club in to the ground and then took the club back from him when they were demoted.

I'd like to know the full role of Tim Murray, who was an associate of Mike, and is still operating in the financial world after presiding over all of this with Mike.

And last, but not least, I'd like to know how the Rugby Football Union allowed Mike to run the club, visited to check that everything was fine on more than one occasion and never lifted a finger, as they were wined and dined by him. How their only action was to punish the club, through demoting them, after the 2011/12 season, but allowing those who were in the wrong to get away with it?

The last I heard of Mike Aland, he had a property in Mayfair, was buying suits on Savile Row, and appeared to have established a company, Blackheath 1858, and it looked as if he was trying to take over the London-based side, who are the oldest open rugby club in the world. Thankfully, that never materialised. Earlier in this chapter, I mentioned Mike's company, The Rugby Construction Group. An online search reveals other allegations by people who hired his company to build homes and extensions. If only we had known this before agreeing to work with him, it would have saved a great deal of heartache. It seems that this man has a lot of questions to answer for his activities against people here, and overseas.

I hope that somehow, some justice emerges in regards to Mike and the others responsible. There is no way that the emotional hurt can be repaired, but if contracts were honoured and people were paid what they were owed, at least it would give those guys a chance to draw a line under matters and move on with their lives. How is Mike living now? He must have funds from somewhere, and do the people involved with him now know about his past and what he has done? I hope so, before it's too late.

I also think that there is a responsibility for the RFU to ensure that not only are Mike and his cronies prevented from doing this to anyone else, but that no club and no group of people in rugby are allowed to go through what we went through. Look at the recent London Welsh case, where conman Neil Hollingshead tricked the club owners in to believing that he was a wealthy individual with the backing of the Saudi royal family, and ask yourself why he has rightly been jailed for seven years, but those involved with the Rugby Lions debacle are able to continue as if nothing has ever happened.

To this day, no one at the RFU has even spoken to me, or offered to help us. I am shocked and hurt that this was allowed to happen and that no one has done anything about it.

When I left Rugby Lions, it wasn't just the death of the club, but for me, in a way that will probably never be fully repaired, it was The Death of Rugby, as my relationship with the game will never be the same again. My subsequent decisions after my time at Rugby Lions have illustrated the effect that my time there has had on me, and on my career. I know that the circumstances have made me a better and stronger person, but it isn't something that anyone in rugby, or in life in general, should ever have to go through again.

My sole reason for writing this book is not financial; it is to tell the story of all of the people affected by the actions of Michael Aland and his cronies. My solicitors are looking in to the whole sorry affair for me and I sincerely hope, for the people who lived through that year, that some form of justice is brought sooner rather than later, so we can all move on with our lives.

12

The Long Road Home

I WAS called by my agent, David Ricketts, who works for Legion Sports as part of the Legion Worldwide Group, as he was looking for any opportunities for me following my departure from the Rugby Lions project. David had been called by Michael Bradley, the head coach at Edinburgh Rugby, which led to me flying up to Edinburgh to chat to Michael and the club's CEO Mark Dodson. The decision to invite me up for a chat came about through a conversation on the training pitch between Michael and their defence coach, Billy McGinty, and once they had done their research and located me, they expressed a desire for me to join their coaching team as their forwards coach, to replace Tom Smith who had left Edinburgh Rugby.

I went through the formal interview process and was offered the job, which I was delighted to accept. Of course, you are appointed by the Scottish Rugby Union in essence, and it was just the kind of challenge I was looking for after the disappointment of Rugby Lions. I had worked in a variety of coaching roles, from player-coach working with younger players, the forwards and in a defence coaching role, through to being a head coach and director of rugby, and the Rugby Lions role was meant to be the one that saw me take three steps forward in my career, but as we know it dragged me three steps back. I felt that I had to get back out there. I loved coaching anyway, and I genuinely felt that I had something to work with and felt I could help to improve the club. I was probably a little naïve in not completely understanding the set-up of the Scottish Rugby Union and the way things were done there, as compared to the English Premiership, but apart from that I was extremely proud to be back at a reputable rugby club and back doing what I loved.

I didn't really know Michael Bradley as such, although I was aware of his career as an international for Ireland through to the 1995 World Cup and his successes as a coach for Connacht and the Georgia national team. While at Connacht, which has always been seen, with all due respect, as the development pool for talent to go on to the more prominent provinces, Michael had taken them to the latter stages of the Amlin Challenge Cup in all but one of his seven seasons at the club. He certainly had some pedigree behind him and had worked as a coach in the Irish international set-up previously, and the season before I joined Edinburgh, he led them to a historic Heineken Cup semi-final appearance, which was a great achievement. Billy McGinty was a coach with a great reputation too, with pedigree from his time in rugby league, in a similar way to Phil Larder and Mike Ford who had both made an impact in union.

In the Heineken Cup pool stages in the 2011/12 season, Michael had led the team to five wins and one defeat, which saw them claim top place in Pool Two. They beat London Irish and Racing Metro home and away, and beat Cardiff Blues at home, only losing the away fixture to the Welsh side. I don't want to take anything away from that achievement, but the draw certainly favoured Edinburgh when compared to the next season. Cardiff and London Irish finished in the bottom half of the Pro 12 and English Premiership respectively, and Racing Metro squeezed in to sixth place in the Top 14. In our Heineken Cup campaign, we lost all six pool matches, but that doesn't tell even half of the story. The Racing Metro side we faced were a much stronger proposition as they began to invest heavily in new talent. Munster and Saracens both reached the semi-finals of the Heineken Cup from our pool, with Munster finishing in the top half of the Pro 12 and Saracens winning the English regular league season and finishing runners-up to Northampton Saints in the Premiership Final. We were faced with the 'Group of Death', so the two seasons were incomparable. Credit to Michael and his staff for the job they had done though.

There were real expectations that the club would kick on after the Heineken Cup success, but my seven months at Edinburgh Rugby were difficult. In fairness, the club did finish tenth in the Pro 12, one position higher than the previous season, but it was still a disappointment for everyone involved. I feel that we did make progress during my time at the club, but obviously the Heineken Cup results didn't look good on paper. I didn't want to come in to the club and organise or dictate. I'd been used to setting the agenda through empowering the players and staff, as at Leeds and Rugby Lions, but now I was more circumspect and made a conscious attempt to integrate myself in to the already established coaching set-up at the club. I listened, learned, talked and built individual relationships with everyone and then at the appropriate time, I would critically feed back, always with a positive view, to the rest of the coaching staff at the club. For example, Billy McGinty's defensive coaching approach was meticulous, and laid out in black and white for everyone to see. I agreed with probably over 95 per cent of the way things were done on the defensive coaching side at

Edinburgh, and to be honest, you would never agree with everything anyway as that's just simply not possible in an industry where opinions and methods are always going to differ slightly.

Through pre-season, I was encouraged by Michael to give my input on training and certain moves, and I felt that we all got on very well; not just the coaches, but the support staff and the players too. Similar to Leicester Tigers with the amazing Jo Hollis, they had a female team manager, Lynsey Dingwall, who was excellent at her job, organising people and the operations at the club. In fact, when you looked at the respective heads of departments, guys like Stuart Paterson, the head physio, and Murray Fleming, the performance analyst, they had the right people there to create success, but some of those people shared dual roles with the Scottish Rugby Union as well.

I rented an apartment in Edinburgh, but didn't purchase like I had done at Leeds. It was difficult in terms of seeing my family but I was used to that being one of the necessary sacrifices within elite sport. If we played at home, I could fly back to Leicester to see my family for one day and two nights every two weeks, but if we played away, with some games in Italy, Ireland and Wales, it was less easy to arrange. I think that by this time, my wife Ali and my two children were used to this element of our lives, and to be honest I know that they really enjoyed visiting me in Edinburgh, much more so than they had when I was working in Leeds. Edinburgh is a beautiful city, with so much history and culture, and Ali used to enjoy frequenting John Lewis for a glass of Champagne before shopping, which was a dangerous combination, let me tell you! The children also loved being in Edinburgh and got on very well with Michael's young children too, so over my seven months at the club I had a good feeling and could have seen myself continuing to work in that environment.

When I look back on my time in Edinburgh, it was a great opportunity and unlike Leeds and Rugby Lions, the way the role was sold to me was pretty much exactly as it turned out to be. The big shame is that seven months in a job is not nearly enough time to make your mark, or have a meaningful influence on the players and the club. I felt like I was getting there, and particularly in my area of responsibility, the forwards, I was beginning to empower them and get to understand their characters and what made them tick. I wanted them to recognise their strengths and weaknesses as players and to improve their approach to the game, but changes can't take place overnight, so we were building towards that, until sadly the coaching staff were dismissed early. I guess one of my criticisms would be that the work ethic wasn't quite where it should have been, and what I was used to, but I think we were addressing that with each week that passed. In terms of statistics, in the Pro 12, for line-outs we were in the top four sides, at the scrum we were in the top six, and for kick-off and reception we were a top four team too, so there were real signs of improvement from the forwards.

I loved having the opportunity to work in the Pro 12, which is a great competition with some quality sides, as well as being able to enjoy the travel as we faced Scottish, Irish, Welsh and Italian clubs. Every other week, you travelled to a place you would only normally visit for European rugby, which was great. I guess that one of the major problems for the league though, was that teams were guaranteed a place in European competition, even if they finished near to the bottom, as Edinburgh had done. The qualification for the new European Champions Cup has been amended and more positively rewards the better, higher-ranked and more consistent teams from Pro 12, Top 14 and Aviva Premiership competitions.

In February 2013, Michael explained to me that Billy was leaving with immediate effect and that he would be leaving at the end of the season as well. The SRU had decided to remove them from their positions as a direct consequence of the team's poor results in the league and in European competition. I sincerely doubt that it would have been a player-led change, as the coaching staff and the players had a strong relationship. I would have thought it would have been the old alicadoos (ex-players associated with the club), sat in their armchairs and just unfairly passing opinion based on results. I had a two-year contract and hadn't been told I was leaving so I carried on supporting Michael with the job. Later that month, I was interviewed by *The Scotsman* and was asked whether I had ambitions to replace Michael and become Edinburgh Rugby's head coach. The following quotes are a direct excerpt from that interview, which was published on Wednesday 27 February 2013, 'Previously, I've been head coach and since I came here as assistant coach, I've done my best to support Michael in his playing philosophy. But I've got my own playing philosophy and I'd like the chance to work as a head coach in the future at Edinburgh Rugby or elsewhere.

'It was disappointing [when Bradley was sacked]. I joined as assistant coach this year and hoped to spend more than a short time together. I think Michael has made some big improvements and, unfortunately, with that platform laid, he's not going to see it through. But, hopefully I'll have an opportunity in the future to progress the work he has put in.'

Only two weeks after the interview, I was informed by Mark Dodson that I would be leaving the club too. Mark explained that Edinburgh would be undertaking a new approach, to employ Scottish coaches and to change the philosophy of the club. I guess that I was therefore a casualty of the results that season and if they were looking to make a fresh start, then it would need to be done with all of the main coaches leaving, not just Michael and Billy. Do I think that the interview I gave had an effect? Possibly so. I was, and still am, an ambitious person and of course, if you've been a head coach and a director of rugby, then you are going to want to experience that again, but I backed Michael all the way and I was loyal to Edinburgh throughout. If they'd have offered me the chance to stay on as head coach then I would have certainly considered it.

I felt that I was thrown out with the bathwater, but in my exit interview with Mark I stated that I felt that there were some key areas that the club needed to address if they were to be successful in the future. I'd accepted the decision that I was leaving, but I felt it was my duty to try and give them some constructive feedback. Firstly, the international development programme, which has a few caveats to it, but basically an international player plays five games and then has to rest one game. That counts whether the player is in the squad and doesn't play, for example has zero minutes on the pitch, or plays in all five matches, which could be 400 or more minutes. I felt that this had a detrimental effect to a young player, who is pushing for a place as deep down he knows that every sixth game, they will get a chance as an international player couldn't be selected.

I wanted players who would work harder than their contemporaries to earn the shirt, who would train on Christmas Day in the snow, just because you knew that your opponent wasn't. I felt that the rules and guidelines were ridiculous. We had experts to analyse the collected GPS and well-being data, but they weren't using any of it. I had a conversation with Andy Robinson, who had coached me for England, alongside Clive, and was the Scottish head coach at the time, before Scott Johnson came in, and I queried it with Andy. I couldn't believe that it was for the good of Scottish club and international rugby.

Secondly, I questioned the issue of player recruitment. The mandate from above was to sign Scottish-qualified players, which I could understand if the players were going to be good enough to play for Scotland, but if they weren't then it was a pointless exercise. Players learn from other good players and we were depriving young Scottish talent of the opportunity to play alongside European and world-class rugby players. Playing rugby football, if you are a good player, is easier the higher you play, as you only need to focus on your job instead of overworking and taking up other players' slack. These lads were missing out on playing next to the best of the best, while other clubs were recruiting from everywhere. It was Michael's job to look after recruitment and obviously I was part of that and supported him and made appropriate suggestions where possible, but we were limited on what we could do.

Then I highlighted the young player development programme. If you are not playing for Edinburgh or Glasgow, then you gain valuable game time to develop from playing in the Scottish leagues. There are some good sides at that level, but some very poor sides too. This is highlighted as the English Championship sides beat them with ease on a regular basis. If the players are not standing out at the Scottish league level, then they simply shouldn't be playing for Edinburgh or Glasgow. What I am saying is that I felt that the gap between Edinburgh, Glasgow and some of these league teams was too much of a leap. I didn't feel that the development level was enough of a challenge for the younger Scottish players and it was hindering their progress. English clubs benefit from good Championship clubs, helping injured Premiership players return to play, or young players to develop, like at Leicester where players like Tom Youngs and Dan Cole would go out on loan and gain valuable experience. Clubs like Nottingham or Bedford play a vital role in the development of players. Some people may take umbrage at what I'm saying here, but

I'm just being honest and retelling what I felt and what I said at the time I left Edinburgh.

Another contributing factor and something which I still feel that they need to look at is the venue that Edinburgh Rugby plays at. Murrayfield is a fantastic stadium, but with most of it closed off for regular games, there is a real soulless feel to the place on matchdays. I've said before that a pitch is a pitch, wherever you play in the world, but playing at the national stadium didn't help the club. At Murrayfield there are a number of pitches on, and a 7,000–10,000 stadium could have been built on site, so there would have been a strong atmosphere, and the club's attendances could have been developed and the new stadium could have been increased gradually. Those 5,000–6,000 fans who regularly attended must have wondered what they were doing sat in a 67,000 stadium. Look at the way Exeter have grown as a club. That's the model to follow. The atmosphere was pretty poor at Edinburgh and that wasn't the fault of the supporters who were great, and incredibly loyal.

I understood and accepted the decision taken to relieve me of my duties, but I wanted to help them to move Scottish rugby forward. I can look back now and be proud of the fact that the players I worked with improved in my time there, as shown by the stats I mentioned earlier, and I do look back on those seven months with fondness. If you take people like Hamish Watson, who was a young kid at the time, and made his debut for Scotland against Italy in the Six Nations earlier this year, it shows that there is some real talent there.

I met some wonderful people up in Edinburgh and I enjoyed every minute of my time there. Murray Fleming, who I often went in to the city centre with to grab a coffee and watch the world go by, and Stuart Paterson, were good guys who I thoroughly enjoyed working with, and also the head of fitness, Andy Boyd, who I got on well with, and my son Fin loved him. I learned plenty from Michael and Billy, and I feel that I became a better coach and a better person for the experience in Scotland, albeit that it was too short a spell north of the border. There may be a few Scots who would disagree after my playing days with the red rose, but I'll let them off!

Soon after leaving Edinburgh, things took a turn for the worse for me. Ali remembers this period well, and having never been one to suffer from illness, what happened next was quite a shock to us all, as she explains, 'Neil had been home for a couple of months to take time to consider his next step. He'd had a normal cold, a runny nose and all that, at the end of a busy week of after-dinner speeches and we were about to go away on holiday. He couldn't wait to go and we were in town just doing a final few jobs, and he suddenly felt some pains in his feet and legs. It was a Friday night, he took a shower, and he couldn't put his feet down without a shooting pain going up his legs. We took him to the walk-in centre in Loughborough and they advised him to keep taking painkillers and he would be fine. The next day he had a rash on his leg and he was off to London to watch a game, and travelled back in the afternoon. He felt terrible and the rash had spread. He spent a couple of days in hospital, and they suspected meningitis, so we all had to have the jabs.

'Anyway, it wasn't meningitis thankfully, so we decided to go away on the holiday and felt that the rest and relaxation would do Neil good. Sadly, he just continued to deteriorate, and it didn't help that we had to trek up and down hills to get to the pool. God love him, but Neil is like any man, and he really seemed to be making a meal of it all. We'd been told he just had a virus, so I was just telling him to get on with it. Unfortunately, Neil continued to be in pain, had the rash and then started to put on quite a bit of weight and was retaining water. Luckily the specialist that we'd seen in the UK was a big rugby fan and he had given Neil his direct number, so we were able to call him from the resort to update him, which meant that we didn't have to get the doctors involved in Greece. I think if we had, we would have struggled to fly home as he was very ill. I became very worried by this stage, and I think that the way I dealt with it was to be defensive and just say to Neil that he'd be okay. I feel so guilty now looking back on that time, as he really was very poorly, and I was giving him grief rather than sympathy.

'When we arrived home at 3.30am, we walked in to the house to a fly infestation, which was all we needed. It turned out that Fin had left a bottle on the side of the sink with juice left in it, and as we were away for two weeks, there were flies, dead flies, eggs and faeces everywhere around the house. It was absolutely disgusting. I sent Neil to bed as there were no flies in the bedroom, so he was able to get some sleep, and the consultant was able to see Neil at 9am. Neil managed to drive himself to hospital, I rang Neil's mum and I was very emotional. Talking of that, Neil was crying the whole time, which was really out of character. I mean, Neil would cry if he sees someone doing well, despite a sad story, perhaps on something like *X Factor*, or *Britain's Got Talent*, but never about himself, as he's a strong guy. I knew that something was wrong. I remember him bursting into tears in front of his mum, and he just blurted out that he thought he was going to die.

'It wasn't until the next day that they realised that the virus had attacked his kidneys, and because of the water retention around his organs, like his heart, he could have had a heart attack at any time. He was in hospital for around ten days, during summer 2013, and I remember the fluid being drained, it was quite a traumatic time for us all. He could quite easily have ended up on dialysis for the rest of his life. He just wanted to know what was wrong with him and what he could do to get better, as that was how he had coped with injuries during his playing career. Neil was diagnosed with Henoch-Schonlein purpura, and he was signed off as fit and healthy again in summer 2014, around a year after first feeling symptoms. Even in 2015, his blood results were slightly out, but they were fine. The virus is more common in younger children, but it was a random reaction and there didn't appear to be any clear reason as to why it happened.

'Having been through all of those emotions, and being someone who likes to be in control, I think his perspective on life really changed and he wanted a break and wanted to be nearer to home. He thought he was dying and that made him sit up and realise that he wanted to be around his family and not away at another coaching role.'

I've made a fairly smooth transition in to my current career and life. During my playing days, I felt as if I missed out on a great deal of time with my family, my hobbies and passions such as cars and other sports, so I suppose that no longer coaching has given me a little more freedom than I had for the last 25 or so years I have spent directly in rugby as a senior player and as a coach. Essentially though, I still need to be able to bring money in to support my family and our lifestyle.

Over the past few years, along with my rugby agent, David, we've looked for the right coaching opportunities, but nothing that felt right has come up for me. I've been somewhat selfish throughout my playing and coaching career, as I always came first, and my family have understood and always supported that. As our children have grown older though, I have now been able to step in and share the family duties a little more, in terms of their academic, sporting and personal development. It's been nice to have the flexibility to help out more at home, and actually to be around Leicestershire, as opposed to working away.

Once my days coaching for Edinburgh were over, I met an old friend, Neil Fletcher, who was at Leicester Tigers between 1995 and 2000, a period which included a great deal of success at the club. Fletch won't mind me saying this, but he was never one of the frontline players, yet he was definitely someone that you would want alongside you and in the squad. He was very supportive of the team and played his fair share of games as well, but had the likes of Johno and Fritz van Heerden ahead of him, who would have kept most people out of the side in fairness. Fletch then moved on to Sale Sharks where he played for a couple of seasons, before playing in France. He eventually moved back to the same village I live in, in Leicestershire, with his wife Debbie and son Louie, and a couple of months after Edinburgh, we got chatting about his plans to form a new insurance company, called Adelphi Special Risks Ltd. He established the company, along with our managing director, Damon Blakey, and I came on board as a director, with the responsibility for helping to introduce new business, and look after those clients and existing clients, in a customer relationship role. It's a role that I'm proud to have and thoroughly enjoy making a contribution to. I have a background in the financial sector from the amateur era days of rugby union, so everything had a familiar feel to it.

I also met with John Hayes, the owner, and his son Matthew Hayes, managing director at Champions (UK) Plc, a brand agency, who among many other services look after celebrities. I knew John from the past and I had done various appearances for them previously. I had been so dedicated to rugby that I didn't want to commit exclusively to Champions in the past, but now that I had more time I was able to make myself available. It was all a case of timing, and it was a great fit for us to work together. I've been looked after by some great people, including Melanie Nocher, who was an Irish Olympic swimmer, Katherine Donnelly and more recently

Amelia Neate, and they have done a great job sourcing me personal appearances, media, leadership and motivational work, after-dinner speaking and brand ambassadorial roles, including businesses and charities. All of those opportunities allow me to meet people and work hand-in-hand with my role at Adelphi, along with my business development management role at TPS Visual Communications, working alongside owner Lawrie Alderman, managing director Mark Adams, and the rest of the team.

I do feel at times like I'm spinning a lot of plates, but I've thrived off the work and have really enjoyed the variety as no one day is the same. Fletch also introduced me to Henry Whale, the managing director of Rybrook Cars, a prestige car company, and with that being one of my passions, I was able to agree an ambassadorial role for them. The role allows me to meet with the right people, while promoting Rybrook's vehicles, and they have been kind enough to allow me to drive some fantastic cars from their extensive range of brands and tour the Rolls-Royce and Bentley factories, all coordinated by group marketing manager Sophie Heptonstall.

Being at home has allowed me to spend more time socialising again with some good friends, in particular Ian and Helen, Bren(da) and Penny, Keith and Nicky, and Andrew and Debs. Thanks guys for your friendship and advice, and lots of good times shared; cars, golf, good food, beers and bubbly!

I've had a number of opportunities to get back in to rugby, at Premiership, Championship, and Pro 12 level and also in South Africa, but they haven't quite been right for me. Having lived in Leeds and Edinburgh for those respective roles, if the next opportunity in rugby does come along, it would have to be right for me and, more importantly, for my family as well. Ali has recently undergone a floristry course, has a real flair for it and would love to do it full-time, but it's difficult as we need to be around to support our children, so maybe it's something that she will do full-time in the future, and I'd love her to do that and set up her own business, which I'm sure she would make a huge success of.

I've really enjoyed going to watch more Leicester Tigers games, being my local and former club, as well as working all of the England home and some away international games and I think that through all of the roles I have now, I'm able to give something back to my family in terms of time, and also through the charities and partners I work with, such as the Leicester Stop Smoking Service and the Midlands Air Ambulance. Both of those organisations mean a lot to me, and I hope that in a small way I'm able to help bring some attention to their work. In fact, within a week of working with MAA, an air ambulance was called to my local school and local rugby club, because of injuries sustained in rugby games.

There is certainly a balance to my life now, which is perhaps something I haven't had in the past, and it's allowed me to enjoy and appreciate my family more than ever, as I've put them second for far too long.

13

A Life Less Ordinary

I WAS the middle son of three boys, born in a semi-detached house, at the end of a cul-de-sac, in my mother's bed, and both of us nearly died at my birth. Having an 18-month-older brother and a four-year-younger brother helped to develop my competitive streak as we fought for every scrap of food on the table. My grandmother was there to help deliver me, while my father went up the road to ring the ambulance as we didn't have a phone in the house. It was 1969 after all. From that day onwards, both of my parents have been very supportive of me, and their life philosophy matched the Mars Bar adage, 'Work, rest and play.' My parents always worked hard to ensure opportunities were available to us as their children. If they were at the beach getting a shell, they would pick one for each of us. When we came home from school, it was always a case of homework first, then food, and then we could play outside until it got dark. It was a happy home life, with the right amount of discipline and a good work ethic.

My mum and dad both worked, and my dad, who was at Rover Cars, ensured we had a new car each year, but not in a flash way; he just worked all hours for us and got staff discount as did my mother from the same company. Maybe that's where my interest in cars came from? Our holidays were in the UK, camping or caravanning, and they were very happy times. I saw first-hand, how hard my dad worked, nights and weekends too, as did my mother, working from nine until five, so I think that given the attitude of both my parents, I was always going to be a hard worker.

I remember walking to our primary school, during my early years, which was around a mile away, and our senior school which was about three miles away. We always walked to school, we weren't dropped off, and I remember waiting for my mum to get back from work at 5.15pm, and I'd always have a cup of tea ready for her when she got in. As a result of their strong work ethic, they weren't always there to take me to play rugby, so a guy called Peter Lloyd who I met at Barkers Butts Rugby Club, as his son played in the year above me, would take me here, there and everywhere. Peter is sadly not with us now as he passed away in 2010, but he was a big influence on me and was a big part of my life, ferrying me back and forth from various representative training sessions and games when my parents were unable to. I don't know what I would have done without him. He was a huge rugby supporter and is someone I am very grateful to, especially as I have two children myself and I have seen first-hand what it takes to provide them with the support they need.

My family is not the type that needs to call each other every day on the phone. There is unconditional love in our family. Ali's family are more likely to send a card and return the gesture with a thank-you phonecall. There's no right or wrong; it's just what your family is like, and as long as there is love there it doesn't matter which way it is shown. As we were growing up, the whole family would go to my grandmother's house on my mum's side, most Sundays, until she passed away, and then my mum took up the role of entertaining for a while, but we don't get together as a whole family these days, often just the immediate family. My parents still live in the house where I was born, in Coventry, so there is a real feeling of going back home when I visit them. I suppose, in some way, because of Ali's influence, I am more affectionate, like I will tell my mum that I love her and give her a hug when I leave their house, which is not something I would have always done in the past. I do love my family, but I guess I just never felt the need to say it.

Without Ali, I can categorically say that I wouldn't be here today writing a book. I simply couldn't have achieved what I have done without her support. My girlfriends before Ali were aware of the fact that I played rugby, but Ali was quite oblivious to it. We worked at the same place, AXA Equity and Law, but it was a big company and we weren't likely to see each other every day, more like once a week once I knew she was there, as we worked on different floors.

We met before the 1995 Rugby World Cup, but we were both with someone else at the time, as Ali explains, 'Neil was a pensions manager, and I worked in a different department. I kept receiving contact from him, asking me how I was and that sort of thing, and he asked me out a few times but I had a boyfriend and I knew he had a girlfriend. He was a bit of a ladies' man, and he pursued me. I was going through a rough time and I suppose I was a little bit anti-men, so I thought, "I'll go out with you, and I'll show you that you can't just have anyone." We went on our first date to Stratford, and I wanted to hate him, but we got on really well. He was very polite in the car, and I turned to him and said, "So where does your girlfriend think you are tonight then?" His face turned bright red and he tried to deny that he was going out with anyone! From that day on, he has been completely honest with me. They say opposites attract, and he is quite quiet, whereas I am loud, so I guess we complement each other. He is a thoughtful person and has a very sensitive side.'

One of the most positive qualities that Ali has is the fact that she is independent and has retained her own group of friends, through school, work and the people she has met through having children and rugby. She is certainly not the rugby widow, sitting at home and waiting for her husband to return from the game. In fact, having been away for a long time with the various roles I have had, I now have to sync in to her diary. She was born in Blackburn, but moved down to Nuneaton when she was about five years old, with her mother as her parents had separated, and then at the age of 16 or 17, she moved out and rented her own apartment, again showing how strong-willed she was. She was good at sport; netball and athletics, and did her A-levels, but had to work, like myself, so didn't go to college. When I look at our children, Olivia and Finley, I see so much of Ali in them, both in their academic ability and their strong characters. Ali would have succeeded in life, whatever she put her mind to, but she sacrificed her own career to support me and to help our children and be there for our family, and I honestly can't thank her enough for everything she has done for us all.

Olivia plays hockey for her school, the Leicester Hockey Club Premiership second team, and was recently picked for the under-16 national squad, so will hopefully be capped before this book is published, and Fin plays football for Nottingham Forest's academy, which people may not expect as I played professional rugby, but it is credit to them for finding their own way. We ferry them both to training and matches, but the day they lose interest in going is the day that we'll stop. There is no pressure on them at all and there never will be from us. We encourage them with their studies, but they are still at an age where sport should just be fun. We are a million miles away from being those pushy parents.

Michael Bradley, during our time at Edinburgh Rugby, noticed and mentioned how strong Olivia was mentally, during a kickabout on one of the training pitches. Now Fin is a little older, you can see his character too, and they both make us so proud. When the children were younger, I felt that Ali probably did too much for them, but what parent doesn't? Now I see that everything that she did for them has helped to make them the people they are today, especially in their mentality, which all comes from her. They have a strong level of emotional intelligence, which certainly comes from Ali. I've learnt a great deal from Ali, as she gives a masterclass in meeting people and getting on with them. Even if she walks in to a room in a bad mood, she can put that to one side and bring through her character for the moment. I mean, when it came to Michael Aland at Rugby Lions, she had him sussed straight away.

All in all, she's not a bad egg, my Ali. In fact, the only thing I would change about her is that our body clocks are totally out of sync. She's a morning person and I'm a night owl. Ali will be up early and share a cuppa with Olivia for some mother and daughter time, then work like a trooper all day, but come 8pm or 9pm she'll be spent and ready for bed, whereas I will most likely get up slightly later and then stay up past midnight. I'll watch anything on television; news, sport, or part of a film, you name it. Ali will be fast asleep and I'll still be watching TV or replying to work e-mails. If we could get more in line it would be nice, but I'm not complaining as life seems to work as it is.

Ali has had incredible support from her sister, Linda, as I mentioned at the start of the book, particularly during the 2003 World Cup and that journey from hell. Now, Linda is the wonderful mother of two, and is also PA to Peter Tom, the Leicester Tigers executive chairman, at Breedon Aggregates. Linda is there for her own family, but always there for our family too, and we owe a great deal of love and thanks to her. When our kids were born she actually moved in with us to help, and with me away at the 1999 World Cup when Olivia was born, her support was invaluable and is something we will never forget.

My father was a golfer and my mother played hockey and netball through school, and they supported me as much as possible on the touchline, and I know that it might be hard for people to believe, but I'm quite reserved at games. Fin had started playing local junior rugby at Syston RFC when he was five years old, and at most of the games the parents from both sides were screaming, shouting and coaching from the touchline, while I simply stand back and just offer quiet support. Pleasingly, when he plays academy football, there are guidelines for parents to follow, with a line drawn and no parent is able to step within five metres of the touchline and only positive comments of encouragement are allowed. It is the same at all academies I believe. Referees are allowed to get on with the game too. As soon as Fin steps off the field, I always ask him whether he enjoyed the game and then occasionally ask him what the coaches have said to him, and what feedback is given to him and the team. I hear parents sometimes sound critical and pick fault, which doesn't help at all.

I bought Olivia and Fin a mini weight-training kit, so that they can learn how to lift correctly, and they are just beginning to work in that area of training at Fin's academy, and Olivia is taking GCSE Sports Science. Watching how self-motivated they are, and seeing them go on the treadmill and do a session on their own is fantastic. They have really invested in facilities and in people within football, with Nottingham Forest spending £1.5m and Chelsea, for example, spending around £13m on their academy. Players and parents are given regular nutritional and psychological talks and support, and the relationship with their school is first-class too. I feel very comfortable with Fin playing football, as he is developing in all aspects, even to the extent where I've watched him drop kick a rugby ball from the 22, with either foot. Seems like I may have passed on at least one skill to him after all!

In the way that I chose rugby as my route in to sport, Olivia has chosen hockey over netball, which she also demonstrated a flair for, playing at county level in both sports. Olivia is playing against the odds, as she is competing against girls in the school year above who are under-16s, whereas she was born at the end of September so is an under-15 at school. I cried recently, just sat in a coffee shop when I called her and she told me she had been named in the national age group squad, and I think that while other girls may be older and more physically mature than her, she is not only talented but also very well-conditioned, and has a great level of emotional maturity. Olivia is aware that there aren't many opportunities for women in sport, especially to achieve a living salary just from sport. She is focused on achieving at school and gaining good grades and we couldn't be happier with both of them. Whatever they choose to do in their lives, we will support them both. I don't mind what their grades are as such, I just want them to give their best in whatever they do, and then the success will follow. Sport is such a fragile career; you could get injured the next day and your career could be over, so it's crucial to have something else to fall back on in case it doesn't work out.

They've coped well with having me as their dad too. I mean, firstly, I wasn't around as much as I'd have liked to have been, during both my playing days and more recently as a coach for Leeds, Rugby and Edinburgh. There was only one incident perhaps where me playing professional rugby has had an effect on them. Fin was in class and they were on the computer, with a task set to look up someone famous on Wikipedia. His friends wanted to look me up online, and some bright spark had edited the page to say that I had two daughters, so Fin was teased and called a girl for a little while. We had to edit that page when he got home from school that evening, and he probably won't thank me for bringing this up again!

I think as a parent now, I can appreciate and respect even more what my parents gave up to support me, as well as other family members and friends who I have mentioned. I now see how much time and effort it takes to do a full day of work, then pick one of the children up from their school, make their tea, take them to their sports training, catch up on work and then bring them home and get to bed, before doing it all over again. Ali and I are like ships that pass in the night sometimes! We love what we do, both in terms of our work and our family, and no matter how many early mornings or late nights there are, it's worth every minute. We live busy, fulfilled lives and our ambition to do the best we can has already rubbed off on Olivia and Fin. That strong work ethic is how I was brought up and I hope it is how the kids will continue in their lives, and they will never fail through a lack of effort.

In terms of coaching, the most influential person in my life was my first coach, Jack Carnell. Our next-door neighbour played rugby at Earlsdon Rugby Club, encouraged me to join and that's where I met Jack, at the age of five. He had started at Earlsdon in 1937 and played rugby himself until he was 63. Jack inspired me not only because he was light years ahead of his time as a coach, but mainly because he made rugby fun and enjoyable. I think that he was involved in the club until in to his 70s, so he was a remarkable person. The fact that he taught me tackling technique, in terms of head, feet, body position, leg drive and that same technique and basic principle is what I would teach people today, shows exactly what a great coach he was.

After Jack's work with me in my youth, the main reason I joined Leicester Tigers was Dean Richards. For me, the opportunity to join a world-class back row and to play alongside Deano and John Wells, was simply incredible. After never really expecting to reach that level of rugby, it was really something to play for a club like the Tigers, and Deano was a huge inspiration and had a great influence on me. I would also like to give praise to the coaching set-up with England. I've spoken of how important Clive and Phil Larder were, but all of the coaches and the backroom team for England were equally important to our shared success. They all created a culture of excellence, which ultimately led us to World Cup glory. I should also mention Kevin Murphy, who was the England physio for over 140 games, and his partner-in-crime, Dr Terry Crystal, who is the only person to ever stick their finger up my backside. I can't exactly remember why, but I can assure you there was a medical concern. He was wearing gloves too in case you were wondering. It sounds worrying, but Terry was excellent at his job so I couldn't have been in safer hands, so to speak. He's now working at Leeds United and has been around for many years in sport.

As I've mentioned previously, cars are a real passion of mine. I learned to drive in my mum's Mini Metro, which wasn't the most glamorous of vehicles. When I was 11 years old, my teacher scribbled on the board something about aspirations in life.

I remember slumping down in my chair, hoping not to be picked as I tried to disappear. Unfortunately, my shock of blonde hair and the fact that I played all sports, meant that I was always going to be noticed in class. The teacher shouted, 'Back, what do you want to do when you grow up?' Rather sheepishly, I replied, 'I want to play rugby for England and drive a Porsche, Sir,' and the whole classroom erupted with laughter, which made me slump back down in to my chair once more, with a bright red face, as I tried to disappear all over again.

The reason I said a Porsche was that I had a remote-controlled Porsche Turbo 993 bought for Christmas, and I said rugby because I'd followed the Five Nations as it was back then. I often think of that day and the influence it had on me as I'm certain it drove me on, excusing the pun, to achieve what I have. I am grateful to the teachers I had, as it was just a normal state school, but they stayed behind late for our training and our matches, across various sports, which they didn't have to. I remember my school bringing in external coaches to help us as well, such as Aubrey Pallett, who coached us to play cricket. He passed away aged 91 in 2004, and dedicated 70 years to the game. Youth sport simply can't survive without people dedicating their time and offering their insight.

I played for the school, the city and in some cases for the county and the Midlands, in most sports, but it was only in rugby where I made it to play for England Schools, and then I bought my first car, which sadly wasn't a Porsche. My family didn't have enough money to buy me a car and I went down to Newquay on holiday with my older brother and his friends, who were around 18 years old, with 11 of us staying in a caravan that slept seven; many of us hoping to find alternative accommodation anyway, if you know what I mean. Not me of course. Anyway, while in a pub, I turned around in the wrong place, at the wrong time and I was glassed in the face. I reported it to the police and they asked me to come out with them in the car the next day to try and identify the guy who did it. After driving around for a while I spotted him stood on the kerbside, with his suitcase, among his group of mates. I had stitches in my face and as I got out of the car he started walking towards me, and all of a sudden the plain clothes policeman walked past me, grabbed him and he was eventually given a six-month suspended sentence. I was given £1,500 in compensation, which was really quite a lot of money back then, and I used that to buy an MG Midget, nothing to do with my size I must add. What a car that was. It was blue, with a rag-top roof and a few holes in it by the end of the sixth form from various stilettos. Only joking Ali! So I suppose I can trace my passion for cars back to then.

I've tried to avoid changing in terms of my nutrition from my playing days, but some elements were bound to alter. I'm pretty consistent with what I eat. If the kids grab the occasional bit of fast food, I'll try and avoid it. I got in to very good habits with food during my playing days, having a routine to stick to and I've managed to retain a lot of those good habits as well. My body composition has changed in terms of the balance between lean mass and fat, but in general I eat what the rest of the family eats now, as opposed to having my own meal when I was a player. During those days I would eat around four meals, plus three supplements, like protein or recovery shakes, so around seven meals in total a day. I get everything in terms of nutrients from my food now, but I will treat myself to foods like bread, crisps and fish and chips from time to time. As a player, I wouldn't take any caffeine during the week, but would down the equivalent of eight shots of coffee before a game, which would help to stimulate my senses. Now, I enjoy a coffee as an everyday drink. I guess I used to be ridiculously strict, and now, while I try to keep fit and struggle to keep up when I go for a run with Olivia and Fin, I do look after myself.

In terms of travel, I've been very fortunate to be able to see a great deal of the world during my professional career, and really, the only downside to that was always wishing that my family could be there and share those experiences with me. We've had some incredible family holidays though, through contacts I've met, who have kindly reduced the fee for us because of my role in the game. I have fond memories of touring Canada with England in 1993, and on the way to Vancouver we went through a beautiful little place called Banff, in the Alberta Rockies. I always said I wanted to take Ali and the kids there, so that's one trip we are yet to take. I'd love to take Ali to Hong Kong, to show her what a mad place that is, and places like Durban, Cape Town and Victoria Falls are incredible. These are all places that rugby has taken me to, but sadly not with Ali, and our children.

One memorable holiday with Ali was when we stayed on the beach in Mauritius, with cottages including people cooking for you nearby. We only looked in the cottages, as £30,000 a week was out of our price range, but you could see just why a footballer on £150,000 a week would spend that much as it was pure luxury. I've had lovely times in places like Portugal as well, and now we take the opportunity to travel either the two of us, or sometimes with another couple, and we've been to Amsterdam, Prague and Florence in recent times, perhaps just for three days and two nights, but it's lovely to just get away and have a break.

Out of every place I've played rugby though, and there are so many great places; Murrayfield where I made my England debut, Parc des Princes where we beat Stade Francais to win the 2001 Heineken Cup, the historic Lansdowne Road where we won the 2003 grand slam, and the fantastic atmosphere of the Millennium Stadium, where we beat Munster to claim our second Heineken Cup in 2002; if I could play one more game anywhere in the world, I'd have to go for the Hong Kong Stadium, which sadly didn't make the cut for the 2019 Rugby World Cup in Japan as an additional venue. In 1992, I played there for the Barbarians and five years later in 1997 I played for England in the Rugby Sevens World Cup, and in one game the organisers arranged a 'Kodak moment', and everyone flashed their camera for a photo at the same time.

As a visual, that was incredible, with the stadium surrounded by all the high-rise buildings, it was a real image to treasure, absolutely unforgettable. People may have expected me to name the 2003 Rugby World Cup Final, but all I could focus on that day was the pitch. I can barely remember the stadium, all I picture is the pitch, and of course, Jonny's kick. However, I do remember the deafening roar as our captain, Johno, lifted the ultimate prize aloft. Sorry to the one or two Aussies reading this book, hopefully you can excuse me mentioning it just one last time.

I suppose, being the good husband I am, I should leave the last words of this chapter on my private life to my beautiful wife, with her own unique and sometimes brutally honest perspective on me, 'Neil is such a hard worker, and he always has been. In fact, a lot of our arguments stem from his attitude towards work, where he will say that his work is 24/7 and I will try and remind him that it's not, and that there are times when he needs to take a break from it. As a player, he was very self-oriented, and focused on making his own game better, but then as a coach and in business, he has become more aware of the people around him and their views.

'As a character, Neil is a real neat-freak, bordering on OCD I guess. I'll never forget going off on holiday with the rugby girls. Our flight was cancelled until the next day, so I asked Neil to come and pick me up from Luton Airport and in the few hours I had been away from home, he had completely cleared out the garage, put shelves up and reorganised everything. That's what he's like. I mean, there's too much clutter in this house for his liking, as it is. He rearranges all the tins in the cupboard, so the labels are facing forward. He is very methodical and organised, and is all about the detail. I criticise him because I think he's too slow answering an e-mail, but he has to have the e-mail written just right, at 10pm on a Friday, before sending it, when no one would be expecting contact until the Monday, but that's his dedication and professionalism coming through.

'He is a thorough person, and that can cause arguments between us, as I just want him to finish, but he won't until it is right. Sometimes he's here around the house in body, but not in mind, as he is focusing on his work. I'm still getting used to having him around, as I've always thought of him being away for his work. Every now and again, we try to sync our diaries, as we have quite a hectic lifestyle, but it's an enjoyable life.

'Neil relaxes when he takes Fin to play football, and watches him, or goes to watch Nottingham Forest play with Fin. He relaxes when we are on holiday, or when we go out for a meal, but even then, he will still make time to go and read his emails and reply to people. At home, he rarely switches off to be honest. He doesn't like to have a lot of things on his mind, he likes to get the work done and move forward, and not always for personal gain either, as he really enjoys helping people or companies to link up. He recently spoke to the person who is writing Phil Larder's book, and the writer commented on how normal, honest and grounded Neil was. I think that really sums him up perfectly.'

14

Back To The Future

WITH the way the game of rugby is run at present, for the good of all sides, and there have been talks about it, I feel that one option would be to abolish relegation and promotion between the English Premiership and the Championship. If you'd have asked me years ago, when I was coaching Leeds Carnegie in the Championship, I'd have obviously said no, but having experienced the problems that clubs face to reach the top flight and to remain there, I think that this is a viable move.

Firstly, the clubs at Championship level simply don't have the budget to survive in the Premiership. Under the current criteria there are only a few clubs who have either the ground or the finances to meet the required standard. Then there is the ridiculous play-off system, where a side can run away with the league title over a 22-match season, have a ground that is fit for the Premiership, yet still not know whether they will be promoted as they have to play a semi-final against the fourth-placed side, over two legs, and if they win, a final over two legs against the other semi-final winner. These games take place during May, but recruitment for players and coaches in rugby tends to take place between November and March at the absolute latest. Any player worth his salt will want to join a club that is assured of their Premiership status next season as a minimum and preferably in Europe the following season, so unless a club is willing to pay over the odds in wages, they are going to have to play catch-up over the summer to drag themselves up to Premiership standards. This antiquated system is placing great pressure on Championship clubs and their budgets, and the quest to reach the top could easily result in grave financial issues for clubs at that level. The only way I can see a club being able to sustain their top flight status, is through a big-money backer, and if that individual one day decides that enough is enough, then the club is left with huge overheads to manage, and could face going out of existence.

One way to resolve this situation would be for the RFU to decide on a Premiership of 12 or 14 clubs, which would offer some stability to the lower-end clubs and allow them to attract sponsorship, as they would be guaranteed for say, three years to play in the top flight. It would also help to build a fanbase. At Leeds, when we wanted to sign a £1 player, we would need to pay £1.30, or £1.40, or even £2, per pound, to attract that player. We needed to pay more as we didn't have that guarantee of playing at that level, and the board weren't prepared to pay the going rate, let alone the excess.

People will argue that a move like this would take away the competitive edge which is brought about through promotion and relegation. I can see that, but if a side consistently succeeds at Championship level then they could be promoted and would be better prepared for the leap in standard, as they would have time to adjust. I think that the move would also encourage a more expansive style of play, rather than the trend of 'winning ugly'.

I'm not claiming to have the answer to this issue, and my suggestion of capping the league may not be popular with everyone, but what I hope people can agree on is the need for more discussion on this and for the RFU to come up with a plan which protects clubs from putting their future at risk, for the dream of playing in the Premiership. I do agree with the play-off system in the Premiership, as teams miss their best players for the autumn internationals and Six Nations Championship fixtures. So this way, the best teams will reach the top four over the course of the season and then with all international players available, they are able to play-off at the end of the season, which provides an exciting spectacle for the fans, as well as additional revenue opportunities for the clubs.

Another improvement to the game I'd like to see made is regarding the transfer of young players between clubs. I think that rugby can learn a little from football here, as when a young player is developed somewhere, there needs to be a greater financial reward for that club, based on the future performance of the player during his prime years in the game. During my time at Tigers, Leeds, Rugby and Edinburgh, one of my great motivations as a coach was to help young players develop, realise their potential, and eventually reach the first team. For the future of our game and our national side, we need to do more to encourage clubs, from top to bottom in the sport, to develop quality players. A greater financial reward would go a long way to helping that happen, rather than resorting to bringing in experienced professionals from overseas.

The salary cap is an issue that is always up for debate. I feel that the cap is where it should be at the moment for the good of English rugby. I don't feel that it should be increased, as it would place too much pressure on the game to generate new revenue streams, and apart from the big clubs, that simply isn't realistic. We should be establishing a competitive league, not leagues within the Premiership. I know there have been calls from the big clubs, but they are just trying to widen the gap and flex their financial muscles. If you look at the French clubs, who are spending a lot of money, that can bring its own problems such as disharmony in the dressing room and the challenge of managing the egos of players who are on astronomical salaries. Just look at the effect it has had on football, by moving the game further away from the average man or woman on the street, to the point where in some cases, people no longer feel that they can relate to the sport they once loved. We need to avoid a situation where players are solely motivated by money, and don't actually care about playing or winning, as they are on so much they can afford to just sit on the bench. When I was faced with that decision, between staying at Tigers as a player, or joining Bristol, I knew I would earn less but Tigers meant so much more to me and I wanted to achieve something, not just count the pound notes.

Having said all of that, it is important to keep monitoring the salary cap, and when it gets to a stage where all of the clubs are in agreement and there is sound financial justification, then an increase is fine. I just worry about clubs over-stretching. Few clubs are able to announce a profit and I shudder to think what would happen if Sky or BT pulled away from their coverage of the domestic and European game. Talking of which, I don't buy in to the adage that we are at a disadvantage against French clubs. It is used as an excuse by head coaches and directors of rugby, who are not competing as they should against French sides, and have the salary cap as an excuse to fall back on. Saracens and Leinster have just demonstrated in the European Rugby Champions Cup, by reaching the semi-finals, that the gap in quality is not as big as the gap in salary budget, and four sides reached the quarter-finals from England; Bath, Northampton and Wasps, along with Saracens.

I think that in England we need to look at the brand of rugby we play in European competition, and raise our game. Maybe a capped Premiership will encourage a better attack philosophy, which I believe is the main point of difference between good and great teams. We have many talented players and there is no reason why our top sides can't compete against the best in Europe. The Premiership feels at times a little more defensive, and has a strong physical element to it, whereas European rugby is played in a more expansive manner. We should also be placing more emphasis on developing young players to come through, rather than trying to buy success.

I have to say that I don't agree with the current stance on English players not being selected to represent the national side if they play their club rugby abroad. I don't feel that it would create an exodus of players, but even if it did, it would help with the development of our elite players, which would in turn be good for the national side. As long as everyone can agree to the same terms for release clauses for those called up to play for England, then I really don't see an issue here. Our players will be more rounded and educated, on and off the field, and we could even see young English players developing abroad, which would create more spaces for players to come through on our shores. I wouldn't change my career, but if I could, then I guess with the benefit of hindsight, I would have liked to have played over in France between 1990 and 1994, before I was capped, as I would have developed as a player and as a person from the experience.

Globally, the game of rugby is growing and I expect that it will continue to grow, especially in America in the coming years and in Japan, particularly with the 2019 World Cup being held there, which I think is great for the game and will do so much for the future of rugby in the Far East. I think that in terms of the World Cup itself, the IRB could look at introducing a second-tier competition for the sides that go home early from the competition, maybe without a win, to help them develop in some form of 'Shield' competition. Again, I think this is worth further discussion and it would create more meaningful games for the lesser nations. I certainly wouldn't decrease the number of teams at the World Cup though. I think it's great that those nations get the chance to compete against the top countries, but there could be something else done for them so they don't return home simply with four defeats from four games to their name.

There was a time when Italy joining to form a Six Nations was unthinkable, and they have now beaten everyone in the tournament apart from England, so they have progressed immensely. I know that there has been talk of another country, perhaps Georgia, who have consistently performed well, joining to make a Seven Nations tournament, but I think it would place a lot of pressure on the fixture list, so I don't think that now is the right time to do that. Perhaps a relegation and promotion system could be an option, but I like the format how it is at the moment, as it is a very competitive league. My old colleague from Edinburgh, Michael Bradley, is coaching for Georgia, so I do hope that soon, when the time is right, they are able to progress just as Italy have done so smoothly. There's no easy answer here though in terms of the limits on how many games a player can play during a season, and with an already packed schedule, something has to give.

At the opposite end of the game, rugby has evolved a great deal at grassroots level from when I played as a youngster. For example, tag rugby is played, which I am wholly against. It is an unrealistic version of the game and helps no one. I understand the policy behind it, from a safety perspective, but the world has gone mad when it comes to this kind of thing. What we should be focusing on is educating coaches in the art of training good decision-making, contact, tackling technique and skill acquisition to young players, so they can hone their skills quicker than players of other nations. Instead, we are teaching youngsters to reach out and tag someone as a tackle, which is as far removed from the art of actually tackling as you can get.

I was so lucky that I had Jack Carnell to coach me when I was a kid. He taught me to tackle with my shoulder, to grip with my hands, and to focus on the positioning of my head, feet and body. He didn't teach me to reach out from arm's length and tag someone for them to hand the ball over to me. We need to also look at schools and at clubs to put youngsters up against other kids of a similar size, not just basing selection on age. If you are playing against kids of an equal size, then the focus is on skill development, not just on giving the ball to the big kid who bashes through for a try because he or she is stronger than everyone else. Results shouldn't be the only focus in those early years either. It should all be focused on enjoyment, technique and attitude. Coaches should be looking at how to win in terms of the way an individual or a team has played, and then every now and then, they should pick their best side and create that winning environment. That way, kids are given the chance to develop, while also understanding the importance of winning. We can't be too soft on kids, as a totally watered-down version of the game doesn't really help kids in terms of preparation for their lives at work or home, not just in sport.

I can't finish this book without giving my views on the current England team. Stuart Lancaster has cultivated an outstanding coaching staff and backroom team, while assembling a talented group of young players, who have a great deal of potential. Through injuries over the past year or so, it has enabled Stuart to experiment with players who may not otherwise have played, and that has given a depth to the squad. Where I feel that England suffer is their lack of experience though. That was highlighted in round three of the Six Nations, where a more experienced Ireland side out-thought England in all the key areas. Once we were beaten at set pieces, we were beaten full stop. We made 58 errors in that game, with 13 of those being penalties, of which five were dull and were avoidable. There was an inability shown to make the right decisions when under pressure, and that is a weakness that England will need to address quickly, with the World Cup on our doorstep. It is unfair to compare this current side to our team in 2003, but we had caps coming out of our ears and so many leaders on the field that almost anyone could have captained, if for any reason Johno was ruled out. That won't be the case when England take to the field against Fiji in their opening game, but they do have time to learn from the errors of the Ireland game and other Six Nations matches. In fact, that defeat may turn out to be the warning that the guys needed, like we had in 2002, also in round three of the Six Nations, when we lost to France in Paris. Hopefully it will inspire them.

There is undoubtedly a great deal of pressure on Stuart Lancaster; England expects and all that. He has created a great environment in the camp, and a connection between the players, the fans and the media. Everywhere I go, people talk about the positives when it comes to England and Stuart, and he should be applauded for that cultural change he has overseen. He has got people excited about our national team, but with that comes the expectation and he and his staff will have to ensure that the players can cope with that. Hosting the World Cup will add to the pressure and the scrutiny levels too, which we saw in Australia in 2003. What has particularly impressed me is the development pathways for younger players to break through in to the full national side. But all of this is the easy part. Let's not forget, the England set-up is extremely well-funded, a good organisation, and what Stuart is yet to do is to turn the side in to a world-class, winning outfit. That is ultimately what he, and every England coach is judged on. Success. We have been runners-up in the last four consecutive Six Nations Championships, and the last time we won the tournament was when Johno was team manager in 2011. Some people will say that it is not easy to achieve the success that we all hope for, but Stuart has been given time and now this World Cup will be the acid test.

There's probably no better place to finish this than discussing any future I may have in the game. Up until I left Edinburgh Rugby, I had a contract and a salary for a minimum of two years, through all of my professional playing and coaching days, which I could plan my life around. Since then, life has changed a great deal and my ambassadorial roles and ad-hoc work is a little more open-ended. Obviously things can change in the blink of an eye, but I'm always looking ahead to ensure that I can plan for my family. This time a year ago, my diary was empty and now I'm busy every day, so it shows how quickly I have immersed myself in to this life away from the bubble of rugby and adapted to the business world. Ideally, one day I'd like to have a substantial stake in a company and build the company to a point where I can step away and retire, having achieved my aims in business. The more that I build my reputation in this area, the less likely it becomes that I'll step back in to a coaching role in rugby though.

A number of people have said to me that all I gained from the game is too much of a waste to not still have an active involvement in rugby. My experiences as a player and then as a coach, have given me skills which are invaluable outside of rugby though. I have the ability to invest in people, help to develop them and get the best out of a team in order to achieve a set aim. As I've said though, things can change so quickly. Only a few months ago, a couple of coaches who I know very well and respect, were in early talks to make a move which could have involved me, but they signed extensions in their current roles and the opportunity never materialised for me. There's always the chance of a butterfly effect, and just one move can open doors to a new career. You just never know what might happen, but if something did happen it would have to be the right opportunity. After the Rugby Lions experience, where the finances didn't happen and promises were broken, it would be very difficult to take on something like that again. I was looking five years ahead there, to create something special, but there were simply no foundations to build anything on. If I return to the game, it would need to be real.

I do miss rugby though and the environment. You are generally with like-minded people, competing together and it's such a thrill to be part of a rugby team, especially one with a winning habit. Having said that, I really do love the environment I find myself in now. I enjoy meeting new people, building relationships and achieving results for the companies I work with. I'm hugely motivated by my work, and like anything I put my mind to, I always give 100 per cent. I would never say never to going back to rugby. I suppose if the kids have flown the nest and gone on to university, who knows? I love having my time back though, and being able to spend time with Ali, Olivia, Fin, our extended family, our dog Sylvester, well I say dog but I wouldn't take him for a walk in the daylight for the first six months as he's a Maltipoo, so not exactly a creature that fits with me, plus spending time with friends, while being able to develop another career and prove to myself I can do it to a high standard. During all of this, I'm able to watch lots of rugby on television, go to lots of Premiership, European and international games in person, do some punditry, work for England Rugby Travel, Green Flag, a key Premiership Rugby sponsor, and Heineken. It's not as if I no longer enjoy rugby. Yes, my relationship with the game has changed, and will probably never be the same again after what happened at Rugby Lions, but I will always love the game, no matter what.

My aims in life have changed now. When I moved from being a player to being a coach, I wanted to emulate what I'd done as a player. Those desires still burn within me, but I gain so much satisfaction from the happiness and love within my family, and I will always be there to support them and help them to reach their goals.

If I had one more wish in rugby terms, today though, I'd hope that this book helps to resolve what happened at Rugby Lions, for all the people affected during that season. We were let down by the RFU, and we were misled by Michael Aland and his associates. If there is any justice in the game, the authorities will read our version of events, open this up again and breathe life back in to The Death of Rugby.

The Back Row

Richard Hill MBE

Saracens, England and British & Irish Lions

I THINK it would be fair to say that at first, Backy and I had quite an intense relationship, as we both battled for the openside flanker role within the England side and the British & Irish Lions in 1997. I wanted to be in the number seven jerseys just as much as he did. Let's just say we weren't as close as we are now!

Fortunately for us, Clive became the England coach, and he saw our attributes and eventually settled on a back row combination of Neil, Lawrence and myself. During the first few seasons playing together we had our critics as a back row unit. We weren't a typical set-up for that period of time, but Clive identified how he wanted to play and we worked well together for many years. As a three, Backy, Lol and myself, we learned each other's strengths and became aware of each other's defaults, in carrying into contact, tackling, on the side on scrums. It became instinctive to react to each other.

We always knew we could easily be replaced as Lewis, Joe and Cozza continued to perform well.

There was never any doubt that when I played next to Neil, I was playing alongside a driven man. With Neil there was never any compromise, and there was always huge pride in everything he did. He was the leader of our defence, working closely with our coach, Phil Larder. In that last hour before a match in the changing rooms, he would be sharing key messages to individuals or howling demands on non-negotiables for the team.

Neil was our terrier; a link player, who would always help to put others in to space, and who would go in to the tackle low and hard and quickly back to feet being a nuisance. In the maul, I can honestly say, I don't know how he came out with the ball so many times, but he did. He would get lower than others, and tackle harder. That is a sign of the kind of person he is; never prepared to accept second best, always 100 per cent driven and always striving to be the best he can be.

Undoubtedly, at times, it felt that we were spending too much time together, including a ten-minute stitch repair job against South Africa at Twickenham. He had received a deep cut around his eye just before I received a lesser version to my forehead. His ability to get to places first meant he occupied the stitch table and I had to revert next door in the dentist's chair.

In the 2003 summer camp, building up to the World Cup, we roomed together at Pennyhill Park. I ended up being more nervous about leaving my socks on the floor than training, given his perfection and precision with folding clothes.

Neil was always committed, always plugging away, always giving his all for the team.

Lawrence Dallaglio OBE
Wasps, England and British & Irish Lions

I**N the early days, I'm not sure anyone really got on with Neil; I mean, number sevens are normally just a bit weird! There was also a bit of a clash of cultures between the Leicester and the London lads, and as we didn't meet up that often as an England side, we had to beat them at club level to earn their respect.

Backy had gone to the World Cup as part of Jack Rowell's squad in 1995, yet in 1996 I was picked for my first Five Nations game at openside flanker, ahead of Neil, despite having only played a handful of times in that position. I pictured him sat up in Leicester, sticking pins in to a voodoo doll of me!

Number sevens, as I've said, are strange and a little eccentric, and Backy was no different. He was single-minded though and a specialist in his position, just like the stars of today such as Steffon Armitage, Richie McCaw and Sam Warburton.

It took a while for the back row of Hilly, Backy and myself to come together. I think the 1997 Lions tour of South Africa changed how everyone felt about each other, and Hilly and Backy were immensely competitive on that trip, constantly pushing each other to the next level in terms of performance. In the second Test, Neil came on as a substitute, and in the blink of an eye we had turned the ball over, Keith Wood kicked us forward and Jerry Guscott's drop goal sealed the series. I had to watch it again afterwards on television to see how we'd won the ball, and no surprise, who was there at the breakdown, doing what he did best? Backy. No one else in world rugby could have done that. Then later that year, Clive, showing how ruthless he could be, even in the early days, hauled Tony Diprose off at half-time against New Zealand at Old Trafford and put Backy on, which I remember being the start of the three of us playing together.

In 1999 we were devastated. Jannie De Beer's drop goals were daggers through our hearts, and we were dumped out of the World Cup. After an intense campaign we went out for some drinks on the Champs-Élysées to commiserate, while also toasting Joe Worsley, who had won his first cap against Tonga during the tournament. We'd moved on to another place and I was drinking with Leon Lloyd, Johno and Backy at around 2am, when an England fan with a St George's cross painted on his face, came over to us to inform us that we'd been below par. He tapped us all on the shoulders, one-by-one, and tried to explain where we'd gone wrong. We all ignored him and carried on drinking, but then he tapped Backy on the shoulder and told him we hadn't played with any passion. I just froze and thought, 'You must have a death wish mate,' and the next thing I knew I was holding Backy's pint, while he sat the bloke down, turned to face me, took the pint back and carried on drinking as if nothing had happened; a priceless moment that would have made national headlines these days.

Our 18-13 Test match win in 2000 in Bloemfontein, over South Africa, showed a great rapport between the three of us. As I'm sure we would all say though, a back row is very reliant upon the tight five ahead of you. We developed a great partnership and became very close. The three of us all had core skills, but there was an almost perfect balance about the things one of us could do, and the others couldn't, that complemented us as a unit. We had our own ways, but that togetherness showed as we began to warm up together, finding comfort and solace in each other's company, and we would talk through the game and our tactics, almost as a ritual. It was an incredible time.

Throughout the time I've known Neil I have always respected him. His fitness levels and his preparation were simply second to none. In the early days, he was, perhaps by his own admission, over-analytical and maybe a little sensitive at times, but he was always a fantastic bloke to work with and he became an integral part of the England side for many years, and the special guy that he is today.

Neil Back is an example to anyone who is told they can't do something, or won't be good enough, or big enough in his case. He just kept coming back, never giving up and always proving people wrong. For me, rugby is not necessarily about your wins or losses, it's about the guys you played with and the memories you create. I think when people look back in 50 or 60 years at the sport, they will remember that England team, and they will remember Neil Back.

Statistics And Honours

Club Playing History:

Nottingham RFC   1988–1990 (37 caps, 10 tries)

Leicester Tigers   1990–2005 (339 caps, 125 tries)

International Playing History:

England Schools	1985–1987
England Colts	1987–1988
England U21	1988–1990
England A	1990–1994
England XV	1990
England	1994–2004 (66 caps, 16 tries, only England forward to drop a goal, plus three World Cups played in)
Barbarians	1990–2005
British & Irish Lions	1997 South Africa, 2001 Australia and 2005 New Zealand

In addition to the above, Neil played sevens rugby for Leicester Tigers, the Barbarians and England including the World Cup of 1997.

Playing Accolades:

RFU Player of the Year – 1998/99

PRA Players' Player of the Year – 1998/99

Zurich Premiership Top Try Scorer (16 tries) – 1998/99

Nominee: European Player of the Year – 1998/99

Leicester Player of the Year – 1998/99

Leicester Players' Player of the Year – 1998/99
Only English forward in history to drop a goal in a Test match
    (v Italy, 18 March) – 2000
Tigers Supporters' Outstanding Service Award – 2002/03
Leicester Tigers Captain – 2003/04
Captained England four times to victory (Australia, Romania,
    Wales and Italy on 50th cap)
MBE for Services to Rugby – 2004
Inducted into the RFU Hall of Fame – 2004
Finished Tigers playing career scoring 125th club try to set
    club record – 2005

Team Trophies:

World Cup Winner	2003
Grand Slam Champion	2003
Six Nations Champion	2000, 2001 and 2003
Triple Crown Champion	1997, 1998, 2000 and 2003
Premiership League Winner	1999, 2000, 2001 and 2002
Zurich Championship Winner	2001
Pilkington Cup Winner	1993 & 1997
European Champions	2001 & 2002
Orange Cup Winner	2002

Coaching History:

1997–2004	Defence Leader with England Defence Coach Phil Larder
2003–05	Leicester Tigers Player/Defence Coach
2005–07	Leicester Tigers Academy Head Coach
2005–08	Leicester Tigers Defence/Assistant Forwards Coach
2008–11	Leeds Carnegie Rugby Head Coach
2011–12	Rugby Football Club (2011) Director of Rugby
2012–13	Edinburgh Rugby Forwards Coach

2005/06 Leicester Tigers
Premiership Finalists
Ashridge Programme 'Developing World Class Coaching'

2006/07 Leicester Tigers
European Finalists
Guinness Premiership Winners
EDF Cup Winners
RFU Level 4 Coaching Award

2007/08 Leicester Tigers
EDF Cup Finalists
Guinness Premiership Finalists

2008/09 Leeds Carnegie
Promotion to the Premiership as Championship Winners

2011/12 The Rugby Football Club (2011) Ltd
National Midlands Division 3 Champions (winning every match)
Warwickshire Cup Winners

Bibliography

Books
Winning: Clive Woodward
Mad Dog – An Englishman: My Life in Rugby: Lewis Moody
Martin Johnson: The Autobiography
Will: The Autobiography of Will Greenwood
Jonny: My Autobiography: Jonny Wilkinson
The Right Place at the Wrong Time: Corne Krige
Engage: The Fall and Rise of Matt Hampson
Leicester Tigers History Book

Newspapers
Leicester Mercury
Daily Telegraph
Rugby Advertiser
The Scotsman
The Yorkshire Post
Sydney Daily Telegraph
The Sydney Morning Herald

Websites
BBC Sport
Lions Rugby

DVD
Rugby World Cup 2003 – England's Story